THE CULTURAL POLITICS OF SUGAR

CARIBBEAN SLAVERY AND NARRATIVES OF COLONIALISM

With the expansion of trade and empire in the early modern period, the status of sugar changed from expensive rarity to popular consumer commodity, and its real and imagined properties functioned as central metaphors for the cultural desires of West Indian Creoles. Keith Sandiford's study examines how the writings of six colonial West Indian authors explore these properties to publicise the economic value of the consumer object, and to invent a metaphor for West Indian cultural desires. Sandiford defines this metaphorical turn as a trope of 'negotiation' which organises the structure and content of the narratives: his argument establishes the function of this trope as a source of knowledge about the creolised imagination, and about its social and political idealism. Based on extensive historical knowledge of the period as well as recent postcolonial theory, this book suggests the possibilities 'negotiation' offers in the continuing recovery of West Indian intellectual history.

KEITH SANDIFORD is Professor of English at the Louisiana State University. He was born in Barbados where he has also taught modern languages at Secondary and University levels. He is author of *Measuring the Moment* (1988).

THE CULTURAL POLITICS
OF SUGAR

Caribbean Slavery and Narratives of Colonialism

KEITH A. SANDIFORD

CAMBRIDGE
UNIVERSITY PRESS

PUBLISHED BY THE PRESS SYNDICATE OF THE UNIVERSITY OF CAMBRIDGE
The Pitt Building, Trumpington Street, Cambridge, United Kingdom

CAMBRIDGE UNIVERSITY PRESS
The Edinburgh Building, Cambridge CB2 2RU, UK   www.cup.cam.ac.uk
40 West 20th Street, New York, NY 10011–4211, USA   www.cup.org
10 Stamford Road, Oakleigh, Melbourne 3166, Australia
Ruiz de Alarcón 13, 28014 Madrid, Spain

H   © Keith A. Sandiford 2000

First published 2000

Printed in the United Kingdom at the University Press, Cambridge

Typeface Baskerville 11/12.5 pt   *System* 3b2   [CE]

A catalogue record for this book is available from the British Library

Library of Congress Cataloguing in Publication data
Sandiford, Keith Albert, 1947–
The cultural politics of sugar: Caribbean slavery and narratives of colonialism / Keith
A. Sandiford.
p.   cm.
Includes bibliographical references and index.
ISBN 0 521 64233 7 (hardback)
1. Sugar trade – Political aspects – West Indies – Historiography. 2. Slavery – West
Indies – Historiography. 3. West Indies – Colonial influence – Historiography. 4. Ligon,
Richard. True & exact history of the island of Barbadoes. 5. Rochefort, Charles de,
1605–1683. Histoire naturelle et morale des iles Antilles de l'Amerique. 6. Grainger,
James, 1721?–1766. Essay on the more common West-India diseases and the remedies
which that country itself produces. 7. Schaw, Janet, ca. 1731-ca. 1801. Journal of a lady
of quality. 8. Beckford, William, d. 1799. Descriptive account of the island of Jamaica.
9. Lewis, Matthew Gregory, 1775–1818. Journal of a residence among the negroes of the
West Indies. I. Title.

HD9114.W42 S26 2000
306'.09729–dc21   99–045511

ISBN 0 521 64233 7 hardback

Contents

v

Introduction

The first phrase of my title is used on two separate but not unrelated occasions in Richard Ligon's *History of Barbadoes* (1657; 1673). In both usages there resonate the unmistakable motives of the discoverer and the publicist. The first occurs towards the end of the principal exposition on sugar production in early colonial Barbados (p. 96). It caps three pages of hard reckonings in which the author makes the case persuasively that handsome profits were to be made investing in Barbados sugar plantations, sweetening the narrative with reports of the success achieved by Colonel James Drax and Colonel Thomas Modiford, two of the colony's earliest pioneers. The second, coming some twelve pages later, concludes a sketch of the personality types best suited for life in this emergent enterprise zone. To men of orderly and 'moderate' tempers it holds out the attractive inducements of the first reference, issuing a stern moral dissuasion to men of dispositions 'too volatile to fixe on businesse' (p. 108).

Besides fitting its immediate contexts with a certain aptitude and felicity, 'sweete negotiation' carries with it a remarkable density of reference, reaffirming the Bakhtinian axiom that the most commonplace of utterances are often found to be inhabited by a multitude of voices. In this particular instance, the 'sweete negotiation' to which Ligon referred was as much a *mot juste* to describe the headiness of his personal discovery of the rare taste of sugar as it was a cleverly telegraphed message to a wider audience about the quality of experience and opportunity that awaited early colonizing populations in the sugar colonies of the West Indies (opportunities available even to perfectly common people). Not only was Ligon attempting to express his private excitement about the possibilities the emergent sugar colony of Barbados offered for enriching his personal knowledge and enlarging the stock of ideas available to a man of letters, he was also (albeit only thinly) disguising the larger publicity

I

function of his book, a commonly used strategy in these early colonizing texts designed to stir the hunger of prospective new settlers for the promise of individual enterprise and prosperity that awaited their exploitation on this new economic frontier.

Still another function, of even greater ideological significance, lies embedded in this dialogic voice: 'sweete negotiation' stands as a complex cultural marker within its own host text, while its allusive coding of sugar production prefigures certain forms of desire enacted in Ligon and scores of other contemporary and later narratives as they pursued similar aims of claiming and defining positive social value for these colonized spaces.

Like Ligon's *History*, the five other narratives that form the nucleus of this study, Charles de Rochefort's *Natural and Moral History of the Antilles* (1666), James Grainger's *The Sugar Cane* (1764), Janet Schaw's *Journal of a Lady of Quality* (composed 1774–6), William Beckford's *Descriptive Account of Jamaica* (1790) and Matthew (Monk) Lewis' *Journal of a West Indian Proprietor* (1834) all manifest a conscious relationship to this multivoiced practice of negotiation. All six texts evidence this activity in the linkages they infer between the process of literary production and the more secular business of sugar production, negotiating that relationship into an argument consciously framed to seek validation for a contested colonial culture. In general terms, the earlier texts are driven by the sheer demands of making these far outposts of empire known to audiences 'back home', domesticating differences in physical nature, and assimilating diversities in manners and mores of both indigenous and colonists. As the texts seek authority for their producers, they simultaneously assume the role of courting legitimacy for the rather narrow special interests of a colonial planter class deriving its wealth and power from slave-produced sugar in the colonies and for their commercial and political allies operating from the metropoles. Faced with the local imperatives of producing value and building community at the periphery while divorced from the certainties and settled traditions of the centre, the slavocrats found valuable allies in colonialist authors.

Most assuredly, in its consumable substance and in the politics spawned by its trade, sugar represented a complex signifying system. Ligon and the early colonizing intelligences evaluated their new-found prospects in a language figuring the discovery of a fruitful, desirable body, ripe for appropriation and assimilation. As one of the 'fruits' of this desirable body, the sugar cane played a central role in developing the material economies of these societies. Similarly, sugar's real and imagined properties are reproduced in textual economies as central metaphors for the idealized desires of those special-interest Creole publics. These texts thus implicate multiple voices in this representation of the desire for a particular kind of civilized order. Typically, these authors and these interests imagined an idealized body politic made up of masters and servants living in serenity, peace and harmony, and handing on their legacy to posterity.

Not surprisingly, the politico-cultural objectives of these texts are complexly constructed. Heavily fraught with ironic ambivalences and contradictions, they oscillate constantly between the polarities represented by the two oddly coupled ideas contained in the defining concept of 'sweete negotiation', and then the further internal oppositions contained in the single locution 'negotiation'. Succinctly stated, it is that polarity which will be the object of this study. The central argument will be that 'sweete negotiation' is a complexly constructed metaphor for the cultural desire that informs these texts. Drawing its energy principally(though not exclusively) from the economies of sugar production, that desire subsumes within itself both the material artifacts and the ideological content of that production. These texts produce negotiation as a desire to win a tenuous and elusive legitimacy for an evolving ideal of Creole civilization, conflicted by its central relation to slavery and its marginal relation to metropolitan cultures. Each of these sources of conflict posed stout challenges to Creole pretensions: slavery aroused moral and economic objections crystallizing in abolitionist and anti-slavery polemics; traditional cultural preservationists (purists) back home continually interrogated the Creoles' desire for social credibility by raising the spectre of cultural pollution and political disintegration.

Reading each text as a distinctive production of antagonistic cultural designs, my critique will illuminate the dynamics of negotiation as a dichotomy between two (ideological) myths, two sets of cultural ethics that inhere in the etymology and ideology of Ligon's usage and retain their force and durability across the 160-year trajectory represented in these texts. Dichotomy and antagonism are rooted in the very origin of the term 'negotiation'. The Latin voice *negotium* is constituted from two roots: *neg-* (not) and *otium* (ease, quiet). Juxtaposed, the separate parts produce antithesis and negation; compounded, their essence yields ambiguity and ambivalence, a fitting verbal correspondence for the kind of tension (referred to earlier) and crisis that were to mark the slave plantation economy as it grew into a mature system. Deconstructed in this way, negotiation also illustrates some of the questions that are raised by the very nature of conquest and colonization, questions bound up with the right to alienate and appropriate physical space and exploit the economic resources of that space. Thus, negotiation begs the very question that these texts were produced to resolve: the uneasy interface between the twin principles of *neg* and *otium* problematizes that very bid for cultural legitimacy and respect which these publicists endeavored to wring from the metropolitan audience. These texts oscillate ceaselessly between the twin poles of *neg* (colonization, slavery and the economic activities related to sugar production) and *otium* (ease, the antithesis of business, the inverse of the active life). The *neg* supported a lucrative commerce and helped to develop the bourgeois capitalist ethic, promoting lifestyles of luxury, consumption, and dissipation. The *otium*, formerly a consummation devoutly to be wished, now becomes distracted by an anxiety that this suddenly acquired wealth and power would sap the very virtue on which the metropole predicated its imperial greatness. *Neg* and *otium* would be the prime factors in the constitution of colonial identities. *Neg* and *otium* would increasingly engender the fear that identities so constituted would bring on political threat, moral enervation and cultural degeneracy. At the focal point of this search for legitimacy and this anxiety over cultural dilution stands the figure of the West Indian Creole. It is typically around the formation of Creole identity that the dynamic tension of these texts is concentrated. For that identity is often embodied in the person of the very author, hence transforming substantial portions of these texts into strategies defensive of the common interests of author and audience. This anxiety and these strategies give rise on the one hand to a recurrent thematic preoccupation, and on the other to a definitive structural property. Together they situate these texts squarely within the defining formations of Caribbean society: the theme is that of purity and pollution, the structure is the dialectic of antagonistic forces, a dynamic which has since attracted significant scholarly analysis from theoreticians in Caribbean history and sociology.[1] I shall return to this theme and structure later in this chapter and in the Lewis chapter where I discuss revolutionary energies.

Reference to Creole anxiety and the writing of Caribbean history demands some prefiguring of a cultural critique within which to probe the roots of that anxiety and a larger historical framework within which to trace the evolution of these texts. In pursuit of its design for a cultural study, this book will deploy the complex *negotium* of Ligon's early conception as a theoretical instrument with which to derive a collective cultural meaning; which might serve as a foundational and diachronic principle of these six texts. Because none of these texts is, by any common measure, standard fare on academic or scholarly menus, I have thought it fitting to locate each work in relation to a specific nexus of colonial–metropolitan historical developments contemporaneous with its composition or publication. Thus the discussion of each text will seek to unfold that pattern of meaning and continuity implied in the preceding chronological listing and later in the sequential relationship of each text to the dynamic of the thesis. The object will be to show that the texts always identify themselves with and promote forms of idealism associated with colonial cultural desire. That idealism will be historicized in its relation to the insidious external forces of scepticism and adverse mercantilist policies which were having their effect from as early as the first half century of sugar production in the West Indies (reflected in Ligon's *History*). Those forces will be shown to shape the content and strategies of these texts, as their subject elites, were pressured, some to reaction, others to reform, when plantation slavery and sugar began to be implicated in political and economic transformations which culminated in the full-blown campaign for abolition and emancipation.

To posit the significant presentation of Creole anxiety as early as Ligon's *History* is to confront two large problems endemic to Caribbean intellectual history and scholarship: how to locate the roots of creolization, and how to define the causes and consequences of that anxiety. What follows will sketch out some historical and theoretical lines bearing on these questions and illustrate their relevance to the present discussion.

In his groundbreaking historical work on creolization in the West Indies, Edward (Kamau) Brathwaite defines that process as the gradual development of a distinct cultural identity by diverse groups of people 'caught up in some kind of colonial arrangement' with a metropolitan European power, on the one hand, and a plantation arrangement on the other, and 'where the society is multiracial but organized for the benefit of a minority of European origin'.[2] In further amplifications on the terms 'Creole' and 'Creole society' Brathwaite identifies and develops the master–slave–plantation nexus, the heterogeneous nature of the society, the persistent struggle with adaptation to local and external pressures and, very importantly, the Creoles' commitment to the 'area of living'. Granted, Brathwaite's work confines itself to Jamaica and focuses on the 'developed' manifestations of creolization there around 1820. Still, because it has stood for such a long time as the most substantial historical study of creolization in the West Indies and has been used for significant extensions and extrapolations, it provides a respectable point of reference from which to re-examine the question over the wider domain of colonies represented here. And since the very morphology of the term 'creolization', like the term 'negotiation', is synonymous with gradual continuous process, and reciprocal exchanges, the effect of my inquiry will be to place the origins of Creole identity and its attendant anxieties closer to the origins of West Indian settlement and sugar production (here represented by Ligon's text), thus supplying some earlier substantive chapters to the record established by Brathwaite. Ligon's gesture grows in complexity the more it is understood (at least in part) as a defensive response to metropolitan attitudes of contempt and calumny. All five of the writers examined here offer their personal experiences self-consciously as credible authorities in the representation of newly incorporated colonial spaces, and the broadest ideological values of their texts as persuasive signs of the existence of culture in Creoledom, tangible proofs against anti-colonialist detractions and scurrilities concerning West Indian character. The noted Caribbeanist Gordon K. Lewis acknowledges this burden of proof as existing 'from the very beginning', a burden imposed by the 'Anti-Caribbean animus' emanating from the metropoles and directed against poor white emigrants and rich white planters: 'what London thought about Jamaica was only matched by what Paris thought about Saint Domingue and what Madrid thought about Cuba'.[3] Geoffrey Scammell adverts to the 'universal contempt' in which colonials were held in the old world because they were thought to be 'imperfectly governed and archaic in their manners'.[4] Likewise Philip Boucher, writing of French colonial attitudes, documents the stereotypes of colonists as 'human refuse'.[5] Understandably, such scepticism and antipathy contributed to obscure the existence of a 'genuine Caribbean historiography, a Caribbean sociology [and] a Caribbean anthropology'.[6] Two years before Ligon's publication, the report of a visitor to Barbados confirms that creolization as earlier defined was already in evidence in the pride and sense of value witnessed in the attitudes of the colonists. Barbados was already accounted one of the 'Riches spotes of ground in the wordell . . . where the gentrey . . . doth live far better than ours doe in England.'[7]

Thus, on the one hand Ligon's 'sweete negotiation' may be seen as providing a more sophisticated (because more complex, more literary and multiply signifying) usage as an abstract metaphor, a snapshot of the self-confidence born of improved material prospects, and the self-consciousness born of cultural adaptations, and the all-round sense of well-being felt by early colonists in the most thriving colonies. On the other hand, it serves as the verbal figuration of that conflict referred to earlier as Creole anxiety that is problematized in colonial Creole desire. Each successive text reproduces its own specific expressions of Creole anxiety. In Rochefort, that anxiety drives the text's recourses to the classical topos of *premiers temps* and the rhetorical strategies of collusion. In Grainger that anxiety appears as diffractions of the desire for cultural monism. In Schaw, a sensibility flushed with the perfect assurance of its own superiority works to deny Creole value and privilege the metropole's. William Beckford endeavours to reclaim the Creole advantage by valorizing the colony's landscape and its elites through the aesthetic of the picturesque. And in Lewis anxiety underlines the persistence of the revolutionary sublime in the struggle to mediate the roles of slave master and romantic reformer.[8] All these connotations of conflict and struggle are the conditioned defensive responses to those calumnies referred to earlier: they are manifestations of anxiety embedded in identity, but for all, they are manifestations of cultural consciousness resonant enough to earn the descriptions of 'emergent Creole identity' and 'embryonic Creole nationalism'.[9]

Perhaps the most unmistakable sign of the Creoles' deep-seated anxiety about their colonial status and the low esteem in which plantation society was held in the metropolis was the high incidence of absenteeism among landowners and slavocrats.[10] Ownership of land and slaves brought with it the perquisites of power and prestige that were to be enjoyed from leadership in local politics, law, trade and religion. However, for increasing numbers the magnetic pull was great to seek a different order of civil society and higher public visibility in the more populous cities and resorts back home in Europe. The historian J. R. Ward identifies this as one important respect in which British West Indian slavery as an institution differed from its classical antecedents, as well as from its even closer counterpart in the antebellum South: 'Most British West Indian slaves belonged to men who chose to live as absentees in the mother country.'[11] He further estimates that by about 1760 close to one-third of British West Indian sugar plantations belonged to absentees, with a steady increase in the proportion into the nineteenth century.[12] Even amongst the most colony-loyal of slavocrats, feelings of disconnection and exile affected them powerfully. Even in Ligon's Barbados, which developed an early tradition for high residency, one finds strong sentiments of nostalgia and firm determination to return as soon as great fortunes could be secured: 'planter outlook was typically one of felt exile.'[13] Judge Edward Littleton, writing in *The Groans of the Plantations* conveys in this reflection those conflicting emotions, that sense of a self divided in its loyalty-relationship between two places: 'By a kind of magnetic force England draws to it all that is good in the Plantations. It is the center to which all things tend: nothing but England can we relish or fancy: our hearts are here, wherever our bodies be: if we get a little money, we remit it to England. When we are a little easy, we desire to live and spend what we have in England, and all that we can rap and rend is brought to England.'[14]

But nostalgia, homesickness and older loyalties do not account totally for the full complex of absentee anxiety. The personal fortunes derived from sugar were inevitably placed on public display to satisfy the need of this new plantocratic class to indulge in emulative consumption, to imprint these forms of ostentation and visibility as signs of their entry into the culture of emergent bourgeois capitalism. The fine clothes, lavish equipages and opulent accommodations were deliberately theatricalized to elicit envy and recognition, without which new wealth typically feels unverified. Not the least among the insignia with which absentee identity and anxiety code themselves in this context is the display of the human body as property in the object relations of the slave to the master or mistress. As a ubiquitous companion in public places, liveried and orna-mented (often in ludicrous mimicry of heroic, classical figures), a slave so displayed could not fail to advertise that anxious desire for higher social recognition in the Old World.[15]

It bears further emphasis that this aspect of absentee behaviour signals more deeply repressed layers of tension and ambivalence that are indivisible from the formation of the West Indian creolized self as it is inscribed in these texts. Physical absence from the scene of bonded labour, spatial distance from shackles and whips, no doubt assuaged absentee guilt; their own social costumes and those of their slaves permitted them to reconstitute themselves by masking and recovering these harsher social realities. Herein is powerfully pro-duced two complementary expressions of that 'sweete negotiation' between the pursuit of subjective self-invention and the pursuit of cultural legitimation. The Creole subject struggles to reconcile the conflicted parts of this new identity by expatriating those complex bodily formations from the physical scene of production on the plantation and reconstituting them as familiarized objects on the constructed scene of bourgeois life.

Likewise this book's representative authors endeavour to natur-alize those increasingly contested scenes by negotiating credibility for their personal and literary authority through aestheticizing the bodies and work of the slaves and the guilt-ridden natural emotions both evoked. The covertness and complicity that mark the colo-nizing apologetics of these texts will establish their substantial role in producing identities for Creole West Indian elites as they attempt to penetrate the larger body of bourgeois elites in Europe. We shall see this diffidence about admitting their true relationship to the violence and brutality of slave-owning and slave-dealing most sharply drama-tized in the writings of Grainger, Schaw and Beckford. In the delineation of the historical framework unfolded in the ideological content of these works, we shall see how carefully orchestrated abolitionist agitation (for example, the anti-saccharite movement) appropriated that discourse of degradation and contamination to affect consumer attitudes towards slave-produced sugar. Later in this introduction, in the context of georgic, I shall return to this discus-sion of the effacing, obfuscatory functions of colonizing narratives.

The pattern of absenteeism on British plantations mirrored a model of engagement that reflected the indirect-rule official policies of the central authorities in London, and was reproduced in popular perceptions about the role of the colonies as dumping grounds. The case of France differed decisively in this respect. It is critical to emphasize this here for a clear and proper assessment of the part Rochefort will play in this book and for a similar understanding of the distinctive cultural politics his book illustrates. The French West Indian model of colonial administration exhibited qualitative differences in the deliberate attention France paid to selecting both political administrators and ordinary settlers. According to Adolphe Roberts, 'The Gallic concept of overseas territory resembled that of Ancient Greece. It sought to make each holding an integral part culturally, politically, and commercially of the homeland. The colonists in Saint Domingue and Martinique so loved their traditions that no new civilizations sprang up.'[16] By the date of Rochefort's *Histoire*, the monarch and his chief ministers were beginning to predicate the country's imperial greatness on the success of the colonies, and by 1678 gubernatorial appointments were being made directly by the Crown. With respect to common settlers, a certain idealism informed official policy: 'Colonies were not to be, unlike those of Portugal and England, dumping grounds for undesirables, but were to be populated, as the Spaniards planned for the Americas, by virtuous and hardworking Catholics and old soldiers from the mother country.'[17] With respect to indigenous Carib Indians, policy tended more towards appeasement and conciliation. French Creole anxiety at this early period (1630–60) arose from a unique cultural desire to incorporate these new territories into an imperial ideal of Greater France, a pointed distinction from British policy. This peculiar national difference drives the specific negotiations (allusions and collusions)that distinguish Rochefort's text from the British texts treated in this study.

Besides the cultural differences that separate French and British colonial policies, there are significant differences to be found in the two nations' political histories during the period spanned by these texts. And since the colonized scenes they describe occupy such widely disparate historical junctures, some attempt will be made next to elucidate a pattern and context in which these texts' contents can be understood.

The 260 or so years bounded by the literary landmarks of Ligon's *History* and Lewis' *Journal* describe a colonial period in which the

British and French slave-sugar properties in the Caribbean experienced early years of rapid growth, attended by optimism about future prosperity, middle years of competition, war and realignment, and later years of intensified trading rivalries, tariffs, taxes, the rise of anti-slavery, revolt, and the beginning of decline for the planter class.

The Act to abolish the slave trade to the British colonies was passed in 1807. Eight years later Monk Lewis made his first visit to his Jamaican plantations during a period of deep concern among members of the planter class and the resident Creole power structure. If the Act's implications caused these persons to fear for their continued political and economic security, it engendered much confusion and raised premature hopes among the slaves that their freedom had been won.[18]

Of the colonial territories represented in these texts, Grainger's St Christopher was the earliest to be settled (1624), and the second to begin sugar cultivation(1640). Ligon's Barbados was the second place to be settled (1627) and the first to begin sugar cultivation (1640). Jamaica came under British dominion during the Cromwellian regime in 1655. From an initial settler party of about twenty Englishmen and forty African slaves in 1627, the Barbados population increased to 18,300 white males and 6,400 African slaves in the mid-1640s.[19] The island was to receive increasingly large supplies of black slaves, their numbers reaching 134,500 between 1640 and 1700.[20] In another, related, respect early landowning patterns in Barbados were to repeat themselves in other colonies (relatively small white populations; high owner absenteeism; large black slave labour force). This profile exacerbated the vulnerabilities of the Creole class; in combination these factors directly affect our understanding of Ligon's, Grainger's and Beckford's constructions of their publics and of their affinities to them; likewise the factors clarify the peculiar nature of Lewis' relation to that class, and why his literary and seigneurial behaviour stands so sharply at odds with antecedent publicity patterns.

In the early years of colonization, the pattern was to encourage immigration of all those opportunity-hungry groups (beggars, transported felons, the idle, the adventurous, assorted fortune-seekers), mostly white people of poor to middling status. Most went as indentured servants, providing the labour on smallholdings, eventually becoming smallholders in their own right at the fulfilment of their indenture. As sugar proved its profitability, wealthier planters increasingly appropriated these smallholders' plots, such that in Barbados between 1640 and 1660 (the first twenty years of sugar cultivation), the number of white landowners declined from 11,200 to 745, the number of white men from 18,300 to 8,300, with a corresponding rise in black slaves from 5,680 to 82,023, until by the 1680s the number of sugar planters had dwindled to some 200. Eric Williams in *Capitalism and Slavery* describes this shift thus: 'King Sugar had begun his depredations, changing flourishing common-wealths of small farmers into vast sugar factories owned by a Camarillo of absentee capitalist magnates and worked by a mass of alien proletarians.'[21] A similar displacement was replicated in Jamaica: according to J. R. Ward, 'by about 1750 about 500 individuals with more than half a million acres between them had appropriated most of Jamaica's useful land'.[22]

The inclusion of a French and a Scottish author in this study makes for some significant conceptual contrasts and relationships. Rochefort's presence could be justified on the general ground that these early colonizing documents, in their function as prospecting instruments for particular imperial objectives at the metropole, and as publicity texts for narrower interests within, persistently make direct (and oblique) references to the competitive relationships of their rivals. Rochefort's *Histoire* and Schaw's *Journal* reflect the continual rivalry of their nations for absolute control over St Christopher. Though separated by well over a century, those works oscillate back and forth as national fortunes fluctuated in that colony. More than any of the six, these two authors' close identifica-tion with the competing imperialist objectives of their respective metropoles is an essential factor in the construction of attitudes to Creole culture and its thematic valency in each text. As the only French author represented here, Rochefort is present,moreover, not merely for the variety or contrast his text might bring to an otherwise Anglophone study, but also because the publication date of his work situates him as a significant link between Ligon and Grainger. More importantly, the extended title of his work includes both Barbados and St Christopher, pushing itself into that arena already heavily crowded with English and Spanish authors, clearing for itself a space to prefigure the emerging challenge France was to pose to British political and economic hegemony in the lesser Antilles, and especially to British dominance in the sugar trade.[23] Situated between Grainger (incidentally, a fellow Scot) and Beckford, two confirmed Creole apologists, Schaw makes a studied assertion of British legitimacy in St Christopher and inserts her own Scottish essentialism to cement the union of aims and identities.

Sugar production commenced in St Christopher around 1647 and in Martinique and Guadeloupe in the 1670s. This activity placed the French settlements in direct competition with English plantations, and the corresponding increase in both white French settlers and black slaves to work the plantations brought them into open hostilities with the indigenous Carib populations.[24] For a five-year period immediately preceding the date of Rochefort's book, the French were engaged in a war for living space with the Caribs: the security of their tenure was continually challenged between 1642 and 1661.[25] To add to their distractions during the 1660s, too, their attentions and resources were also divided by war with the English over possession of Dominica.[26]

In spite of such resistance and hostilities, French populations grew in the early seventeenth century to meet the increasing demands of sugar cultivation and trade. About seven thousand Frenchmen emigrated to the Lesser Antilles.[27] Thanks to the able direction of Colbert, the powerful minister of Marine and director of colonial affairs, those numbers rose to 47,321 by the time of his death.[28]

Estimated at 12,000,000 lbs in 1674, sugar production rose to 18,000,000 lbs in 1682; sugar refineries numbered approximately twenty-nine in France and five in the islands.[29] Once more in the French case, as in the English, the inextricable link between sugar and slavery caused a sharp decrease in the number of white settlers and a corresponding increase in the number of black slaves. As the rapid development of sugar cultivation depleted soils in Barbados, the French islands gained in ascendancy: 'Less exhausted than the longer settled English islands, cultivation was easier and the cost of production less. As early as 1663, a mere twenty years after the rise of the sugar industry, Barbados was decaying fast and the complaints of soil exhaustion grew more numerous and more plaintive.' In 1717 Barbados needed 'five times the number of Negroes and many more head of cattle and horses than the French islands to cultivate a given acreage; one slave in French Saint Domingue was equivalent to four in Jamaica. In 1737 the Barbadian owner of a plantation of one thousand acres, which required a capital investment of fifty thousand pounds, was making a profit of two per cent; a similar plantation in the French islands cost one-sixth as much, and yielded a profit of eighteen per cent.[30] The French islands, so much the focus of Rochefort's interest in the *Histoire*, rose to competitive ascendancy, eventually even surpassing the longer established British colonies' success. By the eighteenth century 'Martinique and Guadeloupe had developed into successful sugar islands'.[31]

Anglo-French conflict over territorial and commercial issues extended from about 1700 to 1815; in 1713 the British won the coveted Asiento, entitling them to almost absolute control of slave-trading on the African coast.[32] Significant issues of this rivalry were contested in the Seven Years War (1756–63), a conflict marking the period covered by Grainger's residency in St Christopher. The centre of gravity was the Caribbean: 'it was there', in the words of Jamaica's leading sugar planter, Alderman William Beckford of London [the cousin of the *Descriptive Account's* author], 'where all our wars must begin and end'. The long see-saw struggle in the Caribbean is sufficient testimony of the importance attached by both Britain and France to that theatre and all that it represented.[33] In 1756 St Christopher had a population of 2,713 whites and 21,891 Africans. Eighteen years later the familiar sugar colony pattern had set in: the white population had declined to 1,900 while the black had increased to 23,462.[34]

Grainger's *Sugar Cane* was published against the backdrop of the critical consequences of that war's end. It appeared in a decade identified by some historians as marking the start of organized opposition to the slave trade. Slave revolts broke out in neighbouring Nevis in 1761, in Surinam in 1763 and in Jamaica in 1765. In the world of ideas, the Quakers passed two resolutions in 1761 and 1763 enjoining severe penalties against slaveholding Friends. In the intervening year Anthony Benezet, also a Quaker and an eminent anti-slavery intellectual, published *A Short Account of that Part of Africa Inhabited by Negroes*. This and subsequent works were to have far-reaching effect on the principal abolitionists. As plantation economies began to decline in the British colonies, planter elites suffered a weakening of their political power and economic security. These contingencies offered an opening to the anti-slavery forces whose rising influence inserted themselves into Grainger's consciousness as subtle and persistent sources of division and contestation.[35]

Ten years later, in 1774, the year Janet Schaw left Scotland to travel to Antigua and St Christopher, and William Beckford returned to Jamaica, British public opinion was further quickened by a major landmark court ruling by Lord Mansfield that slavery was contrary to British law. The judgment delivered in the Somerset case (June 1772) dealt a severe blow to Creole legitimacy, for it denied Creoles any legal standing to recapture slaves who seized the chance to break for freedom while accompanying their owners in England. On arrival in Jamaica, Beckford found a colony suffering from widespread soil depletion. The American Revolution brought with it food shortages that led to starvation and death among the slave populations in Jamaica as well as other islands. The war divided planter attitudes between dissent on issues related to taxation and defence on the one hand, and their prescriptive loyalty to the home government on the other. Janet Schaw would hint at the former in her allusion to the reimportation of refined sugars for fashionable consumption in the colonies, and she would manifest her resistance to American aspirations for independence in the North Carolina part of her journal. The year of Beckford's return to England saw the formation there of the Abolition Society (May 1787). In November the legislative campaign spearheaded by Wilberforce and his abolitionist colleagues was begun: altogether more than a hundred petitions were received urging the cessation of the infamous trade.[36]

By the time of Monk Lewis' first visit to Jamaica in 1815, the number of such yearly abolitionist petitions in England had grown to an average of 900. The Abolition Act had been passed eight years earlier. France had overthrown its monarchy in the Revolution of 1789. In the Caribbean, unrest and instability had erupted in a full-scale revolt in 1791 in Saint Domingue, culminating in the declaration of independence for the new republic of Haiti in 1804. Some of the Jamaican planters' worst fears and the slaves' most fervent hopes must have seemed fully realized in the Maroon War of 1795.

As a critique of cultural practice, negotiation will be shown to be intricately constructed and widely ramified among a number of related theoretical approaches to issues of colonization, empire, creolization, cultivation and the rich figurations of language in which these processes inscribe themselves. As defined in this study, negotiation is inextricably bonded to questions of desire and value. It might be useful here, then, to sum up those questions in such a way as to demonstrate how closely its political, economic and social manifestations are inscribed in some of the major theoretical writings on which this analysis will draw.

The manifestations referred to above all contextualize the several fronts on which the Creole struggle to win and secure cultural legitimacy was waged. Viewed in synthetic relationship to the cultural theories drawn upon later, negotiation may be reduced to two major functions. The first illustrates its use in penetrating the space of metropolitan culture, saturating it with the epistemologies of colonization and its particular productive underpinnings in sugar. In this expression, it effects a reciprocal favour, colonizing the metropole with Creole desire and colonial ethics. The second is evidenced in the representation of sugar as matter and metaphysic, a substance potent enough to transform not only consumptive patterns but also to alter perceptions and invent new aesthetic and imaginative space.

Defined in the language of pursuit and struggle, the negotiations by which these texts model symbolic action encode the very lucid historical archaeology Anthony Pagden performs in his *Lords of all the World*. There these questions of value are traced back to their ancient and modern sources and reduced to the central question, as Pagden frames it: 'how to sustain certain kinds of cultural value over time'.[37]

That issue emerges very early in the conceptual design of this study: Ligon's preoccupations with the foreignness and novelty of life and landscape opens up a narrative of epistemological expansion while also proposing creolized solutions (this pattern persists from Ligon to Lewis). Similar occurrences have been given extensive attention in cultural studies from Kolodny (1975) to Pratt (1986).[38] While these very valuable contributions concentrate on North America and Africa, the present study complements and extends the field by supplying a long-unwritten chapter for the colonial West Indies. Where they focus on the strategies of erasure and exclusion, *Sweete Negotiation*, by virtue of its definitive concern with sugar and the heterogeneous bodies linked to its production, reveals how such bodies collude to infiltrate and defy those strategies.

My theory of negotiation pays due respect to the totalizing tendencies of imperialist desire. But my reading of these early colonizing texts privileges the desiderative rather than the naturalizing voice of colonialist discourse, emphasizing the persistent interrogation of antithetical constituents (African slaves and Carib indigenes). Mediated by negotiation, the superordinate power of colonizing is continually contested by those antithetical factors: Caribs and Africans are always elusive, never attaining total presence, therefore never accommodating themselves to full apprehension. Together they ensure that Creole desire is always problematized and decidedly contested. One additional factor in the definition of negotiation's antithetical character must be acknowledged here. It is the very egoism of the authors themselves. That trait is especially acute at the terminal points of the study, where Ligon confronts the challenges of settlement and Lewis the resistances of a mature system. In the middle, Schaw opposes her own nationalist chauvinism and the presumptions of her class to the pretensions of creolization. Persistently riven by their own subjective anxieties, the authors (Grainger and Beckford notably in this respect) mirror the fragile, uncertain prestige of an emerging resident elite.

These egoistic positionings engender certain striking effects when placed in historical and political confrontation with subject groups in colonial settings. There are cogent enough warrants for defining colonialist authorial egos on the one side, and African slaves and Carib indigenes on the other, as antithetical (even dialectical) forces. We could begin with the considerable body of critical discourse, spread widely across the human sciences, that bears persuasive testimony to the persistence of allegorical constructions in historical narrative. A major source for this approach are the theories of Hayden White, which demonstrate that historiographical narratives typically yield a meaning 'other' than that expressed in their linear chronicling of events. I shall attempt to understand the problem of this 'other' and its elusiveness by extrapolating from Michel De Certeau's ethnographic theories that the object of the narrative discourses in question may be attainable only within symbolic and metaphoric structures (I shall argue that collusion is one such structure). For my argument that the figuring of heterogeneous bodies in creolizing and creolized narrative structures is socially symbolic and discursively significant, I find apposite foundation in Louis Mink's theory that the propensity of narrative to figure bodily economies is a 'cognitive function' whose purpose is 'not just to relate a succession of events but to body forth an ensemble of interrelationships of many different kinds as a single whole'. Edward Said's propositions about how 'exile, immigration and the crossing of boundaries' work to produce 'new narrative forms' supply a partial buttress for my mediatory approach to the familiar constructions of exclusion and erasure: Said's theory intimates that my texts may be uncoupled from their links with conventional history and conventional interpretation, and redefined at their intersection with Vlad Godzich's formulations about the repeated shifting of subject-object relations from one 'hegemonic mode of cognition to another'. Lewis' modelling of displacement both in himself and in his reform of institutional structures enacts a concrete gesture of this shifting. To understand certain key terms of order informing Rochefort's notions of natural and moral history, I shall explore the extent to which the historical nature of these texts may be recovered via Roland Barthes' position that conflict exercises a 'collusive power' to yield a profound version of history. By deriving inferential extensions of Godzich's hegemony and modes of cognition, and intersecting the same with Barthes' profound version of history, Lewis' situation at a point of crisis in West Indian Creole history and at the terminal point of this study can be more efficiently negotiated out of mere romantic enigma or egoistic indulgence.

The reference to 'collusive power' leads to my second category of negotiation, collusion. While the linear logic of this study tends towards evolution and transformation *over time*, it will be critical to recognize the tendency of negotiation as a creolizing function, uniquely related to Caribbean cultural history, to shift and play even as it seems to aim for stable essence. Edouard Glissant, the eminent Caribbean intellectual and theorist, elucidates this tendency, located in the mythic values of the Caribbean as place, by defining the essential local ethos of the Caribbean as a place of 'dissensus', 'the sea that diffracts'.[39] That dissensus and that diffraction are uniquely creolizing factors. Collusion is the distinctive formation of negotiation in which this ethos is produced. And though I locate its central formation in Rochefort, it may be shown to be present as early as in Ligon's work.

Together with other colonialist authors, Ligon, his contemporaries and successors, pursue a myth informed and empowered by the characteristic flux of the *negotium* and well suited to the perceived imperatives of culture-making. Homi Bhabha calls these pursuits 'strategies of naturalization and cultural assimilation which make our readings unwillingly collusive and profoundly uncritical'.[40] Bhabha therefore anticipates my second category of negotiation both in naming the strategies as applied to critical attitude and in providing a caveat against a reading that might otherwise collude in the mimicry.

Colonizer in its own right, mimicry persists, embedding itself in the third category of negotiation, the aesthetics of a crisis subsumed chiefly in georgic, picturesque and sublime discourses. Constituted as colonial subjects, these authors pursue their defined desires to comprehend, translate and even transform the colonized 'other' by deploying these discourses as containment practices or revisionist aesthetics. In the first three texts Bhabha's familiar axiom 'almost the same but not quite' unmasks the extent to which the desire for hegemonic authority is contained (restricted). Mimicry and hybridity unfold the doubleness that marks georgic praxis: they inhere in those insoluble enigmas that diffract Grainger's vision, and they persist in Beckford as a struggle between the constraints the Jamaican land-scape impose upon his consciousness and the Creole designs he pursues, forcing him to alternate between georgic and picturesque modes in different parts of his *Descriptive Account*. Barbara Bono's observations on literary imitations and their relationship to destabi-lization and transvaluation are especially apposite to this struggle as it is experienced in *The Sugar Cane* and the *Descriptive Account*.[41] Thomas Kent suggests the potential of the georgic label to hybridize and mask itself in collusion with other genres.[42] Such filiations of critical and theoretical methodologies will illuminate how the aes-thetic practices of these texts are made to serve larger cultural ends, how the texts' ostensible objects become obscured by strategic digressions or outright retreats to ideology.

It would have been difficult to talk about the relationship between the embedding of ideological objectives in aesthetic discourse without invoking Terry Eagleton. His insistence that aesthetic discourses contain within themselves a broader range of social, political and ethical issues is borne out pre-eminently in Rochefort's collusions; in the full scheme of the present study they produce these texts as ideological negotiations.[43]

At the intersection of my negotiation critique and Eagleton's thesis stands the very important contribution of Kurt Heinzelman to georgic scholarship. As that critic so lucidly demonstrates, when traced back rigorously to its Roman roots, georgic makes a striking departure from a simple loose association with pastoral and didactic purposes, vindicating Terry Eagleton's thesis. Georgic evinces a resistant attraction not simply to the activities of agriculture and work in general, but also to the politics and ideology of these activities within the human sphere. Kurt Heinzelman enumerates three premises about the way georgic manifests and transfigures itself in eighteenth-century practice. One of these, which he calls 'entailments' of the form, stresses georgic's enabling, originary power and its capacity to generate myths of civilization. These 'entailments' hold obvious coherence with my conceptual principles here because they define georgic's potential to generate 'diverse strategies for negotiating poetry's public role of defining cultural values'.[44] The close coincidence of this analysis with the one I am applying to the discourse on civilization in colonizing narratives is of critical consequence to this study. Alastair Fowler's essay on the beginnings of English georgic and Annabel Patterson's study of pastoral literature illuminate some of the dimmer pathways encountered in trying to understand georgic's deeper political and cultural bearings.[45]

Its specific European references notwithstanding, the aesthetic of the picturesque proves an invaluable auxiliary to georgic in prosecuting the interests of the landowning elites whose desires animate these texts. Equally with georgic, the picturesque offers itself as an antithetical guarantee, a reactionary praxis that naturalizes the slaves to the landscape of labour and low social privilege while also suppressing and effacing any semblance of particularity or protest on their part. Ann Bermingham's very fine art historical study of the mode in England added clarity and insight to my own recognition of the devices in the specific context of colonizing space.[46]

With Lewis, Creole desire is forced to accommodate itself to the fourth modality of negotiation, a highly individualized romantic desire, differentiated from narrow plantocratic interests, a version of the sublime identified with radical egoism and dissensus. In Monk Lewis' *Journal*, the major evolving themes of anxiety about cultural legitimacy, the concomitant desire for ideal order, political conflict and ideological contestation find a congenial habitation. Both the eighteenth-century traditionalist theorizing of Herder and the modern exposition of Anthony Pagden underline the role that anti-expansionist ideology played in checking imperial aspirations (and by extension colonial–Creole desire). Together, they provide durable buttresses for the evaluation of historical forces already traced in the growth of abolitionism. Though my definition of contestation and production as sites of tension in colonialist texts accords closely with Terry Eagleton's ideas about the distinctive relation of these processes to colonization, the Creole–West Indian context demands specific revisions to his aesthetic theory. By rethinking his inferences about the interaction of ideology with aesthetic, I develop my theory that the focus of Lewis' reformist impulses was directed towards a highly egoistic ideal of order arising from his encounter with the forces of contestation, production and colonization, and that the otherness of his colonial experiences combined in these forces to decentre his subjectivity from its regular ordering principles.

By means of literary critical and theoretical practices my book reaches conclusions similar to those Edward Kamau Brathwaite reaches through historical methods. The Creole impetus toward undiluted cultural construction was effectively stymied by the very problematics of purity in colonized environments. But this book supplies a necessary and substantial antecedent to Brathwaite's study, suggesting, with the significance it assigns to Monk Lewis, the specific negotiations that might have been necessary to reproduce Lewis' tangible, if idiosyncratic, production, on a larger social scale. What Brathwaite elucidated by means of chiefly historical and sociological methods is here amplified and redefined in the light of subsequent critical and theoretical approaches current in literary study. These approaches compel us to theorize an earlier onset for creolization and to see that process through the prism of narratives which assume the important philosophical function of imaginatively building a viable polity out of complex, widely diversified colonial embodiments.

As a discrete literary category, colonial discourse exhibits a remarkable range of themes and variety of forms. Even the most cursory perusal of full titles in any relevant bibliography would be sufficient to intimate the sheer intellectual breadth of some chroniclers and the vaulting ambitions of others. The authors under discussion here are not atypical. Publicists for early West Indian cultural construction, these authors advance similar intellectual ambitions to apprehend, know and make known a new world and the pretensions their Creole publics forged within it. Both publicists and publics are embodied in textual contents which aim to validate new emergent selves, and to stir readers' emulative desire for that emergence and for the attendant processes of knowledge-making, production and consumption. In their broadest ideological significance, the texts really constitute some of the earliest chapters in the construction of a history of ideas for the Caribbean, the beginnings, as Gordon Lewis puts it, of a 'genuine Caribbean historiography, a Caribbean sociology, a Caribbean anthropology . . . a movement of ideas'.[47]

Defining the nature of these texts, then, through the functional concept of 'negotiation', establishes their role in identifiable cultural practices. In Ligon and Rochefort the activity is marked by the incidental practices of ethnographic representation: each text historicizes, in varying degrees of emphasis, the emplacements and displacements of different races in these apppropriated environments. The problematics of negotiating formal authority for text and context are most fully displayed in Grainger and Beckford, for example, as they wrestle with questions of adapting traditional discourses (georgic, picturesque, the sublime) both to claim personal credibility as well to suggest some continuity between an emergent creole culture and the cultures of classical and contemporary Europe. Schaw dissents from this attempt at creolized hybridity by treating that concept with a studied scepticism often bordering on contempt. Her negotiations displace the pattern of continuity with notions of essence and purity that promote decidely British class and colonialist ideologies. In Lewis, by comparison, each expression of those aesthetic practices listed is subjected to forms of ironic subversion or revision: his romantic and revolutionary impulses drive his text to consciously disrupt those Creole master/African slave dichotomies so steadfastly naturalized in the other four writers. While I identify these impulses most centrally and strategically in Lewis' *Journal*, they insinuate themselves often unwittingly, sometimes perversely, in all of the other texts. It is one of my major positions that the whole recurring discourse of bodies in these works is an expression of the overarching cultural desire for a complex mythic body. I read this desire as an idealizing gesture (a reformist impulse in Lewis), whose object was to imagine and invent a veritable alternative social system (Monk Lewis actually implemented his ideal). In their literary emanations these impulses worked to mediate (even destabilize) the increasingly powerful voices of anti-slavery and anti-colonialist opinion in the case of the first four authors, and to supplant Creole pro-slavery publicity by a new colonizing apologetics in the case of Lewis.

Just as the pursuit of material value in the colonies was predicated on maximizing the production of sugar, so the pursuit of cultural value in each work but Schaw's is hinged to the transformation of those raw productive processes into a highly constructed myth of creole civilization. This myth-construction appropriates the sugar cane, its products and processes, to inform and legitimate an emerging category of creole social economy. The present book explains how sugar's sweetness, its universal utility, its vaunted essence and its mythicized perfection shaped a number of discernible variants of utopianism, all of which imagined a harmonious social polity and a philosophical ideal of alternative civilization. In these authors this ideal vision is typically manifested by a preoccupation with purity and perfection, singleness and integrity on the one hand, and with their antitheses, imperfection and putrefaction, on the other. This close connection between modes of cultivation and modes of discourse has been given classic treatment in Herder's reflections on cultural development: it is an apposite coincidence that Herder singles out natural histories as one of the categories typically implicated in this process by which societies emerge from a state of nature to a state of culture.[48]

From Ligon to Rochefort, from Grainger to Beckford, these texts endow the sugar cane with values of purity and perfection; in their rhetorical economy both plant and product are negotiated into aesthetic objects of transcendent mystical properties whose essence was vaunted to produce a wholesome moral economy. Schaw stands alone in diminishing the narrative profile and figurative value of sugar, but invests its beneficiaries with a social and moral worth whose lineage is traceable to the very Creole antecedents she desires to deny.

The pursuit of purity in sugar manufacture itself was always predicated on the triumph of artifice over nature. The Creole pretensions to a culture built on the originary idealism of its 'sweete negotiation' was continually interrogated by the cynicism and snobbery of metropolitan detractors. These disruptions are personified in Ligon's quarrels with West Indian nature, Grainger's struggle with his intractable muse, Schaw's dissent from prevailing Creole orthodoxy, and Beckford's need to aestheticize the horrors of history from his idealized georgic and picturesque landscapes.

CHAPTER I

Ligon: 'sweete negotiation'

In common with so many contemporary examples, the full title of Ligon's *True and Exact History of the Island of Barbadoes* intimates an ambitious project, both by virtue of the scope and the heterogeneity of the matters it promises to cover. In common with other texts sharing this specific identity (colonizing histories, travel, colonization and settlement narratives), Ligon's project signals its distinctive dialogism in the exposition of analyzed contents on its title page as well as in some of the early pages of narrative preceding the author's actual arrival in Barbados. Far away and exotic, the subject location was a natural draw to curious audiences. More compelling still, as we will see in the ensuing chapters, was the text's unusual admixture of the digestible (sugar) with the industrial (the ingenio, or sugar mill), its ordered catalogue of structures related to production (grinding-room, boiling-room, filling-room etc.) and the strategic placement of three allusions to the combined economies of profit and purity so germane to sugar culture. The full value of the desire implicit in that strategy will be more fully appreciated in the forthcoming treatment of the profit–purity relationship as a site on which the credibility of sugar culture (in both its senses)was persistently contested.

Though the voice of this book's organizing principle, 'sweete negotiation', does not appear until rather later on in the actual representation of early plantation life in Barbados, that voice is also prefigured and dialogized in an early part of the narrative where Ligon reveals certain details about the occasions that set him on his travels. Those occasions, too, encode some cunningly interwoven negotiations, mirroring at once motives personal, social (with specific reference to Creole class construction) and national (with specific reference to the larger political, economic and cultural context of contemporary British history).

The various functions of negotiation that will provide the impetus for inquiry in this chapter are to be found, then, in that aggregation of forces attending the text's production and the author's relation to its contents and context. First, the relationship between Ligon's immediate personal history and the larger cultural moment of his country is produced as a moment of crisis for whose resolution negotiation offers a serviceable metaphor of exchange. Insofar as the voice *negotium* is always already polarized, the second structural movement in this chapter will turn on the conflicted problematics of that voice, marked by dichotomy and antagonism. To the very definitive extent that Ligon's history inaugurates the apologetic discourse on the origins of Creole identity and the search for legitimacy mediated by its own anxiety and the denial of its detractors, negotiation will offer a key to tracing cultural foundations and recuperating the forces that subverted those foundations. And because all these intentions converge and seek resolution in the commercial and metaphysical economies of sugar, negotiation is produced in Ligon's work as a mode of symbolic action and as a rhetoric pressed into the service of representing material culture, aspiring to apprehend the aesthetics and metaphysics of that plant described by Ligon himself as 'noble' (202) and 'benign' (51) in its faculties and capable of supplying virtue, purity and health to this emergent cultural entity (87).

As a metaphor for the specific exchanges involved in the relation of Ligon's *History* to a moment of personal crisis and a larger evolving process of cultural change, Ligon manipulates negotiation as a device to re-establish control over his own threatened personal security and to mediate the publicity for a soon-to-emerge political entity (Creole interests) and the cultural exchange (creolization) they would make between the crises they left behind and those they would encounter in sustaining the sugar economies of the West Indies.

The biographical record on Ligon is spare, but this much we know. Like many who embraced the hazards of a sea voyage and the rigours of colonial settlement, Ligon's own report of the circumstances surrounding his visit to Barbados describes a familiar scene of crisis in the narrative of colonizing: having lost his livelihood and material possessions in a 'barbarous riot', Ligon pictured himself as 'stripped and rifled of all I had, left destitute of a substance, and brought to such an Exigent, as I must famish or fly . . . I found myself a stranger in my own countrey'. A refugee from England's post-Civil War turmoil, he attached himself to Thomas Modyford, a Royalist exile, and sailed to Barbados in a ship called *Achilles* on 16 June 1647. The author arrived in Barbados in September to find that fledgling colony barely recovering from a recent plague (some bodies still remained unburied) and gripped in the throes of food shortages (Ligon 21). Notwithstanding these inauspicious conditions, he assisted his patron Modyford to build a highly profitable plantation holding in partnership with another early Barbados settler, William Hilliard. Ligon himself seemed to have reaped less brilliant personal success, for after three years in the colony he returned to England in 1650 to face arrest and imprisonment for debt.

Enfolded in the narrative economy of his account are both his story (replete with obvious classical and biblical resonances) and the history of countless other colonists. In addition, that same narrative economy encodes wider vibrations of political turmoil and radical economic change back at the metropole. In conjunction, they stand as metonyms for the socially constructed nature of Ligon's 'sweete negotiation.'

As the nation struggled in the aftermath of civil war to redefine its identity under a new constitutional dispensation (Cromwell's Commonwealth and Protectorate), social and economic thinkers increasingly reflected on the composition of the body politic, recognizing at once the value of the colonies not only as profitable economic investments but also as social escape valves for persons rendered expendable either by extremities similar to Ligon's or by transgressions that rendered them a risk to the public weal. The Lord Protector himself exploited the very favourable exchange value Barbados provided to the realm: he used that frontier land to expatriate all sorts and conditions of British felons – particularly Irish and Scots – ('to Barbadoes' them, was the euphemism) and in return extract from their planting and industry the produce and taxes so advantageous to the nation's imperial ambitions. One of the earliest instances of excess used for exchange can be found in Ligon's revelation that on board his ship was a consignment of prostitutes from Bridewell prison and Turnbull Street in London, also bound for Barbados.[1]

This is a dramatic foreshadowing of those bodily exchanges that Ligon will detail further on in the *History*; but they are worth noticing here to foreground certain pretextual sources of cultural construction, in effect to mark and qualify the genesis of creolizing community in Barbados. War, exile, social and economic dislocation throw individuals together indiscriminately, disrupting the old rigid structures of class and race that once held them apart. Under such exigencies the givens of life, knowledge and culture are sharply defamiliarized.

The concatenation at this early juncture in the narrative of radical reversals in individual fortunes, of national crisis mediated by colonial opportunity, and colonial growth threatened by natural disaster preconditions the moralized modes in which Ligon couches parts of his narrative. It is out of just such contingencies that dissonance, diffraction and (at least potential) dissensus spring. These argue the necessity of a mediatory structure: in Ligon's *History* that structure is negotiation, which rationalizes and gives them form. From this source may be located the very seeds of nascent creolizing culture.[2]

The etymological and ideological history of the concept 'culture' in Western thought manifests an oscillation between disparate poles not dissimilar to the term 'negotiation'. For 'culture' Raymond Williams unearths both sacred and secular origins. The religious sense of the word derives from the Latin root *colere* (= to worship) which splits one way into *cultus*, to yield the sense of 'honour with worship,' and another into *colonus* (= colony, farmer) to yield the sense of inhabiting and cultivating. Williams synthesizes this disparateness in these words: 'Culture in all its early uses was a noun of process: the tending of something, basically crops or animals.'[3] From this reference to 'tending of natural growth' culture extends to the process of human development, the dominant sense from the eighteenth century onward. What this linguistic archaeology discloses is the use-value:exhange-value economy immanent in the very genealogy of culture, an economy that reproduces itself in the cultural practices of Ligon's *History* (where history is exchanged for the new values of colonizing capitalism) and in Creole desire (where marginality is exchanged for political legitimacy).

The traditional tendency in historical studies has been to define cultural creolization in gradualist terms, predicating its emergence on the accommodations, adaptations and negotiations that colonists must necessarily make with their new environments *over time* before they call it home. Standard definitions also assume the maturation of a few native-born generations to invest the concept with a sense of home- and group-consciousness. However, the presence in Ligon of certain actions (objective and symbolic), structures (concrete and aesthetic) and thematic preoccupations with direct relevance to identity and cultural consciousness in early colonial Barbados makes more compelling this book's premise of an earlier onset of Creole formations.

'Sweete negotiation' wears that identity and consciousness as a proud publicity slogan, imaging the sheer pleasure of individual experience extrapolated to the consumption ethos of a whole class. The consumption is advertised for its own sake but more importantly for its value as emulative consumption, for the value it rendered in raising the cultural stock of Creoles on a veritable frontier economy. In addition to the demographic categories discussed earlier, this display is to be witnessed in both the verbal and pictorial representation of life, in advertising the economies of nature and business. Ligon's first impression of Carlisle Bay, the main commercial shipping port, paints a scene of bustling purpose and enterprise, of boats 'so quick, stirring and numerous as I have seen it below the bridge at London' (21). The apparent intent of the comparison is to place the colonial harbour on a parity of prestige with its larger metropolitan counterpart. This assimilation of small to great encodes a significant gesture in staking Creole claims, placing the narrative fully within the text of relations McKeon calls the 'homogenization of use values' (215).[4] The gesture is extended to this picture of the flourishing beauty and vegetative harmony of nature in Barbados producing an image of that 'wealth, beauty and all harmony in that Leviathan, a well govern'd commonwealth where the might, Men and rulers of the earth, by their prudent and careful protection, secure them from harms' (Ligon, pp. 20–1).

The signs of emulation are even more richly encoded in the cataloguing of creature comforts, an unabashed publicity for the enviable style and standard of living available to immigrants: the following gastronomic display advertises all manner of beverages, familiar and exotic, and a sumptuous variety of food (reportedly only one course from a typical planter's feast [in this case, Colonel Drax's]):

A Rump boyl'd, a Chine roasted, a large piece of breast roasted, the cheeks baked, of which is a dish to either mess, the tongue and part of the tripes minc'd for Pyes, season'd with sweet Herbs finely minc'd, suet, spice, and currans; the legs, Pallets and other ingredients for an *olio Podrido* to either mess, a dish of marrow bones, so here are fourteen dishes at the Table and all of Beef. (Ligon 38)

And as if this were not evidence enough of variety, he further lists these additional meats for the emulative public's consumption: pork, boar, bacon, turkeys, chicken, duck, fish, custards, cheese cakes, puffs. To secure the due and proper valorization of the Creole colony in the new liberal world ethic of trade and commerce, he takes pains to enumerate the diverse countries of origin for consumer staples imported into Barbados: beef from Holland, from Old and New England, Virginia and some from Russia, cod, mackerel, neat's tongue, pickled herrings from New England and pickled turtle from the Leeward Islands (37). And so the text deploys this negotiation to publicize the altogether flourishing prospects of this growing colony, while at the same time identifying the place with the larger interests and historical process of England's growing imperial power. This places negotiation squarely in the vanguard of that process of secularization which McKeon calls 'the cheerful challenge of the marketplace' (215).

The indisputable motives located in this rhetoric of the colonizing advertisement campaign underscore the continual appeal these texts make to the metropolitan audience: to stir the hunger of prospective settlers, and to awaken the envy and respect of metropolitan readers for the cultural project under construction. Catalogues like the above have a way of altering perceptions and expanding desire. Those that detailed the taste, uses and products of sugar itself not only stirred hunger and fomented consumer markets, transforming culinary habits and gustatory appetites, they also, as we shall see later, penetrated aesthetic space and raised imaginative possibilities. The striking self-consciousness about the rewards of bourgeois enterprise in the New World and the use of textual stimuli to excite consumptive responses have been remarked in Defoe's colonial narratives: Shinagel's critical comments in reference to Robinson Crusoe serve to place in clear historical context this reproduction of the marked pleasure of consumption, possession and security expressed in Ligon:

Defoe's prose betrays his [Crusoe's] self-consciousness about terming Crusoe's plantation an 'estate' but the idea of having a plantation worth thousands of pounds was a delicious concept to contemplate, particularly when the overseas plantation was the equivalent of an English estate worth 1000 pounds a year . . . Defoe employed the colonial theme as a way of showing his middle and lower class readers how they could better their fortunes, regardless of their ancestry or birth, through industry. . .[5]

The authenticating practices Ligon uses to argue Barbados' value to England were transparent enough. His optimism for the colony's thriving and potential successful growth was a glowing one. In one of his common rhapsodic effusions he declares that by 1650 sugar had become the 'soul of Trade in this Island', attributing to its economic success the rise of property values in the island, and citing the particular example of Hilliard's plantation, which increased its 1647 value from £400 to £7,000, the value of half of the plantation in less than five years (87).

In hard economic terms, the most astute observers conceived the nexus of bodies constituting the colonies and maintaining the supply lines between them and the political centre as a single comprehensive economy. The anonymous author of *The Present State of the British Sugar Colonies Consider'd*,[6] in a vigorous and reasoned admonition against excessive taxation on the trade, showed plainly that sugar produced mainly by slave labour in remote colonial locations provided work for ship-owners and their families, factors, shipbuilders, ropemakers, sailmakers, and other shipping trades – besides many thousands of poor artificers and manufacturers in Britain (24). Jacques Bellin, naval engineer, cartographer and Inspector of the Royal Academy, prospecting the British islands for intelligence useful to the French imperialist information order, recorded the impressive contribution the small island of Barbados made to the national wealth of England (that colony's input grew sharply from 46 million pounds sterling between 1636 and 1656, to 138 million between 1676 and 1756, adding an overall total of 276 million pounds in that 120-year span): 'This trade gives employment to seamen, merchants, works of all kinds.' One English author affirmed the truth of Barbados' disproportionate value thus: 'This little island is for our nation an abundant mine of gold; it has fed endless mouths, kept busy great fleets, employed extraordinary numbers of seafaring men, expanded considerably the national wealth of England.'[7]

If the value of this young and thriving colony was not lost on him, Ligon wanted to be sure that his production of history would serve to impress that value on readers, policy-makers, would-be immigrants and would-be detractors.

The narrative selection of content reconfigures negotiation as a mode of symbolic action. The search for value is taken to another level, negotiated by a similar pattern of exchange mediation. In a very neat crystallizing of sugar's qualities in the manner and conditions of its production, Ligon apprehended the precise talisman he needed to invent the transcendent value he desired. Desirable in its sweetness and universal in its utility, sugar's natural body could be exchanged, at the level of rhetoric, into an object of mythic, essential purity. In Ligon this myth of purity is always structurally related to the erotic. As a structure for imagining Creole identity, sweete negotiation is already complexly eroticized, both at the level of figured language and at the level of literal objective reference. Ligon demonstrates that the negotiation could be sweetened from the widest selection of sources available in the immediate landscape of the exotic. David Richards in *Masks of Difference* recovers from related colonial narratives their use of conventional forms 'as a means of domesticating the erotic.'[8] I find this insight remarkably apposite – and not only for its direct correspondence with my own theoretical proceedings. An exchange of this order is contained in one of those pre-textual scenes from the Cape Verdes; stricken with sexual desire for the bodies of pubescent African females, the white male subject transforms their presence into an almost fetishized fixation. The young 'Negro virgins' struck him as 'creatures, of such shapes, as would have puzzled Albrecht Dürer, the Great Master of Proportion, but to have imitated, and Titian or Andrea del Sarto, for softness of muscles, and curiositie of colouring'. He spends a further page and a half rapt in eroticized gazing at twin sisters

wanton as the soyle that bred them, sweet as the fruits they fed on . . . [such] young Beauties force, and so commit rapes upon our affections. In summe had not my heart been fixed fast in my breast, and dwelt there above sixty years, and therefore loath to leave his long kept habitation, I had undoubtedly left it between them for a Legacy. For so equal were there Beauties and my Love, as it was not nor could be, particular to either. (17)

This scene will reproduce itself as a subsequent revision later, as similar bodies are revalued for slave labour and aesthetic purposes. But Richards is suggestive too for the way in which Ligon inverts his reading of how colonial discourses '[transform]cultural and sexual difference into modes familiar and digestible'. In sugar and sugar culture Ligon transforms what is fast becoming familiar and digestible into the transcendent and the mythic.

Sugar offers Ligon a complex signifying system that assimilates both the imagery and material facts of the enterprise, novelty and plenitude of a creolizing locality into the corpus of European symbolic consciousness and imaginative economy. In this aspect, negotiation may be seen as a mode whose function is to infiltrate (to colonize) the familiar epistemologies of the metropole with those very features of novelty, exoticism and plenitude particular to the colony. By that act of reciprocal colonizing, the forms and usages of plantation life could be displayed and indefinitely reproduced textually both within individual consciousness and within the received discursive practices (by the numerous official, literary and ethnographic sources who typically exchanged these 'true and exact' accounts for wider imperial purposes). This negotiation enables those subsequent uses of its textual body one encounters in diverse disciplines: in economics, subserving imperialist desires and enhancing colonial aspirations,[9] in a variety of texts reflecting on the potential of plantation infrastructures to serve as proving grounds for emergent ideas about social, economic and materialist formation,[10] and generally for rhetoricizing modes of practice and belief which at Ligon's 'creolizing moment' were as yet un-incorporated into the mainstream of orthodox thought.[11]

And this constant originary element that now so absorbs Ligon, as the first author in this study, will extend through and beyond the remaining five writers of our immediate interest into the work of Fernando Ortiz, whose *Contrapunteo del Tabaco y Azucar* (*Cuban Counterpoint*) certainly ranks as the most philosophically significant work to deepen and amplify the tradition.

Ortiz elaborated the first comprehensive critique of the semiotics and metaphysics of sugar and their relevance to social formation. Though grounded in the specific historical conditions that made sugar a seminal force in the development of Cuban society, Ortiz's work treats sugar and tobacco as complex signifying systems, 'visceral' forces in the historical formation of the Cuban economy. The *Contrapunteo* constructs sugar as a profoundly resonant signifying body within a universe of social, moral and political signs. Ortiz systematically and definitively interprets the production of sugar as a master signifier whose signs could be shown to permeate the entire body politic of producers and consumers.[12] It is precisely those semiotic values of the plant, of its productive processes and of its manufactured body that are prefigured in Ligon's negotiations for a definitive Creole social form in early colonial Barbados.

The moralized modes referred to earlier find significant expression in Ligon's search for a myth of purity on which to found his cultural vision. Endued by the creator with the perfection of all sweets, 'this noble plant' is extolled for its efficacy as a source of virtue and purity. Sugar is credited with a 'virtue' of promoting and enhancing economic as well as physical well-being: 'As this plant has a faculty to *preserve* all fruits, that grow in the world, *from corruption and putrifaction*; so it has a *vertue*, being rightly applied, to preserve us men in our *healths and fortunes* too' (emphasis mine). The italicized words are typical of Ligon's rhapsodic claims for the plant; their oscillation between the *neg* of putrifaction and impurity and the *otium* of preserving 'healths and fortunes' situates sugar culture at that boundary between the old alchemical pursuit and the new secularizing exchange. Their conflation of anxieties about physical wholeness and personal economic integrity (financial solvency) suggests the invention of a new panacea. Inherent in the myth of purity is the issue of human agency. The myth of purity is by definition a highly constructed concept. Creolized structures are always already compromised by hybridity. Thus the question of human agency is highly contestable.

From among a category first eroticized in the Cape Verde Islands, and later in Barbados rejected as aethetically undesirable, Ligon makes a paradoxically deliberate selection of the 'cleanliest of slave women' for work around the cane mill and in the processes that clarify the canejuice and crystallize the sugar. This appropriation is at once consistent with the historical roles women played as primary producers for the colonizing machine and also with certain well-defined anthroplogical functions in the production of culture. In mythicizing the meaning of women as producers, Ligon performs a ritual gesture that would appear to bear some symbolic relation to Mary Douglas' explanation of the way purity and impurity rituals create cultural order: this abstraction of the women from the category of contempt and defilement approximates what she calls 'a creative movement, an attempt to relate form to function, to make unity of experience'.[13] A similar gesture undertaken for similar purposes has been remarked in Aphra Behn's treatment of Imoinda in *Oroonoko*, another foundational text in the discourse of colonizing cultures of the West Indies. Richards writes, 'Behn softens the presence of

Imoinda's body. Her erotic strangeness, sensuous and patterned, is
domesticated; her exotic and erotic threat is redefined as virginal
purity . . . Behn's text transforms Imoinda's cultural and sexual
difference into the model of European artistic production.'[14] In
Ligon, the racializing of sugar's body exists in tandem with an
emphatic gendering of the 'sweete negotiation'. In Ortiz 'sugar is *she;*
tobacco is he . . . if tobacco is male, sugar is female'.[15] One further
parallel links this reproduction of sugar as superordinate myth with a
larger colonialist myth in which precious commodities are ascribed
metaphysical value in exchange for colonial respect. Just as sugar was
used as specie (an exchange currency), and reconceived in the
language of alchemy, a mystical rhetoric appropriated to serve an idea
of cultural integrity, so, Anthony Pagden reminds us, the Spaniards
and others between the fifteenth and seventeenth centuries invented
an 'eschatological association between gold and godliness'.[16]

This desire for an ideal of cultural purity in a manifestly hybrid
environment carries with it the seeds of its own contestation. The
foregrounding of slavery, labour and the processes of production in
the narrative occasions anxieties similar to those intimated in the
discussion of slave women. Nostalgia, guilt and moral compromise
enmesh the very authorial self in the antithetical trammels (the *neg*
pole) of the text's negotiations. Factors of landscape difference,
heterogeneous human bodies and an authorial self indivisibly identified with Creole cultural aspirations bring even that self's presumptively purer objectives of imagining a revisionist aesthetic under
hopeless subversive threat.

But this very positing of cultural foundations in close identification
with the slave body and with emergent modes of industrial production brings the *History* into violent collision with sources of
division and conflictedness inherent in its very object. In Ligon's
most fulsome enthusiasm may be located the very seeds of social self-
doubt, the nascent fears about cultural contamination which were to
intensify in succeeding authors.

Some of the most profound anxieties that divided Creole
consciousness originated in the sources of corruption and degeneration the Creole classes feared would dissolve their culture and its
pretensions. From those very female slave bodies abstracted for the
pursuit of cultural purity would spring anxieties about their proximity to Creole perceptual consciousness. While, judged by Dürer's
standards, the male slave physique earned Ligon's approval, the

African female (slave) form, on the contrary, drew a critique markedly less flattering. The size of their hips, their young women's breasts ('which stand strutting out so hard and firm') and the breasts of mature women who had borne so many children 'their breasts hang down below their navels so that when they stoop at their common work of weeding, they hang almost down to the ground, that at a distance, you would think they had six legs . . .' (51) – all these drew mixed reviews of lust and loathing. What would at least by Grainger's time become the subject of anti-saccharite polemic (anti-slavery political agitation against sugar consumption based on sugar's pollution by human wastes) is in Ligon refigured as an anxiety about the proximity of the sweating odoriferous female slave body to Creole aesthetic sensibility, associated in his mind with the potential for producing authentic culture.

There [in Barbados] the bodies of women are so sweaty and clammy as the hand cannot pass over, without being glued and cemented in the passage or motion; and by that means little pleasure is given to, or received by the agent or patient: and therefore if this sense be neither pleased in doing nor suffering, we may decline it as useless in a country, where down of swans or wool of beaver is wanting. (107)

But lest this might be thought a prejudice the historian held exclusively against African slave women, it must be observed that Ligon found colonial West Indian climates especially harsh on all female bodies: in his refined sensory estimation those bodies diminished in value to the degree that intense tropical heat rendered them less attractive as objects of male desire and hence of broad social respect. This part of Ligon's *History* is marked by an explicit ambivalence about the relative capacity of different natural sources in England and Barbados to heighten physical sensation and nurture aesthetic sensibility. Ligon's compulsion to enumerate and categorize differentially the values implicit in these sources reflects the colonist's deeply ingrained anxieties over the nature of colonial identity and its cultural legitimacy.

Those grotesque images of misshapen female slave bodies bring Ligon's aesthetic close to phantasmagoria. At the same time, it must be noted that the physical attributes so negotiated placed these constituents of Creole culture decidedly beyond the pale of Dürer's ideal feminine forms: the aesthetic anxiety could be normalized within common racial attitudes. Since a critical objective of the male gaze in such colonial contexts is to secure hegemony (and here clearly the desire is to cement Creole cultural integrity), this production of failed desire profoundly disrupts the notion of a civil polity founded on an economy of the 'desire for sweete things'.[17]

Here the anxiety is displayed as a desire to separate the cultural ideal from one of its constitutive elements. This disgust for the slave body can be viewed in the wider terms of bourgeois capitalist ideology. Francis Barker shows this behaviour to be common in the textual practices of bourgeois formation, where the writing self endeavours to separate the material self 'silently but efficiently from the spectacle, covering its own traces, the bourgeois subject substitutes for its corporeal body, the rarefied body of the text' (62).[18] This behaviour also has its mirror image in the absentee Creole landlords' dissociation of themselves from the physical space of the slavocracy and the corrupt body of sugar. Back home in Europe the Creoles recuperate all these by reconstituting them for their own exaggerated status as fetishized signs and codings on the body of the slave.[19]

At the colonial scene of production, the deployment of slave and indentured servant bodies in direct juxtaposition to the machinery of production further problematizes Creole cultural pretensions. The labour-intensive nature of sugar production argued its value and respect, but also laid the ground for the subterranean forms of 'agonising conflict' and dissensus.[20] This passage from Thomas Tryon stages the scene as one of conflict between persistent human labour and insatiable mechanistic appetite: 'the servants night and day stand in the great boiling houses, where there are six or seven large coppers or furnaces kept perpetually boiling and from which with heavy ladles and skimmers, they skim off the excrementitious parts of the canes till it comes to its perfection and cleanness, which others as Stoakers, Broil, as it were, in managing the fires; and one part is constantly at the mill, to supply it with canes, night and day, during the whole Season of making sugar; which is about six months in the year'.[21] Tryon's pictorialization captures in one place all those disparate and dissonant energies contributive to culturing sugar. Virtuous industry produced capitalist value but that value was earned only in ironic juxtaposition to violence. The pure body of sugar is achieved only by abstraction from its 'excrementitious particles', but some of those impurities are inseparable from lower grades of sugar and rum. Purity and impurity coexist equally in the production of economic value. Purity and impurity equally engender Creole anxious desire for culture.

Keith Ellis lists three categories of images sugar generates in Caribbean literature: the pragmatic, the idealist and the dialectical. Associating sugar's figured body with 'several levels of ambivalence' and with 'pervasive oxymoron,' Ellis hints at something of the anxiety it engendered in the principal parties to its production: 'Sugar also irritates by the intensive labour it demands and by its occupation of the best lands.'[22] Tryon's vision, then, dramatizes a 'dialectical' struggle between the dissonant energies situated at either pole of the *negotium* and mediated by Ligon's aesthetic preoccupations.

The picture of servants standing 'night and day in the great boiling houses' tending huge coppers (cauldrons), and of 'stoakers' being broiled 'as it were alive, in managing the fires' transmutes the scene of sugar manufacture into an enshrining allegory of violence and sacrifice. Here the categorical function of negotiation is to exchange the sacred for the secular, and to accommodate oscillation between the two: a solid demonstration of Rene Girard's contention that the notion of sacrifice '[applies] to even larger arenas of human activity' than literally construed.[23]

In the reflective parts of Ligon's *History*, the discourse normalizes oppression and violence as the linchpins of Creole plantation culture. The author's distaste for the pains and disfigurements slaves suffered at the hands of overseers arises less from any sense of moral outrage than from his anxiety for the survival of sensibility itself in what he calls an ethos of 'coercive feeling' (107). Girard writes: 'Cultural artifacts are structured so as to hide the mechanisms of violence, and the mechanisms are designed so as to conceal themselves' (7).

Normalization, then, works together with sundry other coded evasions to produce another mode of negotiation in Ligon's text. We shall return to it, deployed under changed circumstances, but for essentially congruent purposes, in Rochefort's ethnographic discourse.

Massy and powerful, the great mill rollers stand as the incarnate signs of an implacable god, to whom slaves feed ritual stalks of sugar cane. The great boiling houses are temples of sacrifice, the cauldrons sacred vessels, the stokers vestals and votaries, some standing in ceaseless offering and adoration, others destined to become the unwilling human victims of this all-consuming capitalist engine. All of these signs and ceremonies embody disciplinary regimes in which the body itself is the controlling intelligence, harnessed to yield of itself and to extract from other bodies economic value, to offer its limbs and, if need be, its very life in the ultimate sacrifice. Both Michel Foucault in his *Discipline and Punish* and H. Orlando Patterson in his magisterial work *Slavery and Social Death* have defined the meanings the body yields under major forms of coercion and duress. By the light of Foucauldian analysis, slavery may be seen as a 'machinery of power', one of those 'strict powers' which impose upon the body 'constraints, prohibitions or obligations'.[24] Patterson's comparative method elucidates the widespread use of the slave body to imprint the signs of the unfree while increasing the value of its inverse.[25] The totalizing power of the slave-master and his symbolic extension in the proto-industrial technologies of sugar production were constant reminders to the slave of the absolute alienation of his body; the common sight of maimed or dismembered slaves was a graphic reminder, to all who would take heed, of the power of these sources to inflict bodily punishments, to leave the imprint of power on their object, to encode the body with meaning.

We have seen how Creole planters used that body and those imprints to publicize and obfuscate their cultural aspirations. Ligon indelibly encodes both the publicity and the obfuscation in his facetious coinage 'saccharocracy' (105) to signify sugar plantation society. The label bespeaks that deep-seated scepticism (and not a little contempt) which persisted in the minds of older, well-established elites and reactionary mandarins for the notion of establishing and sustaining a viable, authentic civilization in the sugar colonies. Their voices are dialogized in the political manoeuvering of the text between secular and sacred poles. Their antagonistic consciousness mediates the workings of the machine just described, efficiently interrupting its putative unitary flow. Creole desire for cultural authenticity and greater political autonomy is exposed as fantasy (witness the images used to represent the labour force: idealized male physiques, degraded female bodies). Instead of a machine serving the narrow special interests of a Creole planter class, the means of production are exposed as 'a desiring machine,' one merely subservient to the desire of the larger capitalist–imperialist machine, thus only 'a machine of a machine' functioning as 'a break in the flow in relation to the machine to which it is connected, but at the same time to the machine connected to it. This is the law of production of production.'[26]

The project of Creolizing autonomy is thus dethroned from the univocal presence it commanded in those parts of the narrative suffused with idealism for the promise of colonization, and with glowing plaudits for the Barbadian planters' impulses toward building social virtue and political harmony. Conflicted by issues of its own identity and contaminated by association, the project is efficiently co-opted by colonization's detractors. Cheyfitz identifies the origin of this anxiety as cognate with colonial culture, positioning it in a specific historical relationship: 'with the intensification of the transition to capitalism as a mode of production, [when] status as a function of wealth rather than family made the class structure practically and potentially volatile.'[27]

As an economic refugee, an emigrant fallen on hard times, Ligon knew personally the forces that occasioned that destabilization. As a Royalist exile in Barbados, he would become the enthusiastic historian of an emergent polity where the partisan labels of 'Round-head' and 'Cavalier' would be studiously avoided, where the old factional occasions would be ritualized and domesticated within a new Creole consensus:

Loving, friendly and hospitable one to another; and though they are of several Perswasions, yet, their discretions ordered everything so well, as some of them of the better sort, made a Law amongst themselves, that whosoever nam'd the word *Roundhead* or *Cavalier*, should give to all those that heard him, a Shot and a Turky, to be eaten at his house that made the forfeiture; which sometimes was done purposely, that they might enjoy the company of one another; and somtimes this shot and this Turky would draw a dozen dishes more, if company were accordingly. So frank, so loving, and so good natur'd were these Gentlemen one to another; and to express their affections yet higher, they had particular names one to another, as, Neighbour, Friend, Brother, Sister . . . (57)

Still, as we have seen in the exposition of historical contexts, the seeds of diffraction and dissensus were present from quite early in the establishment of the young colony, though Ligon's publicist apologetics tend to diminish their significance. Once again, Tryon provides us with the best cautionary counterpoint. His formulation of the problems systemic in slavocratic economy and his proposals for reforming it were at once mindful of the slavocrats' vested interests and cognizant of the slaves' well-being. He does not call for the abandonment of the plantations, only for the removal of women and children from sugar cane field labour: 'I must tell you that nothing hath more hurt and injured the Plantations, than the hard labour and unkind usage towards your Black women, for the whole preservation of mankind as to Encrease, Health and Strength, resides in the prudent conduct of women.' Remarkable for its appearance so early (1701) in the development of plantation societies (just a brief four decades after the commencement of sugar production in Barbados), such reformist ideology imagined a veritable alternative social system, thus disrupting the unanimity of colonialist apologetics. Developing an argument based on moral and religious objections and informed by a distinctive critique of retributive justice, Tryon pointed to the signs of economic decline already apparent in the plantations: 'for the groaning of him that suffereth Pain is the beginning of trouble and misery for him that caused it; and it is not to be doubted, but under this black Character of Oppression and Violence, the Sugar Plantations do now lye under; is not this manifest by many, and some of the chiefest note?'[28] Tryon drew an ominous picture of that 'black character of oppression and violence' to caution his audience against the inevitable influence of unreformed plantation culture on the mores of English youth and, hence, on the quality of England's future leadership both in politics and culture.

The 'sweete negotiation' of Ligon's *History* publicizes an optimistic frontier myth, and within that myth furnishes a discursive space for the Creole desire of cultural legitimacy. However, Tryon's reformist vision stands as a sharp reminder of the internal conflictedness that lay at the root of both the creolizing impulse and the formal *negotium* which framed and mediated it. Tryon's contrarian polemic dialogically disrupts Ligon's idealism, accommodating the discursive space to further literary invention and ideological formations. The legacy for a revisionist Creole myth in the British sugar colonies is therefore passed directly to Grainger. His negotiations for building culture from georgic appropriations and his mythic creation of the idealized Junio and Theana imagine a new Creole order hardly plausible in Ligon's historical scheme.[29] The *History*'s impulse to know the land, appropriate its contents, and envision the profit-motivated exchange of peoples for productive functions upon it, is a desire to comprehend all negotiations, but that impulse is itself comprehended and subsumed beneath the very constructed nature of all this negotiating.

CHAPTER 2

Rochefort: French collusions to negotiate

In spite of his place in this study and his indisputable significance to the comparative study of colonialist culture in the Caribbean, the author of the *Histoire Naturelle et Morale des Antilles* (*The Natural and Moral History of the Caribbean Islands*) remains familiar only to specialists in the field: the *Histoire* itself has so far not received any extended scholarly attention.[1] It is proper therefore to provide here some biographical data and some contextual bearings that will further illuminate the discussion to follow.

Information about Charles de Rochefort's life and career is sparse and inadequate. He was born in Belley (eastern France), studied law in Rome, and was honoured for his public service. He is reported to have produced several notable literary works, the best known being the *Dictionnaire générale des mots les plus usites de la langue française* (Lyons, 1685).

A few sources identify him as 'Cesar de Rochefort', and a few bibliographies name Louis de Poincy, a French Antilles colonial governor, as the co-author of this work.[2]

Following the dual structure prefigured in its advertisement, the work is divided into two books, each of twenty-four chapters, the first treating the natural, the second the moral, history of the colonies concerned. Chapters 1–5 of the first book sketch the principal geographical features (location, size, temperature, populations) of each island in turn, beginning with Tobago in the south, proceeding northward through the French Antilles (St Lucia, Martinique, Guadeloupe) to the Leeward Islands and terminating with St Martin and St Croix. Significantly, the author devotes comparatively more space to the islands then held by the French. The remainder of this book is devoted to descriptions of the flora (chapters 6–11) and fauna (chapters 12–24) of these islands, liberally illustrated with pictures of the various plant, animal, bird, insect, and fish species native to the region. Book II describes the inhabitants, both native and immigrant, of the islands in general, once more placing particular emphasis on those locations of especial interest to the French; sugar cultivation and manufacture is covered in half of one chapter; and a similar small apportionment (three-fifths of chapter 5) is given over to the African slaves imported to work the plantations. By contrast, the largest allotment in this section (chapters 7 and 9–24) is given to representations of the physical appearances, the bodies, clothes, religion, customs, rites and ceremonies of the Caribs. Chapter 8 digresses into a highly allegorized history of the Apalachites (Apalachees).

This profile of the *Histoire*'s contents illuminates the burden of Rochefort's interests; with respect to sugar and slaves, it discloses, among other things, an inversion of the priorities established in Ligon, though Rochefort emphatically affirms the existence of 'an infinite number' of slaves, and calls sugar the 'silver mine' of St Christopher. For obvious economic and political reasons, Rochefort lays out in careful and deliberate detail the locations and productive potential of natural resources like salt pits, silver mines and sulphur springs. But in emphatic contradistinction to the relative early English neglect of such matters, Rochefort underlines the importance the French attached to promoting a high level of moral and social civilization on these islands. He takes particular pains to list the religious and educational institutions which the French established early on their islands, making especial reference to the first communities of Capuchins, Jesuits and later Carmelites in St Christopher, and to a college of Jesuits and a Carmelite monastery in Guadeloupe.

In an otherwise mainly Anglophone project, the French author Rochefort represents a distinctive and valuable study in contrasts. We have seen how Ligon's enthusiastic apprehension of 'sweete negotiation' was strongly conditioned by his personal experience of political alienation and economic adversity. We have seen too how his role as cultural publicist was influenced by official and popular attitudes in England to colonial identity; those attitudes intensified feelings of isolation and promoted nostalgia and absenteeism. For his part, Rochefort appears enabled in inverse proportion by a markedly different concept in France of the colony's relation to the metropole. Further, his particular ethnographic interest in the nature of indigenous populations still surviving on the French possessions of

St Christopher, Martinique and Guadeloupe furnishes an important additional dimension to the content and conceptual structure of his work that is missing in Ligon's. True, he had the advantages of both history and geography: he set himself a much more inclusive task (proposing a wide survey of natural and moral subjects not of a single colonized island but of some twenty-seven). However, the nature of the negotiations reflected in his *Histoire* is constituted as much from subjective factors of the author's design as from the paradigm and arena of cultural politics with which the content and composition of his book are circumscribed. To the critique of political, military and diplomatic affairs he brings the sophistication of an educated mind privy to purposes and reasons of state. To the promise and problems of nurturing young colonies he brings the perceptions of an intimate who is well-connected with the official agents of colonial power. In his narrative focus, selection and emphasis on the French relationship to the colonies' specific human and material contents, he succeeds in creating the fiction of a perfectly benign, civilizing endeavour, mitigating or suppressing the kinds of coercive and mechanistic effects that punctuated Ligon's cultural production. In all these three categories he achieves his objectives by imprinting on literary method some very clearly calculated cultural strategies designed to publicize differences in French colonialist practice. Such strategies seek ratification for a purportedly more enlightened French attitude toward indigenous populations, normalizing the alterity of savage customs, and negotiating a myth of peaceful coexistence.

Thus, where in Ligon the objective of negotiation is to invent a Creole identity in close conformity with wider bourgeois aspirations (and sometimes in direct conflict with metropolitan hegemony), in Rochefort the fluid properties of negotiation are exploited to conform closely with a unitary vision of culture sanctioned by monarch and state. In Rochefort's practice, negotiation becomes a technical instrument, distinctly heterological and deliberately versatile.[3] In the *Histoire*, the prevailing mode of negotiation is collusion, a fluid conceptual instrument of cultural politics, eminently suited to French colonialist ideology. Collusion serves the ends of appeasement and pacification which France adopted to reconcile the indigenes to sharing their patrimony with interlopers, and to consolidate its own imperial power in the face of fierce European competition. This text's refiguring of negotiation (into a collusive strategy) places the Creole settlers in close collusion with clearly articulated nationalist aims, assimilating the Carib Indians into that flexible cultural framework while still pursuing the familiar myths of purity and origins. In common with other colonialist discourses, the *Histoire* also deploys both human and material contents in representational economies of exchange/translation, practices of appropriation, production, consumption and knowledge expansion.

Here it must be said that the intent of Rochefort's negotiations extends beyond the competing strategies of rival imperialisms. Within the intellectual community of French authors on the West Indies, his writing met with polemical dissent both on points of fact and of philosophy. His disposition to validate or rationalize Carib mores and beliefs, otherwise considered barbarous or heathen, placed him at odds with the traditionalist ethnographies of the Jesuit Jose de Acosta, whose systematic hierarchialization of Amerindian aborigines ranked the Caribs quite low on the scale of primitive peoples capable of civilization and Christianization.[4] That he was known to be an ally of Louis Poincy, the anti-Catholic Governor-General of the French Antilles, made him suspect of Huguenot sympathies and brought him into direct controversy with Catholic chroniclers, especially Jean-Baptiste Du Tertre, on the nature of Caribbean peoples.[5] His mixture of narrative and descriptive modes in representing the history and culture of the Caribs has drawn criticism from some scholars.[6] Admittedly, he often blurs the lines between historiographical method and myth, but Lévi-Strauss has so succinctly debunked the traditionalist assumptions of that division that Rochefort's persistent forays across the lines do not of themselves discredit his procedures as 'history'; indeed, his accommodationist ethics of diversity makes them an antecedent analogue to Lewis in the design of this study.[7] In fact, they serve to reinforce the persistence of negotiation as a mediating structure in colonial discourse and to display the extent to which Rochefort experimented with its possibilities not merely to serve the expedients of cultural politics, but also to negotiate an identity for himself and respect for creolizing modes of empirical thought within the developing institutions of colonial Caribbean historical and ethnographic writing.

That identity is at once the agent and the effect of specific constructions of negotiation comprehended under the rubric of the mode of collusion defined earlier. In one of its most crucial manifestations, Rochefort established himself as the only author in this study to accommodate so directly the authentic voice of the Carib indigenes. And that voice assumes force and potency not from any deceit of patronage or ethnographic flavour, but because in more than one place it interrogates and contests the very designs of imperialist collusion that have both validated and compromised it. In a stinging reproach against the civilized sense of justice, this voice pronounces its indictment against colonialist cruelty, malice and victimization:

thou hast driven me, says this poor people, out of St Christophers, Mevis (*sic*) Montserrat, St Martin, Antego, Gardeloupe, Barbouthos, St Eustace, & c. neither of which places belonged to thee, and whereto thou couldst not make any lawful pretence: And thou threatenest me every day to take away that little which is left me: What shall become of the poor miserable Caribbian?[8] Must he go and live in the Sea with the fishes? Thy Country must needs be a wretched one, since thou leavest it to come and take away mine: Or thou must needs be full of malice, thus to persecute me out of a frolick. (268)

Two properties of collusion emerge from this speech; one illustrates the reversible nature of the mode as an instrument of discourse. In that dramatic effusion cited above, the Carib voice demonstrates the indigenes' capacity to engage in rational process, one of the highest of Enlightenment values. The voice asserts command of the word and exhibits the ability to unmask European pretensions. The other property is to be found in the potential of this discourse to erode the ethnographer's exclusive power to inscribe, a potential that places both the Carib voice and Rochefort's documentarian persona in active complicity to supplant the old conditions of historiographical production. This moment in the *Histoire* strikingly defines collusion as a major organizing structure, at once negotiating a retreat from the monologic myth of certain aspects of Ligon's conceptions and the decidedly more pronounced obfuscations of georgic in Grainger and Beckford. The moment fashions its own myth of alterity empowered, repudiating the older myth in the name of a new cultural politics that affects to negotiate or exchange liberal ideology for political and economic advantages. In Book II Rochefort asserts the self-consciously nationalistic claim that the French sought the 'consent' of 'most considerable persons of the Caribbians' before establishing themselves in Martinique, Guadeloupe, and Grenada. 'It was done,' he proudly insists, 'with the consent of the most considerable persons among the Caribbians, who thereupon disown'd those of their Country-men who would have obstructed the said establishment: Nay, such was their earnestness therein that they employed all their Forces and Councils to oppose the designs of the others, and to secure the French in the peaceable possession of what they had before granted them' (159). In those disciplines of historiography which attempt to recuperate literary constructions from narrative history, two theoreticians have called attention to similar contingent practices that bear relevance to the mode of discourse exhibited here. Hayden White speaks very much to the matter in showing how narrative may be used to claim community in a way that Rochefort's collusions seem to desire here: 'what it [this kind of historical narrative] does is to test the capacity of a culture's fictions to endow real events with the kinds of meanings that literature displays to consciousness through its fashioning of patterns of "imaginary" events . . .'[9] Earlier in this chapter I characterized Rochefort's extraction of the mode of collusion from negotiation as an enabling resource, and I identified his historiographical practice with fashioning truth in a way that places his practice on the liminal space between history and myth. Both of these definitions are intuited in De Certeau's critique on how Western historical practice assimilates the New World into the European consciousness. That precise factor of negotiation which facilitates its flow between polarities enables Rochefort's collusions, and is echoed in a construct which De Certeau compounds by borrowing from Vlad Godzich and Raymond Williams.[10] Labelled as 'the hegemonic tendency of the cognitive realm', the construct defines certain kinds of intellectual/ideological interplays that may occur in historical–cultural narratives as they negotiate between 'emergent' and 'residual' impulses.[11] De Certeau designates these impulses as 'the enabling conditions for living in relation to these hegemonic forces'.[12] By extrapolation to Rochefort, these interplays are identifiable with collusion in its etymological dimension (forms of play), and in its figurative function as a politics of deceit: while it plays with a retreat from monologism and hegemony, its very identity with play, like negotiation's ambiguous etymology in *neg* and *otium*, allows it to play around simultaneously with 'emergent' and 'residual' modes, one foot in the camp of nationalist–imperialist designs, the other in the camp of enlightened revisionist ethnography.

Precisely at the intersection of these two modes, precisely between the truth values of Rochefort's proud claim and the Caribbian's plaintive remonstrance, are to be found the defining principles of collusion in this work. The higher profile accorded to native inhabitants and the lower profile given to slaves and sugar prompt critical inspection of the principal continuities and divergences that exist between the *Histoire* and the other texts in this study.

Besides its immediate declared concern with the colonial subject, the *Histoire* figures an identity with and complicity in the crisis climate of mid-century French history and politics which parallels Ligon's relationship to the English colonizing enterprise. Religious wars in the sixteenth century, and challenges to royal power in the Fronde revolts of the seventeenth all left the country so preoccupied with securing internal stability, it lagged far behind its counterparts in establishing footholds in the colonial West Indies. Further, commercial interests suitably qualified to underwrite colonizing expeditions were so divided by factional alliances that they were at best diffident, at worst risk-averse, towards foreign investment.[13] France therefore came comparatively late to sugar manufacture in the West Indies. And when it did, its public policy was less than wholehearted. These attitudes were rooted in part in its lack of expertise, but also in its cultural predisposition to frown on the workaday activities of tropical agricultural production, plantation management, bookkeeping and the sundry other particulars of trade and commerce necessary to sustain a profitable sugar economy. The early initiative in expanding colonial power was thus ceded to France's rivals Spain and Holland. French colonial policy did not benefit from coherent articulation or singleminded political support and direction until Colbert.[14] These conditions engendered a sense of crisis and urgency that are profoundly felt in Louis XIV's pronouncement on his accession that 'chaos reigned everywhere'. The monarch's anxiety translated into initiatives to refocus the nation's imperial objectives from Continental designs to competitive colonial standing with its neighbours.

Rochefort's *Histoire* participates in that climate of crisis. If consolidation of state power at home proved such a stout political challenge, gaining a foothold among hostile native populations proved even more so. Rochefort chronicles the persistent squabbles between the French and the Caribs in Dominica, Martinique and Guadeloupe. He sketches continual collusions (power-plays) between the English and the Caribs to undermine French territorial rights in St Christopher. The early years of colonial rule in Dominica were met with resistance and complaints of 'injustices and affronts'. By Rochefort's account, settlers were living in fear of surprise attack by 'savages' and under the threat of material scarcity: 'life grew wearisome to them, and death was the object of their wishes . . . [continual fear obliged them] 'to be always in arms, and to leave their Gardens and Plantations uncultivated' (180). These adjustment and acculturation problems are similar in nature to those Ligon records for early Barbados.

But while Ligon subsumes the problems beneath the 'sweete negotiation' that lay in the promise of slave-produced sugar, Rochefort negotiates away the narrative emphasis of sugar and slaves, subordinating the productions associated with these entities to a collusive politics of narrative which mimics the statecraft of the monarch and his chief ministers. Where Ligon's Royalist sympathies alienated him and many of the Barbados exiles from the Commonwealth government, Rochefort associates himself with and gives publicity to a model of cultural politics uniquely associated with France in the latter half of the seventeenth century. His narrative assigns a high value to a number of diplomatic negotiations: French and Indian leaders exchange sons as a sign of amity and peace. The Caribs release prisoners they held from previous wars. The French even join the Caribs in wars against their traditional adversaries, the Arawaks, exchanging trade in food supplies and tools (*Histoire*, 184–6).

These negotiations are collusive in that they encode in the narrative and telegraph to France's categorical rivals (the English and the Dutch) the broader national–imperialist desire for political and cultural hegemony. They are collusive, too, in a still more insidious sense: they create a self-legitimizing fiction largely inaccessible to illiterate native populations. That sense of collusion as trickery was inaugurated from the very beginning of colonization with the Spanish *requerimientos*: written legalistic authorizations and injunctions presented to unlettered Indians by the Spanish conquistadores.[15]

Two thematic continuities persist in these collusions that are recognized as legacies from the narrative of desire initiated by Ligon: the desire for authenticity and the desire for purity, inextricably linked to the search for origins.

We have already seen how Rochefort self-consciously validates the French practice of translating their paradigm of cultural politics to the colonies by establishing religious communities to ensure the continuance of moral order. Where Ligon narratively imagines a Creole identity largely decontextualized from any formal institutions of morality (recall his enthusiasm for the planters' self-regulation), Rochefort responds to the implied calumnies of colonial detractors by clothing French Creole evolution in the cultured ideals associated with Gallic national identity. He is emphatic in assuaging the anxieties of putative critics about the dangers of stereotypical colonial laxity and moral decay. Creole society, he insists, is not composed exclusively of 'vagabonds' but also of 'many [persons] of quality and descended from noble families'. Likewise, Davies in his preface endeavours to 'undeceive' those so 'ill-informed' or prejudiced against the colonies as to think them only 'the refuges and receptacles of Bankrupts, and debauch'd persons' (Preface, np).

That Creole social structure had been established on the same basic principle of class stratification which Rochefort himself acknowledges as a feature of French Continental society is a further proof advanced in the argument for authenticity. The work was done by servants, slaves and others 'whose necessities have forced them to earn their own bread with the labour, and sweat of their brows'. Others, privileged by higher social means because they can afford servants, 'lead pleasant lives and want not those enjoyments thereof which are to be had in other Countries'. Here the collusions reside in the capacity of Rochefort's narrative language to naturalize social inequality, to exchange the old value of such social mixtures as vagabonds, bankrupts, nobles, and slaves (coded as a dreaded form of promiscuity), for the new Creole value of diversity coded as wealth-producing and health-sustaining.

Not far behind are equally self-conscious advertisements for the leisure activities of the French settlers ('hospitality, fishing, hunting and enjoying one another in entertainments'): and the unabashed response of an emerging bourgeois elite to publicize their emulative consumption of beef, mutton, pork, wild fowl etc., 'all in as great abundance as at the best Tables in European parts of the world' (199).

Selectivity in immigrant settlers did not completely erase scepticism about the maintenance of secular civil order. To reassure readers that the proper institutions for the preservation of that order and the rule of law exist in St Christopher (so that 'no man should be guilty of so great a weakness as to imagine that people live in these Countries without any order or rule, as many do' (203), Rochefort documents the administration of justice there by reference

to a Council, particularizing the facticity of its operation by speci-
fying the location of its sessions and authenticating its local character
and relevance by veiled biblical/classical allusions (collusions): It
'assembles under a great Fig-tree, which is about the bigness of a
large Elm, near the Court of Guard of the Basseterre, not far from
the Haven' (203).[16] Under just such a tropical tree, other and alien
to European consciousness, the urgency of the crisis that drove the
French colonists to seek the New World other is recuperated as a
search for true self-consciousness. The crisis is negotiated here as a
collusion between the imagined similitude of the fig tree to an elm,
and between the use value of the tree as food, lumber or shade-
producer and the tree as a seat of justice. Through the collusions of
'emergent' and 'residual' the subject, now mediated by a creolizing
transformative power, experiences both itself and the world, 'transforming difference into identity [discovering] the strange and novel
as familiar'.[17]

Thus, on the strategic ground of the *Histoire*, these facts collude
together to negotiate the French desire for a new consciousness, an
identity which, for all its alignment with a pre-existing ethos of
French cultural politics, now radiantly embodied in the Sun King,
experiences itself as incomplete, creolized by its access to the history,
practices, discourses and ethnology of things novel and other. In
pursuit of Carib nature and mores, that identity rediscovers and
experiences its own nature and mores, only now transformed as an
emanation of the bourgeois self, a body in the act of becoming.
Butler, in her discussion of desire as a subject-making mode, suggests
a theoretical basis for this interpretation. She writes that 'Desire
does not indicate a ready-made self, but reveals instead a self having-
to-be formed; desire is the mode through which the self comes to be
– a mode of realization.'[18]

Once again the text's relationship to the monarch's speech of
crisis suggests further dimensions for its definition and interpretation
within the scheme of this study. In taking its cue from the instance of
the monarch's words, the text assumes the burden of the imperial
theme sounded here as a desire for the other or, in James Clifford's
terms, a search for an authentic self: 'every imagined authenticity
presupposes, and is produced by, a present circumstance of felt
inauthenticity'.[19] And so the author of the *Histoire* inscribes a kind of
self-reflexive ethnological history into this discourse that differenti-
ates it from Ligon's if only because his *History* so resolutely aestheti-

cizes (or elides) its authentic ethnological subjects. By embracing the Caribs, Rochefort chooses another route to pursue the pure Enlightenment ends of knowing and translating the exotic world of alterity for an audience back home. The means to that end are located in the way his text predicates its essential difference on a search for authenticity through domestication and naturalization of difference itself. So, the *Histoire* diffracts the monarch's anxieties, mediating them through its advertisements for diversity, predicating their resolution on the fulfilment of the text's central collusions.

Implicated in the sense of crisis reproduced in the monarch's meaning, Rochefort's work negotiates further practices of exchange and translation which will be decoded next to serve as an heuristic for the major acts of collusion, whose analysis has been reserved for much of the remainder of this chapter. Before turning to those acts, though, some insight into the ordering principles that rationalize their defining structure is in order.

Unlike all the other authors of this study, Rochefort assigns a relatively low profile to sugar and slaves. In this respect, the *Histoire* situates itself in a kind of counter-pattern to Ligon's *History*. It therefore prompts the tentative hypothesis of an inverse relationship between the lowered profile of sugar and slaves and the thematization of purity. As we saw in the preceding chapter, the narrative emphasis given to these essential bodies in Ligon interrogates purity as a founding myth of Creole culture. That will continue to be so in Grainger and Beckford. But the minimalist representation of these essentials in Rochefort immunizes him from the anxiety of purity that preoccupies Ligon. By the same token, Rochefort is also able conveniently to gloss over questions of religion and morality raised by the nexus of slaves and sugar in Ligon. After all, both sugar cane and slaves were imports; neither sugar nor Africans were native to the place. Slave-holding and sugar-making could be displaced from the scene of production by switching the quest for authenticity to flora, fauna and indigenous inhabitants. Measured in terms of allotted discursive space, slaves and sugar occupy together a little over one chapter (about six pages altogether). By contrast, flora, fauna and Caribs occupy thirty-six chapters. Viewed in this relational context, Rochefort's selective narrative strategies collude to negotiate away the true value and function of slaves in this Creole economy: by discursive effacement they are artificially consigned to use value, their true commodity value upstaged by the greater space allotted to flora and fauna and to that most bourgeois-capitalist tool, the list of objects with consumption value. In this case Rochefort has forcibly expropriated value from one of his interlocutors' intellectual capital. He has strategically positioned Breton's vocabulary list of Caribbian words and phrases in two key places in his text.[20] It will be recalled that Ligon mediated the problem of purity by aestheticizing the black male body and marginalizing (or holding them in a kind of sensibility quarantine) the black female body by association with deformation and natural odour. Rochefort obviates this uneasy ambivalence by predicating his idea of cultural creolization on the domestication and assimilation of native inhabitants, animals and plants. What descriptive content he gives to slaves is limited to brief conventional sketches on complexion and other physical features. A very pointed (and all too common) assimilation of African slaves to animals is typified in the narrative economy of this phrase ('they are bought and sold after the manner of Cattle in other Places'). Some sparse reference is made to positive qualities, albeit demonstrably for their exchange value as labour: 'They are very strong and hardy, but withal so fearful and unwieldy in the handling of Arms that they are easily reduc'd to Subjection' (201). Here the positive is so closely juxtaposed to a qualified grammatical negation that it disqualifies Africans from any assimilation to implicit Gallic ideals of bravery and honour. Such ideals, as we will see later, are reserved for and lavished on the Caribs whose origins, remapped on to mythicized history, will negotiate for them a status of fictive equality with the Europeans.

Sugar is caught in similar narrative collusions. Again in emphatic contrast to the greater quantum of detail and discursive reflection Ligon gives to its production (not to mention his tendency to indulge in rhapsodic flights and mystified rhetoric), Rochefort is objectively concise, utilitarian and suitably (but by no means excessively) mindful to supply an uninitiated audience with information on sizes, shapes and colours relative to cane cultivation and sugar production. Like other early chroniclers, he is properly respectful of the cane stalks as 'precious reeds' and gives due credit to the 'miracle' role sugar played in the economic growth and prosperity that accrued to the islands as a result of the shift from tobacco-growing. In paying tribute to the role his associate Poincy played in aggressively and efficiently pioneering sugar cultivation on St Christopher, Rochefort is negotiating publicity for the quality of leadership available in the colonies (as Ligon did for planters Drax and Hilliard in Barbados), and the quality of life the 'sweete negotiation' of sugar afforded to French colonials as well as to their trading associates and consumers back at the metropole: 'it may be easily inferred that extraordinary advantages accrued to the inhabitants of that Island by means of this sweet and precious Commodity, and what Satisfaction it brings to their Correspondents in other parts of the World, who have it at so easie rates' (196). Rochefort's erasure of imported slaves and manu- factured sugar in favour of Carib indigenes continues a well-worn fiction that the civilizing mission were more concerned with Chris- tianizing the latter than negotiating them into compliance and collusion with the designs of an evolving productive economy. And on the collusive ground of the *Histoire,* that fiction negotiates the idealized primitives into a mythicized cultural union of Greater France. The calculation that Africans were more amenable to religious conversion and more susceptible of acculturation to the ethics of a Creole slavocracy ratifies their diminished urgency as a discursive project. Rochefort's text therefore redefines the idea of Creole culture as the pursuit of union (assimilation) with exotics, establishing community with them by imagining common mythic origins in the classical past, recuperating a shared heritage from common sources in the Bible and antiquity.

It may be enunciated, then, as an axiom of this book's ordering logic, that the business of cultural production diverges from its focus on slaves or definition in sugar to the extent that the focus of each text's production shifts to accommodate native themes and the native voice. De Certeau, in his exegesis of Montaigne's production of the savage word, illuminates this exchange of productions in a formula he defines as 'the moment when the savage word draws closer to the place of production of the text that "cites" it'.[21] In the collusive nature of exchange involved here, 'the text that cites it' is also the text that sites it: fixing and stabilizing the savage *ethne* is clearly the prologue to the greater drama of cultural politics that will exchange indigenous authenticity for a Creole constructedness and, in the French case, consecrate them all to the greater glory of Greater France. The centrality of sugar and slaves to the business of economic and cultural production is negotiated away in the collu- sions that Rochefort devises for the Caribbians.

Negotiating away the presence of one set of narrative objects in exchange for another, drawing the savage voice into the inscribed discourses of the West and engaging this voice and their presence in the text's definitive practices of citing and siting call our attention back to the generative kinship that exists between collusion and negotiation. Once more the etymological derivation of 'collusion' reveals key parallel properties which elucidate its essence and functional properties as a mode of cultural practice which will control the ensuing analysis. Given the highly textured qualities of the exchanges, transactions, and complicit practices the mode enacts, given its previously demonstrated semantic and political implications in notions of play, allusiveness, elusiveness and oscillation between diverse layers of reference and meaning, the recuperation that follows will greatly enhance our understanding of collusion within the colonial–creole nexus.

The Latin term *colludere* (to play with, act collusively) suggests three main ways in which the mode of collusion functions within the complex cultural practices of Rochefort's narrative. In the primary sense of 'playing together', we may recognize the interplay of antinomial modes of cognition represented by the colonizing subject and the Antillean Other respectively. This sense underscores yet one further respect in which Rochefort's *Histoire* proclaims its epistemological departure from the pattern of colonial discourse initiated in Ligon's *History*: collusion, because of its definitive connotations with reciprocity and exchange, represents a distinct shift in the trajectory of the texts under present study. Rochefort's practice diverges from the presumption of unmediated (monological) authority in the construction of knowledge and consciousness towards forms of knowledge-making earlier identified with De Certeau, finding their most radical expression in the culture of experimental consciousness imaged in Lewis' *Journal*).[22]

In effect, collusion brings to bear on the encounter with the Carib other a new practice of cultural politics pressed into the service of imagining Creole formation. Another extract from that powerful production of the Carib voice dialogized between plaintive and accusatory modes (at once) illustrates the kind of historicist progression represented in Rochefort's pursuit of ethnographic truth. In that pursuit, Rochefort opens up the privileged space of his text, permitting the Caribs the authority to interrogate the ethics of European imperialism:

how miserable art thou thus to expose thy person to such tedious and dangerous Voyages, and to suffer thyself to be oppress'd with cares and fears! The inordinate desire of acquiring wealth puts thee to all this trouble and all these inconveniences; and yet thou art in no less disquiet for the Goods thou hast already gotten, than for those thou art desirous to get. Thou art in continual fear lest somebody should rob thee either in thy own Country or upon the Seas, or that thy Commodities should be lost by shipwrack, and devour'd by the waters: Thus thou growest old in a short time, thy hair turns gray, thy forehead is wrinkled, a thousand inconveniences attend thy body, a thousand afflictions surround thy heart, and thou makest all the haste thou canst to the grave: Why dost thou not contemn riches as we do? (267)

Two kinds of collusion display themselves in these alternations of civilized colonizing with savage voice. The Caribs demonstrate their capacity to engage in rational processes, one of the highest of Enlightenment values. As they document the charges of cruelty, malice and victimization against the colonizing interloper, they question the whole project of civilization, and the immediate project of creolizing, at the same time as they erode the ethnographer's exclusive power to inscribe and supplant the old conditions of historiographical production. Clifford postulates this moment thus: 'It is no longer possible for the researcher to act as if he is the sole or primary bringer of culture into writing. In fact, the field is already filled with intertextual presences.'[23]

Whether we ascribe to the Carib verbal onslaught the status of privileged speech or something more akin to paternalistic accommodation, it is certain that this text can never remain the same, can no longer retain its uninterrupted relationship to the omniscient Western historicizing subject, an entity Said sceptically denominates as an 'authoritative, explorative, elegant, learned voice' which assumes the prerogative to speak, analyze, amass evidence, to theorize and speculate about everything – except himself.[24] What was unmasked in Ligon, though not acknowledged, that dissensus factor which is so fundamental to creolization, is here fully accommodated and openly valorized.

In keeping with its reciprocal character as a discursive mode of cultural construction, collusion implicates the author himself in a way that forces him to revise his role self-consciously. Thus collusion negotiates a legitimacy for Creole cultural consciousness, separating it from prior monological assumptions. As witnessed in his defence of colonial morality, the progress of Rochefort's history is regularly broken by heuristic digressions or plea-like cautions to those readers who might come to the text with preformed notions about the nature of the Caribs in particular and of savages in general, notions derived from sources whose collusions are out of joint with his present purposes. The point-by-point delineation of physical features, customs and manners – universal black hair, beardlessness among the men, chastity and modesty among the women, nudity among both sexes, with assiduous evaluations and validations of these mores – refute and deconstruct those pre-existent discourses that retailed horrific images of the Caribs. Drawing on the time-hallowed repute of ancient authorities, Rochefort establishes an authentic ground for Carib mores by comparing them with the views of Lycurgus on juvenile morality and of Pliny on the antique legitimacy of ritual body-painting. Together, Rochefort and these revered classical sources collude to redeem this group of autochthonous peoples from the disrepute of savages, to immunize them from the calumnies heaped on other 'barbarous' peoples.[25] 'Most savages are thieves', he confidently affirms, 'But the Caribbians have so natural and so great an aversion to that sin, that there is no such thing [thieving] found among them, which is very rare among Savages . . .' (269).

Situated within the context of Rochefort's avowed concern for affirming the moral integrity of an evolving Creole cultural community, these collusions purchase legitimacy for colonial institutions by aligning Carib beliefs and practices with those of ancient peoples, then translating them forward in time to seventeenth-century France, there to be grafted on to an emergent collusive liberalism, theorized in postcolonial cultural studies as mimicry (almost like this, but not quite; grafted on to this, therefore like this).[26]

This bringing the Caribs home, this investing them with the garb of philosophical familiarity by effacing their exotic difference, belongs to a practice of collusion which can fittingly be called domestication. It gets its most self-conscious inscription in Rochefort's repeated references to the indigenes as 'our Caribs', and his flat declaration that 'our Caribs are not barbarians'. His painstaking and perfectly reasonable explanation for this proprietary and exclusive designation is to differentiate the insular Caribs, or those inhabiting the islands of the Lesser Antilles, from those Caribs living in South America.[27] 'Our Caribs' are distinguished for their mild manners, supple bodies, smooth language and cleanly habits from their continental counterparts about whom he knows considerably less but who he assumes, from diverse reports, to be warlike, fierce and inhospitable. Apart from identifying them and establishing his familiarity with them, this patronizing reference has the effect of domesticating the objects of his discourse, isolating them out of the amorphous universe of savages and barbarians about whom readers would most certainly hold certain preformed ideas of brutishness, ignorance and outlandish morals. Rochefort endeavours to eradicate these notions from the minds of his readers by a resolute strategy of domestication, underscoring his design by frequent 'advertisements' and a steadfast purpose to 'give the reader satisfaction' (reassurances) in contrastive descriptions of this order:

> Most of the people whom we call Barbarians and Savages have something hideous and deformed or defective, either in their countenances or some other part of the body, as Historians affirm of the Maldiveses, the Inhabitants about the Magellane Streights, and several others which we need not name here. But the Caribbians are a handsome, well-shap'd people, well proportion'd in all parts of their bodies, gracefull enough, of a smiling countenance, middle stature, having broad shoulders, and large buttocks, and they are most of them in good plight, and stronger than the French: Their mouths are not over large, and their teeth are perfectly white and close. (251)

Perhaps foremost among the uses of domestication is Rochefort's stout defence of the island Caribs, especially those of St Vincent, against the smear of cannibalism. The name 'Carib' was misappropriated by the Spaniards to describe a diverse assortment of indigenous Antillean peoples who resisted their dominion, and whom the Spaniards expediently defined as anthropophagi without any verifiable evidence except their own fears and the need to rationalize their intent to subjugate them.

In the face of such a widely disseminated but tainted history, Rochefort stressed that the island Caribs were not classic cannibals: they did not devour human flesh as a dietary staple, but only savoured choice parts of their enemies' bodies after capturing them in battle as a mark of the victors' ultimate power over the vanquished and a just retribution for the miscreants' past wrongs and offences. In this form of cultural advocacy, Rochefort is almost certainly signing his accord with the ironic cultural relativism of Montaigne: domestication becomes another name for translation in Cheyfitz's historicist usage: certainly, by Cheyfitz's lights, domestication may be seen to act 'equivocally to destabilize [the] univocal value' of culturally weighted concepts like 'cannibal' and 'barbarian'. Cheyfitz writes: 'The force of this kind of reading is to loosen the absolute hold of a term over a particular referent by playing with its propriety.'[28]

To further allay the fears of his audience and make the Carib even more palatable to European sensibilities, Rochefort addressed the other most important source of distaste among barbarian habits, the delicate business of nudity. He admits this fact without the slightest trace of prudery, announcing with the barest candour that 'They go stark naked, both men and women, as many other Nations do: And if any one among them should endeavour to hide the privy parts, all the rest would laugh at it.' But he also records their deference to the Europeans: '. . . sometimes when they come to visit the Christians, or to treat with them, they have comply'd so far with them, as to cover themselves by putting on a shirt, drawers, a hat and such cloaths as had been given them'. Collusion manifests its ironic resources most potently here in the obvious Carib parody of European manners. The Caribs deliberately exceed the minimal civility of covering the pudenda and perform a ridiculous travesty of their conquerors' dress habits. The passage continues,

yet as soon as they were returned to their own habitations, they strip themselves, and put up all in the Closets, till some such other occasion should oblige them to put them on again: To requite this compliance of the Caribbians, some among the French, having occasion to go among them, made no difficulty to strip themselves after their example: This defiance of cloaths reigns in all places under the Torrid Zone, as every one knows. (255)

A variety of collusive forms may be discerned in the discourse just illustrated. Both Caribs and Europeans engage in a kind of role reversal, a cultural exchange, in which they adopt each other's mode of dress for occasional diversion or for sociopolitical resistance. In both cases the role reversal of cross-dressing materializes as a site of resistance: in the Caribs' case a resistance to the intrusion of foreign ways; in the French case 'a defiance of cloaths', a transgression of a defining norm of their own 'civilized' manners. Each party domesticates the image of the other by assuming and appropriating it to his own person. This is especially manifest in the matter of costume exchange, and, in the most extreme mimicry of all, emulative nudity, where an evolving creolization is dramatically signified. We shall inquire further into the cultural values of such collusive mimicries in the illustrations of extreme modelling and theatricalization of identity that follow. By all these means – the patterns of reversal, the naturalizing of nudity and other exclusive or culturally alien behaviours – Rochefort's text displays the capacity of collusion to advance the discourse about the dynamics of adaptivity and reciprocity so fundamentally at the heart of creolization, a source which Ligon at best abhorred by erasing this source and its potential contributions from the scene of production, and which Rochefort appears to privilege for reasons not wholly unrelated to the local interests of creolizing settlers and to the express expediency of French imperialist politics.

Whether we define these tactics under the rubric provided by De Certeau (heterological) or by Cheyfitz (exchanging the univocal for equivocal), it is not difficult to discern how the versatility of the mode allows Rochefort to exploit collusion's capacity for double duty: collusion allows him to play the cultural identity politics of serving two interests which, together, may coalesce to produce their own new identity. Each of these interests may be discerned in Rochefort's manipulation of historical truth to serve cultural ends. Abstracted from its dense narrative ambience and reduced to strict plot sequence, the relevant 'historical facts' emerge in a pattern that describes a strategy of deliberate sanitizing for the purposes of consumption. Earlier in this analysis, we saw how the author felt compelled to morally sanitize the site of colonial production so that that activity could go forward immunized from the detractions of potential critics back home. For similar motives, Rochefort inserts certain assurances of France's scrupulous integrity and plain dealing to legitimize that country's political and cultural diplomacy for the consumption of its imperial rivals. And then, advancing to the last familiarizing practice discussed, he secures the Caribs for domestic approval (consumption) by linking their genealogy with *premiers temps* (and hence with a familiar set of European traditions and values).[29] All this very deliberate ordering of rhetorical defences is an exercise in laying the ground, setting the cultural table for a major activity of assimilation and consumption.[30] In fact, this assimilation–consumption nexus will be the final modulation of collusion this chapter will cover in analyzing Rochefort's strategies of cultural identity politics.

The logic of this form of identity politics runs something like this. Since the nations and tribes of *premiers temps* were now quite fully assimilated into European consciousness, it was a very short and easy step to identify the Caribs with them. This comparative technique is a common practice in European cultural history of

primitive peoples. Michael T. Ryan's insistence that the practice had
a 'self-validating' motive is consistent with the foregoing logical
interpretation, and illuminates what is to follow. 'Establishing that
commonality,' Ryan continues, 'was the first step toward assimilation.'[31] The collusions contained in the assimilation–consumption
serve both political and cultural ends of gathering the Caribs into a
unitary vision of history. This vision serves primordially national–
imperialist aims. And the concurrent business of seeking validation
for an evolving colonial identity or culture retains its presence and
urgency. The assimilation–consumption nexus re-emphasises the
extent to which Rochefort's *Histoire* is about the invention of a
Creole subject and the pursuit of accommodation for Creole ways of
knowing and being. Butler's gloss on Hegel's definition of desire and
the subject is instructive here, especially as it bears on the assim-
ilative and consuming tendencies of that subject in the presence of
difference: 'desire to discover the entire domain of alterity as a
reflection of itself, not merely to incorporate the world but to
externalize and enhance the borders of its very self'.[32]

The extent to which Rochefort's history of the Caribbians is about
self-extension defined by distance and alterity has already been
established by the author's identification with his country's imperialist enterprise. Likewise, Rochefort's preoccupation with the natural
and moral economies of the French Antilles (sometimes with profound defensive anxiety) constitutes itself as an expression of an
emerging Creole consciousness. His history therefore struggles to
situate itself in a mediative capacity with respect to the conflictual
economy produced from the poles of metropolis and colony (metropolitan centre and colonial periphery). How this conflictual
economy continues the reproduction of the creolizing process init-
ially located in Ligon may be gauged from a more concentrated
inquiry into how collusion encodes Antillean nature and mores with
consumptive value.

The primary deceit of collusion (the literariness of this history
also defines it as a conceit) is to construct the Caribs as equal
partners in the text's defined negotiations. Revising Ligon by raising
the Caribs to the status of significant narrative objects, Rochefort
can more efficiently reap the intrinsic sweets of negotiation. Established on the much-contested claims of an ethnography which
accords with and extols the work's authenticity by citing the Caribs

as native informants in the production of their mores, he takes advantage of collusion's capacity to facilitate easy movement back and forth across cultural boundaries. In his critique of anthropological practice and method, Edward Said has defined boundaries as 'permeable' lines between cultures; viewed as such, they become highly susceptible to the kind of stealth through which collusion performs its practices of assimilation–consumption. By a deceit of negotiation collusion permits a slippage across boundaries that is the foundation on which the creolizing identity grounds its authority. That authority empowers it to critique Carib moral character and social values, to recuperate Carib history, to meditate upon their ancestry, and to negotiate a complex interplay of signs manifesting themselves in the creolizing arena.

Deployed for these ends, collusion exhibits its assimilation–consumption dynamics by the authorizing modes it adopts to publicize the Caribs to consumers of the *Histoire* and to potential colonists and settlers. More than any other author in this study, Rochefort feels driven to consult the presiding genius of the place personified in the Caribs' ancestral spirits, to explore some (at least imaginative) basis for an *entente cordiale* with the legitimate indigenes of Guadeloupe. This ancestral theme is given a close generic alignment with the text's preoccupation over evidences of Carib moral virtue. The pious attentions accorded the elderly and the total absence of parricide interrogates the moral authority of civilization's bearers among a people who are capable of 'all the care' and 'all the expressions of love, honour and respect that can be expected from a nation which hath no other light for its direction, than that of corrupt Nature' (347–8).

Since culture by definition (and in particular Creole forms) is constantly being forced into that interrogatory or conflictual stance in order to validate itself, this deployment of collusion validates creolizing identity by linking its authenticity to an evocation of *premiers temps* (ancestral worship) and declaring its differentiation from civilization (the allusion to corrupt nature).[33]

Elsewhere, I have shown how this cultural narrative in Rochefort's *Histoire* evidences a distinctive allegorical character: the linguistic and functional relationships that bind collusion and negotiation together are also fraught with allegory.[34] Publicizing Carib mores and social values to a civilized European audience is a collusion to place the two cultures in effective reciprocity: an allegory on how 'over here' can function as a moral exemplum to 'over there'. The insertion of Europeans into this pristine moral universe facilitates the self-extension and self-renewal alluded to earlier: this opportunity to create themselves anew colludes in the production of creole ways of knowing and being. The dialogized voice of 'corrupt nature' evidences the text's gradual assimilation and consumption by incriminating that Carib voice prominently admitted in Book 2, Chapter 9. This practice of collusion blunts anti-colonialist censures directed against both settler and native communities, censures that generate so much of this text's anxiety.

If the above sharply illustrates how collusion works to recuperate an emergent Creole sensibility from the moral part of the *Histoire*'s binary, we can now turn to evaluate the text's representation of material diversity to show how that same purpose is recuperated from the natural part. That the Creole sensibility is constituted from the expanding knowledge of abundance and diversity existing in the colonized space may be deduced from the profusion of word pictures and visual illustrations of the flora and fauna of the islands Rochefort visited. The ethnographer–historian's commitment to reliable evidence is clear enough in Rochefort's determination to render these with objectivity, visual acuity and verisimilitude. In fact, his illustrations are some of the most naturalistically drawn (almost palpable in their visual effect) to be found in the texts under discussion.[35] (He systematically catalogues size, shape, colour, height, what soils are best for growing, how individual species are propagated: the colour, flavour and consistency of edible and medicinal plants; the habitats and feeding habits of animals.) The collusive structures embedded in this narrative and the visual display of specimens negotiate between two main forms of consumption: the one empirical, the other material. The first has already been suggested in reference to how such displays of the variety and fecundity of New World nature functioned as objects for both economic and scientific consumption.[36] The other is a fairly constant commonplace in these colonial accounts and function as publicity and display, stirring the appetites of readers for the same, awakening emulative desire for the natural produce of colonized space. Inscribed in this production, the assimilation–consumption nexus gathers into one collusive unity the methods of the new scientific and information orders (strategically appropriated to imperialist purposes) and the fruits of artistic labour (now made available for visual consumption) in a compelling image of bourgeois emulation.

While that construction of collusion would appear to privilege the interests of two dominant constituencies back at the metropole, the valorization of those interests in the *Histoire* should not be construed to supplant or negate the special interests of that emerging creole identity whose developing consciousness is the ultimate object of these texts' subjective desire. In fact, this is a function of collusion whose specific deceit it is to mimic consensus, while in fact individuating and differentiating its own needs, identifying them with the *dissensus* that is so much the sign of creolization. I treat this concept as an approximate synonym to Young's term 'dissension'.[37] My earlier critique of the 'cross-dressing' episode stages theatrically and consumptively the outward visible signs of that process in Rochefort. There, collusion works to contain Carib difference within the French colonial political need for cohesion, to assimilate the creolizing subject to new cultural norms which would otherwise remain inward and invisible.

One final narrative structure of collusion in which the body and the gaze are locked in this topos of desire will serve to solidify the argument for creolizing. Just as Ligon negotiated legitimacy for the inherent metaphor of cultural construction by assimilating the African male to Albrecht Dürer's models, so now Rochefort deploys the Carib body in a similar structural negotiation. In a characteristic collusive narration, Rochefort assimilates the natural strength and physical integrity of Carib bodies to the purposes of Creole cultural constitution. Since 'our Caribs' are distinguished for their attractive physiognomies and their loving, obliging dispositions, any blemishes or bodily defects must be mitigated and rationalized to the Caribs' advantage: 'They have large and thick feet because they go barefoot, but they are withal so hard that they defie Woods and Rocks', or, in conceding the rare incidence of blindness, baldness and other physical infirmities, rationalized and revalorized: 'But if any among the Caribbians are thus deformed, or have lost, or are maimed in any limb, it happened in some Engagement against their Enemies, and so those scars or deformities being so many demonstrations of their Valour, they glory in them . . .' (251). The rationalizations and apologies are clearly intended to domesticate the Caribs to the author's interlocutors but, more importantly, the creolizing voice of his own dissensus valorizes these differences for local consumption.

Two ostensibly alien practices, like body-painting with roucou[38] and anointing the skin with herbal oils, are rationalized in point of their utility for covering, ornament and beauty in the first case, and for the practical benefits of protecting and furnishing lustre and smoothness to the skin in the second. Having satisfied his perceived historian's obligation to provide empirical proofs for these claims, he returns to a pervasive rhetorical pattern which begins by affirming the existence of diversity and difference among the savages: 'Most Savages do thus paint and trick up themselves after a strange manner; but they do not all use the same colours, nor observe the same fashion: For there are some who paint their Bodies all red, as our Inhabitants of the Caribbies do . . . but others make use of other colours, as Black, White, Chestnut, Ginglione, Blew, Yellow, and the like. Some use only one particular colour; others paint themselves with several colours, and represent divers figures on their bodies' (255). The analysis continues to provide other evidences of variety and diversity and ends with this matter-of-fact but instructive observation: 'There is sufficient choice of all these modes' (255–6). Next, in one broad collusive swath, Rochefort collapses the triple heterologies of Carib native customs, his own ethnographer–historian's practice and his contemporary European readers' primitive antecedents into a negotiated cultural assimilation. Through reference to reputable classical authorities identified with his own, he rationalizes:

But this is to be noted, That the painting of the body is a very ancient kind of Ornament; and among other Monuments of this piece of Antiquity, Pliny and Herodian affirm, that certain people of Great Brittany, not using any kind of cloathing, painted their bodies with divers colours, and represented thereon the figures of certain living Creatures, whence they were called Picti, that is, Painted people. But among the Savages who at this day paint themselves, the Caribbians have this advantage, that they adorn themselves with a colour which the Ancients honour'd most of any; for it is reported, that the Goths made use of Vermilion to make their faces red; and the ancient Romans, as Pliny affirms, painted their bodies with Minium upon the day of their Triumph . . . (256)

Analogues in meaning, motive, and function to the interrogating Carib voice ('thou hast driven me out . . .' etc.), those extended citations constitute a profound organic relation to the text's ethnographic desire. They mark a critical narrative moment in which desire engages in exchange for very calculated, if ambiguously expressed, purposes. The motives are at least self-interested. The presence in those passages of Butler's two qualifying markers, 'the sensuous and the perceptual', define them as self-reflexive desire, a category she isolates as required for consumption and for reproducing life (33). The voice of early French Antillean consciousness, Rochefort is in fact engaged in an exchange that is meant to fashion and reproduce a new identity, an early French Creole identity. The obvious attempt to authenticate Carib practices by invoking Pliny and Herodian places collusion in that same category of imperialist practice which Cheyfitz calls 'translation,' except that here the metropole has been eluded (if not elided); the natives' customs, mores, practices, and imperial ideology itself, have been 'translated', appropriated as a 'usable fiction',[39] a collusion to call a constructed consciousness into being.

The play of elusion/elision stages a scene of constructive incertitude, a season of trickster politics which verifies the specific essence of collusion as a cultural practice. Its persistent recourse to the negotiations of desire encoded in exchange and translation returns us inevitably to its master source. That return to origins helps us to measure the *Histoire*'s achievement and fix conclusively Rochefort's relation to the project of creolizing culture. Collusion makes clear that the literary construction of Creole consciousness proceeds by a kind of entity rotation, a code-switching that accords more or less presence to metropolitan/hegemonic entities or to appropriated peoples, to the extent that either entity assists in or impedes the production of activities related to the myth of frontier culture. A very decided kind of risk-taking is encoded in this, but it is a risk 'cheerfully assumed' in the name of production (here cultural) by subsuming conflictual or interrogating forces.[40] De Certeau associates this kind of entity-disruption with the Enlightenment processes of industrializing and production, so that the exchange is a fluid juggling or switching of selves (he calls it an 'internal division of the subject between the kind of self one needs to be in certain situations [generally linked to one's means of livelihood] and the kind of self that one is in other settings'.[41] The bargain is to exchange or negotiate away the old stable privileges of the civilized ego for a new self-consciousness forged in 'diverse zones'.

In his relation to immediately adjacent authors, Rochefort looks both before and after. Where Ligon's optimistic vision is sharply conflicted by Tryon's dire cautions, Rochefort has effectively elided the sources of that conflict (African slaves and sugar cane), displacing those potential sources of contestation with sources of collusion (accommodating the Carib voice and assimilating their practices). Questions of cultural dilution raised both in Ligon and in Grainger have been pre-empted by proofs of moral foundations and the authority of *premiers temps*. Where Ligon depends on imported entities for the aesthetics of his idealism, Rochefort negotiates collusive alliances with the native inhabitants to secure his frontier myth. In the characteristic ambiguous nature of negotiation, collusion permits Rochefort the equivocal privileges of assuming, that is, taking on the risks of cultural dilution and taking them for granted. James Grainger will have the certainly more intractable negotiation of repatriating formal myths and human embodiments of those myths to give this ideal continuity.

CHAPTER 3

Grainger: creolizing the muse

For all Rochefort's concern about potential sources of cultural contestation and his desire for metropolitan approbation, these sources do not materialize in the contemporary record with any greater specificity beyond the author's misgivings about a too-critical audience. James Grainger's challenge, on the other hand, was altogether a more stout one because of his close intimacy with what was arguably the most powerful literary establishment of his day. An intimate of Samuel Johnson (and by association known to Boswell), William Shenstone and Oliver Goldsmith, Grainger won the admiration of several figures in Johnson's circle. The most notable of these, Thomas Percy, Bishop of Dromore, very generously promoted Grainger's literary ambitions, wrote reviews of his work and maintained a considerable correspondence with him.[1]

The influence of that circle on *The Sugar Cane* may be inferred from major aspects of the poem's formal features. Grainger's self-conscious struggle with literary form was an obvious attempt to win the approbation of those powerful arbiters of knowledge and culture in eighteenth-century England. The anxiety Grainger evinces about his treatment of and relationship to the slaves is (at least in part) engendered by Johnson's well-known animus against the colonies and their slavocratic culture (slaveholding).[2] The apologetic tone Grainger commonly adopts in his role as publicist bespeaks an understandable sensitivity in the face of growing contempt for Creole cultural pretensions and opposition to their economic interests.[3]

Born in Berwickshire, Scotland (in either 1721 or 1724), Grainger studied medicine at Edinburgh University for three years, breaking off that pursuit to practise as an army surgeon in the 1745 Rebellion and in Holland from 1746 to 1748, taking his M.D. degree formally in 1753. The practice he established in London in 1753 seems to have enhanced his public reputation without making a commensurate contribution to his financial success in medicine. Besides his authorship of a few medical papers which appeared in the 1750s, he contributed reviews and essays on a variety of literary subjects to the *Monthly Review* (May 1756–8). Before *The Sugar Cane*, his most distinctive works were translations of Ovid's 'Hero to Leander' and 'Leander to Hero' (*c.* 1758) and his *Poetical Translations of the Elegies of Tibullus and the Poems of Sulpicia* (London 1759). These latter productions drew acrimonious criticism from Smollett, more, it seems, on account of Grainger's association with the *Monthly Review*, a rival journal to Smollett's *Critical Review*, than from any serious literary demerits.[4]

Considerably improved prospects for Grainger's medical practice and his personal fortune beckoned when, in April 1759, John Borryau (a former pupil, now a wealthy property-owner in St Christopher) engaged Grainger to accompany him to the colonies at an annuity of 200 pounds for life.[5] Through that connection the doctor met and married Miss Daniel Mathew Burt, a wealthy heiress of the island. During the first four-year stint (1759–63), he practised medicine among the slaves of various plantations, including those of his wife's brother. *The Sugar Cane* was composed during regular rounds through the country, and the manuscript sent to Percy and Shenstone for revision (June 1762). Grainger returned to England for his brother's funeral in late 1763, during which visit he read his work to Johnson and some other 'assembled wits'. The poem was published just after his return to the West Indies in May 1764. He died in St Christopher in December 1766.[6]

The Sugar Cane is written in four books, after the design of Virgil's *Georgics*, and consists of some 2,500 lines, with an approximate distribution of about 600 lines to each book, copiously annotated with information on the natural history, topography, and colonial arrangements of St Christopher, and helpful explanations on local customs and learned allusions. The first book describes the ideal soils, seasons, and other physical conditions favourable to the cultivation of sugar cane. Book II mixes locusts, rats, mongooses and earthquakes with hurricanes and other pestilences that threaten crops in these parts, sprinkled with regular negotiations with the muse and ending with the romantic Creole vignette of two star-crossed lovers. The activities of harvesting and grinding bring sugar, slaves and the poetics of labour into sustained perspective in Book

III. The final book enters into detailed ethnographic analysis of the provenance, temperaments, manners, mores and diseases of the slave populations, with good-faith instructions for their proper care and management. A vision of West Indian slave society reimagined on the *negotium* values of sugar and the liberal idealism of a Creole polity closes the work.

Grainger's poem figures its continuity with the preceding authors both by its traditional georgic form and in its deliberate foregrounding of certain content formations. In these respects, as well as in others that belong to the author's peculiar conception, the work stakes out its distinctive ground in the unfolding process of change that would radically alter modes of imagining a Creole future. The choice of georgic permitted Grainger to continue the aesthetics of erasure practised in Ligon and Rochefort: this poem obliterates the aboriginal subject, while privileging sugar and slaves as alternative (constructed) subjects, whose collective value could promote material progress, and whose aestheticized potency could supply the sinews and promote the dream of Creole cultural idealism in St Christopher.

That island supplied a further common link between Grainger and Rochefort. Both authors lived there and made it the subject of their writings. The colony's prior inscription in the *Histoire* initiated a paradigmatic narrative of relationship between centre and margin which will be categorically revised in *The Sugar Cane*. With Ligon and Rochefort Grainger shared the common challenge of representing colonial difference, but by mid-century to an audience markedly better informed, its attitudes increasingly politicized by the publicities of dissenting anti-colonialist and anti-slavery voices. We may defer until later Grainger's primary audience's (the Johnson circle's) aesthetic objections to the anomalies of a West Indian georgic. Johnson had expressed his very forceful repudiation of the slavocrats in these terms: 'Sir, they are a race of convicts, and ought to be thankful for anything we allow them short of hanging.'[7] Thus more than a century of social and philosophical interrogation made it impossible for Grainger to immunize the Creole slavocracy from the contagion of moral evil. Not even the aptitude to infect readers with the commercial value and ideological power of sugar and the opportunity for inventing new cultural paradigms on the colonial frontier could negotiate their full unproblematized respectability. By mid-century the historical developments outlined in the introductory chapter had transformed the climate of moral opinion. The expansion of the sugar trade had crystallized partisan interests but polarized their antagonists. Power relations in St Christopher shifted constantly, placing British control there under continual test from the joint and several threats of Caribs and French.[8]

Still, a century's elapse was not sufficient to change the fundamental issue for these texts of mediation between colonial difference and metropolitan desire. Grainger's scheme of inventing resourceful negotiations from georgic remains faithful in categorical structure, though different in formal mode. Like the preceding texts, *The Sugar Cane* must negotiate its author's and his public's changed relationships – compromises and appeasements occasioned by colonization and slavery. Simultaneously, too, it must participate in that economy of desire and exchange inherent in the 'sweete' factor of the ambiguous binary that is our theme. Georgic is ideally suited to these disparate functions by its originary relationship with colonizing and cultivation, displacement and desire. As a response to the changing demands of creolizing culture in Grainger's St Christopher, georgic becomes the perfect instrumentality of negotiation: it must oscillate between the desire for truth in representing the world of natural objects and the desire to exchange these natural constituents for economic and cultural value. And above all it must be adaptable to those coercions imposed by the author's divided allegiances to the clubbable ethos of Johnsonian politics and the Creole ethos of bourgeois capitalism.

Grainger's practice of natural description echoes some of the sheer sensuous delight of discovery found in Ligon. He is largely exact in his depictions of West Indian natural scenery and vegetation. His copious footnotes on the use of indigenous plants as food and of herbs in the practice of tropical medicine are valuable indices of the interests of a man of science and letters. At his hands, the sugar cane (and tropical vegetation in general) gains the most extensive legitimacy ever conferred on them by any of his contemporaries in English letters. Sugar itself is elevated beyond its common household uses to the level of an elixir that 'dilates the soul with genuine joy', rum is described as 'heart-recruiting', and rum punch outstrips the best burgundies and champagnes of France:

> For not Marne's flowery banks, nor Tille's green bounds
> Where Ceres with the God of vintage reigns

> In happiest union; not Vigornian hills,
> Pomona's loved abode, afford to man
> Goblets more priz'd or laudable of taste,
> To slake parch'd thirst, and mitigate the clime. (III, 501–6)[9]

On the other hand he negotiates from georgic's adaptivity the power to invest the sugar cane with superordinate value and philosophical meaning (surpassing Ligon's achievement by virtue of thematic concentration and poetic licence). In their full-bodied effusiveness these rhetorical libations (of the lines quoted above) ascribe to the sugar cane a value analogous to the grape–wine nexus of antiquity and contemporary Europe. They imagine in sugar a capacity not only to fulfil material need but also to transcend it. Like Ligon, they appreciate its capacity to exchange the products of differently constituted nature for the market values of monetary and consumptive desire. But what separates Grainger from Ligon (who, seemed almost paralyzed by the image of those 'sweaty' black female bodies) is that he anticipates and addresses the inevitable scepticism head-on and early. Within the first thirty lines of the poem he historicizes the validity for literary discourse of the word 'sugar' and its derivatives, citing its use with positive connotations from Chaucer on through to the seventeenth century. Armed with that authority and with a self-confidence born of the experience of alterity, he finds the courage to call his putative critics 'squeamish'.[10] This is a significant valorizing gesture. It claims for the alterities of sugar cane and its cultural matrix the natural privileges of language- and meaning-making without too much genuflection to metropolitan authority.

True, Grainger suffers his own bouts of diffidence (we will examine his aggravated negotiations with the Muse later). But the discourse begun in Ligon on the possibility of inventing a Creole aesthetic is here distinctly transformed and advanced. According to Judith Butler, this claim is linguistically based. In Grainger's terms, the construction is cultural. His georgic may be read as one of Butler's 'narratives', imaginary works enacting their meaning not only in 'telling about desire' but in the telling itself. From a rarity to a contested idea, sugar here undergoes what in the referenced theory of desire is described as an 'essential transformation from nothingness to a linguistic and imaginary presence'.[11]

By claiming for sugar the legitimacy of Chaucer's positive usage, Grainger advances that discourse considerably, in that where Ligon seemed helpless before the imagined threat of female pollution of the aesthetic, and is only able to sustain his vision of survival only by coding women with the sign of the impure, Grainger effectively displaces the old classical–Western prerogative to define value by affirming the sufficiency of sugar cane and its products to cater to appetitive desires and constitute its own myth of superior worth.[12] In like measure, his relation to specific strategies of discourse coded with cultural valency repeats this identical pattern of linkage and disjunction. In an interesting coincidence with Rochefort's exchange negotiations, he singles out the St Christopher fig tree as a symbol from which to invent place. Here, as in Rochefort, the tree figures a *locus amoenus*; but Grainger refrains from pursuing similitudes. His fig tree stands nonpareil, because it is 'enormous size, / Wondrous in shape, to botany unknown, / Old as the deluge' (I: 381–3). In a region where the regular succession of the seasons is not so clearly demarcated as in northern latitudes, the empire of difference holds its sway over his intent. Instead of relying exclusively on the well-tried topos of assimilating the landscape to *premiers temps*, as Rochefort did with Carib place and people, Grainger exploits the oscillating potentials of *neg* and *otium* to appropriate novelty and to exchange it for the transcendent values of diverse signs embodied in St Christopher's natural phenomena. The sugar cane is more than a specimen of exotic colonial nature, more than its exchange value in fiercely competitive economic markets: through the poem it assumes a transforming presence over people and place that establishes the text's desire for a comprehensive creole economy. Thus, georgic assimilates itself comfortably to the demands of *negotium*, allowing the poet to construct an idea of Creole civilization by transforming the great diversity of natural objects figured in Book I into a whole new treatise on signs: new signs for rain, new signs for planting. Instead of superimposing the old stable norms of British value, he proffers this *blazon* of difference as a codex of New World signs for Britain to read and profit from:

> Thus all depends on all; so God ordains
> Then let not man for little selfish ends,
> (Britain remember this important truth!)
> Presume the principle to counteract
> Of Universal love; for God is love
> And wide creation shares alike his care.   (I: 462–7)

The paradigm of colonial priority is hereby inverted: the colony

assumes the leadership in illuminating the empire: a radical enlightenment gesture has been negotiated.

This emphatic affirmation marks a critical point of departure
from the two preceding narratives. *The Sugar Cane*'s continuities with
the newer tradition of colonial narrative and its identification (albeit
contested) with the older Western literary conventions yield to
constructed change, tentative and destabilizing.

That adept use of local signs to subvert the older order of
authentication bids fair to enthrone West Indian nature. But since
that prospect is entertained with only a very brief subjective
authority, the proposition demands specific qualification. While in
imaginative time the event appears to be accomplished in relatively
short order, it must be acknowledged that in the poem's narrative
duration this reversal is not quite so explicitly dramatized, nor is it
accomplished without much tedious searching, diffidence and
anxiety. The notion of abandoning aesthetic decorums and philo-
sphical allegiances sorely taxes Grainger's newly acquired Creole
sympathies (he calls them his 'acculturating sentiments').

This source of tension in the poem is but part of a broader and
more pervasive set of preoccupations that spring from the nature of
the literary project itself (a georgic on sugar cane). Its origins are to
be found in the disconnection among methods of agriculture developed and practised in temperate climates, some of which had now to
be painstakingly adapted, and newer ones evolved and implemented
by trial and error in tropical localities. The poem has to negotiate
these questions at the intersection between two cultures: how to
apply old rules to new husbandry (agri-culture or the culture of the
earth) and still make this 'sweete negotiation' palatable to a sceptical
audience (the culture of letters).[13] Contributing to this tension, too,
are the issues of how to acculturate the author's own metrocentric
poetic sensibilites to a creolized social order, slavocratic, propelled to
increasingly reactionary postures by abolitionist attacks, and consumed by rampant bourgeois exchange values. The critical challenge
facing Grainger, then, was to negotiate the 'terms of art' (his usage)
necessitated by this very secular, exotic subject, and to translate
them into a poetic form acceptable to all parties in his audience.

With respect to form, these are issues that belong familiarly
enough to the aesthetics and poetics of the text. Grainger's challenge
was to negotiate a version of georgic capable of comprehending and
revealing his own moral value, and of winning acceptance for his

proposal of a sugar-cane plantation economy as the root of a new civilization (the recurring confluence of *neg* and *otium*), a mirror by which could be reflected prophetic images of England's future. We shall give these georgic negotiations fuller rendering later on in this chapter.

With respect to ideological function, the evidence is ample that this challenge defines itself as one of those dilemmas of translation we witnessed in Ligon and Rochefort – the fitful searching for form, the troublesome logistics of migrating the Muse to unfamiliar locales – are all bound up with the procedures of imperialist narrative politics, interposing their peremptories through the commonplace figure of the *translatio imperii et studii*.[14] Consistent with its modal relationship to the *negotium*, the *translatio* exhibits in its very linguistic structure a divided (or dialogized) voice, oscillating between the *imperium* of political dominion and regulation and the *studium* of the life of the mind, the domain of letters. In a historicist sense the issues here are analogous to those that entered into the debate about the proper method of translating the classics in the seventeenth and eighteenth centuries.[15] Writing on this subject, James Kinsley observes that both Dryden and Pope aimed to make Virgil and Homer speak good English, as though they were good Englishmen living in Restoration and Augustan London. In the terms of colonization and empire pertinent to the conditions of Grainger's composition, it is essential to pursue the implications further. With the indigenous effectively erased from the scene of discourse (if not entirely from the scene of historical action), it is essential to ask what is the reconfigured role of translation now that its primary function of 'figuring out', or bringing eloquence to the savages, has been obviated. The answer lies in the rhetorical culture war embedded in those disputes raging in Johnson's (or Sir Joshua Reynolds') rooms over the aesthetic propriety of matters like Grainger's introduction of rats into the georgic.[16] The preservationist impulse of literary authority interposes its voice to assert the primacy of a universalizing imperium. For Grainger, though, the matter is rather more complex. Even without the savage, he still has to reckon with savage nature, the 'other' of the landscape, and the exchange values colonization hoped to extract from it.

The commonplace invocations to the Muse he attempts at various points in the poem prove far more perverse than might have been anticipated. The hired muse proves curiously reluctant, if not downright sullen and uncooperative. The tropical heat of West Indian climate seems to throw her into sustained bouts of somnolence, necessitating frequent cajolings. And no wonder: she is called upon variously to sing mosquitoes, sandflies and cockroaches (I, 334); to celebrate the native soils of 'deep dark mould with clay or gravel mix'd' (I, 217); to inveigh against monkeys and rats that devastate ripened crops (II: 46–48); and to depict the awesome spectacle of tropical storms during the hurricane season (II: 270–5). Grainger's besetting temptation is to translate West Indian landscape into an English scene (the dynamic of his *negotium* must be coded with a dialogism efficient enough to help his readers picture what they cannot see, as well as to aid them to see what he wishes they could see as he thinks they would want to see it (III, 526). The *translatio* therefore persists. In his desire to bring savage nature into a new colonialist *oikoumene*, his poem turns the centrally defined ideas of nation and empire into new occasions for negotiation – to the colony's advantage.[17] Translated, this idea is constituted of a *neg* of metropolitan desire for economic progress (exchange values) and an *otium* of post-pastoral, colonial alterity (use-values). I want here to restate the suggestiveness of Cheyfitz's and McKeon's readings as well as to establish how my own construction of negotiation subsumes and deconstructs those readings to the specific references of a developing mid to late eighteenth-century debate between the protagonists of empire and the anatagonists of slavery. The propositions to the Muse stage a variety of scenes of translation whose function may be produced in an oppositional relationship to Cheyfitz's critique (Cicero's unruly schoolboys metamorphose here as St Christopher's exotic and resistive nature) and McKeon's critiques (the 'post-sacral' devolution of sovereignty to private interests) metamorphose here as the Creole desire for sovereignty over the discrete domains of discursive and political economies (Cheyfitz, 114; McKeon, 113–14).[18] Both the resistance and the sovereignty claim are figurally illustrated in the poem's subtle creolization of Johnson's objection to Grainger's original line, 'Now, Muse, let's sing of rats.' According to Boswell's anecdote, when first read to certain members of Johnson's circle that line was the occasion for great risibility, and, on subsequent revision, deferentially emended to:

> Nor with less waste the whisker'd vermin race
> A countless clan despoil the lowland cane   (II: 62–3)

Grainger's deference could not erase entirely the creolizing obligations to represent other equally exotic phenomena (mongooses, chigoes, cow itch). What Johnson feared most, expressed as the pollution of georgic's pristineness, was ideologically amplified in his dogmatic antipathy to colonization, and in a very determined resistance to imperial expansion expressed as a threat to cultural integrity.[19] Grainger would reproduce similar anxieties later in *The Sugar Cane*, but the poem's interior programmatic scheme suggests some experimental solutions.

Against this background of contested legitimacy, Grainger's counter-intuitive pursuit of an ideal of creole civilization can best be understood as a negotiation of georgic's capacity to mediate that ideal and constitute its myth from these thematics: the transvaluation of sugar, the naturalizing of slavery, the invention of a landscape aesthetics from the possibilities of local place, and the micro–meta-narratives of exceptional Creole figures. What Grainger apprehended, and Johnson could or did not, was a continued concretizing of the Creole dissensus: the gradual transformative effects on consciousness exercised by the colonial experience. His immersion in the process of Creolization, aesthetically over the course of the poem and historically over the period of his residency in St Christopher, worked a 'thwarting' effect on his 'sentiments', a diffraction engendered by the Caribbean sea itself that gradually liberates him from the totalizing imperium of his authenticating references – the community of kindred minds – Johnson, Shenstone, Percy.[20] What emerges from the linkages to be examined in the ensuing discussion is an allusive 'crystallization' that yields meanings which Mintz shows to be consistent with the diachronic socially constituting power of sugar.[21] Stuart Hall proffers a pertinent heuristic key to theorizing this complex paradigm of negotiation in his formulation that new subjects are constituted *somewhere*, and that somewhere offers the ground on which those subjects struggle for a new epic.[22] Indeed, it is Grainger's consciousness of the centrality of that myth of struggle to the imagination of his West Indian georgic and to the invention of a culture of West Indian colonizing that gives meaning to his ideas.

The pursuit of georgic holds the traditional kinship community at the metropole and the adoptive Creole community on the periphery in negotiated tension. Grainger's role in providing publicity for Creole desire rests increasingly on the transhistorical facility of georgic to make itself hospitable to diverse cultural formations in the name of well-defined political objectives.

Grainger's desire to reproduce St Christopher as an ideal of Creole civilization was signalled quite early in the poem, in two notes to Book I. The first, a long gloss on the the history and colonization of the island, is a dual figure of material value and philosophical idealism: 'St Christopher has gradually improved and is now at the height of its perfection.' And the second is an endorsement of a quotation from Sir Hans Sloane: 'The inhabitants of St Christopher look whiter, are less sallow, and enjoy finer complexions, than any of the dwellers on the island' (notes labelled *ver* 71 and *ver* 206 respectively). These reflections on the social landscape of the poem's setting continue the narrative of purity established at the outset of this book as one of the key predicates of the Creole cultural ideal; here in Grainger they are no longer conditioned on the contested bodily sites of Indians or Africans but rooted in the beauty of the white ruling class and their women's virginal purity – both posited as irrefutable facts – on the probity of the Creole social sphere, and the fertility of St Christopher's soil. When Grainger is able to distance himself from the Johnsonian imperium as the poem proceeds he attains a clearer vision of the poem's and his subject's integrity: the old myth of the authenticating muse loses much of its paralyzing urgency. A new myth evolves from the image of cultural progress reflected above.

When further rationalized, the sketch of analyzed contents given at the start of this chapter reveals a four-part symphonic structure. Though the parts do not occur in this identical sequence in the linear movement of the poem, their meaningful relationship may be recuperated on this order: first, the themes of sugar and slaves occupy a position of centrality to Grainger's myth; then there are the metaphoric uses of natural description to invent a setting, an architecture of purposeful human exchange. Less prominent, but organic to his structure of Creole desire, is the deliberate mythicization of the figures of Montano (at the end of Book 1) and Junio and Theana (at the end of Book 2). The symphonic pattern is complemented and resolved by further themes of human action linked to generalized Creole profiles so constituted as to produce an ultimate vision of civilizing progress.

Consistent with predecessor publicists, Grainger inscribes his poem and the expanding information order with distinctive factual

contributions as well as individual insights based on his objective
experience of the sugar cane. Like earlier authors, he recognizes
sugar's pivotal role in the continuing economy of exchange that
would enrich Creole planters and fulfil the emulative desires of their
families, associates, and wider bourgeois consumers, yielding them
'well earn'd opulence'. The work of a medical professional, this text
witnesses its author's natural interest in the therapeutic economy of
sugar, especially its usefulness in the treatment of slave diseases.
Directly linked to this natural interest are the careerist purposes for
which georgic was traditionally employed: a very particular kind of
negotium offers itself to Grainger's desires here, an echo of his mixed
or unspectacular fortunes in medicine and the brighter promises that
beckoned in the Creole milieu of St Christopher: both the promise
of property-ownership and the promise of self-reconstitution from
the authority of *The Sugar Cane* itself. Heinzelman's point comprehends all the major categories personified either in Grainger or in
his ideal Creole invention: as a model for a career poem, georgic, he
writes, 'defines writing as a vocation within the largest possible
political economy that includes farming, soldiering, statesmanship,
artisanal   production,   poetic   mythmaking'.[23]   The   diminished
urgency of the problem of acculturating the Muse to a Creole colony
can therefore be resolved by the incremental growth in Grainger's
self-confidence and his consciousness about the sufficiency of Creole
ideas and experience. That confidence and consciousness are pain-
fully won from the defining association of georgic with constant
labour (of which his struggle with the Muse is an apt metaphor), a
struggle to wring health and well-being from the ever-encroaching
predations of perverse nature – locusts, rats, blast – 'Gainst such
ferocious, such unnumber'd bands, / What arts, what arms shall
sage experience use?' (II: 237–38). 'The georgic situates writing as a
vocation within the larger political economy of acculturation.'[24]

Where his distinctive contribution to the discourse rests is in his
use of the plant and its products to institute the liberation I
mentioned earlier, a necessary rhetorical gesture that responds
antiphonally (more in form than in fact) to learned scepticism and
anti-Creole detractions. Just as he establishes St Christopher's
distinction from the outset, so he makes early an unequivocal claim
for sugar that negotiates its unexceptionability as a natural specimen
for the bolder, somewhat mystified claim of its 'independency'. That
is a claim for moral autonomy that translates the plant out of the

sphere of everyday natural growths into a natural paradigm whose growth and thriving do not, like so many other crops, depend on celestial vagaries:

> 'Tis said by some, and not unletter'd they,
> That chief the planter, if he wealth desire,
> Should note the phases of the fickle Moon.
> On thee, sweet empress of the night, depend
> The tides; stern Neptune pays his court to thee;
> The winds, obedient at thy bidding, shift,
> And tempests rise or fall; even lordly man,
> Thine energy controls.-Not so the cane;
> The cane its independency may boast,
> Though some less noble plants thine influence own. (I: 468–77)

The cane has claimed ('translated', in our present terms) its autonomy from the empire of the moon. Its idiosyncratic self-determination figures the restive desire of Creoles to derive their own respectability and independence from those forms of imperium jealously coveted by this book's subjects: political and economic power for bourgeois-capitalist classes, ideological and discursive power for figures like Grainger and Lewis. In fact, this desire has been so strongly encoded in the politics of the poem it negotiates away from the metropole the prerogative of central sovereignty over the uses of imperium, translating that privilege to the periphery and implanting it in the construct of 'the imperial cane' (III: 100). By a direct line of succession that imperium is devolved to the planters and their class. And the devolution, Grainger assures his Creole audience, is attained not by supplication to some totalizing power but is derived from their individual experience with the land and their collective involvement in its productive processes:

> Planter, improvement is the child of Time;
> What your sires knew not, ye their offspring know.
> But hath your art receiv'd perfection's stamp?
> Thou can'st not say – unprejudic'd, then learn
> Of ancient modes to doubt, and new to try.   (I: 278–82)

The procedures for instituting the thematics of slavery are cut from that same cloth of structural compatibility between georgic and negotiation. In *The Sugar Cane*, georgic performs its definitive work of naturalizing slaves to the conditions of colonial acquisition, making them indispensable agents (though not beneficiaries) in the work of building civilization, while obfuscating the rigours of pain and loss that are inherent to their experience in those contexts. Negotiation colludes with georgic to naturalize slaves to bonded labour, muting the consciousness of their loss in exchange for the illusion that the loss of cultural and social identity (the *neg* of commodification) could be cheerfully surrendered for the *otium* of their aesthetic assimilation to the landscape of labour and to Creole status symbols. Depicted as engines of labour, the slaves personify alacrity to every call, gratitude for the occasions of service (to extinguish a cane fire 'they pant to wield the bill') and a 'glad barbarity' in their musical and kinaesthetic expressions. To ennoble this cultural ideal, the disagreeable sound of whips and familiar tortures is erased from the poem by the disingenuous evasion that it would displease the Muse:

> Nor need the driver, Aethiop authoriz'd
> Thence more inhuman, crack his horrid whip;
> From such dire sounds th' indignant Muse averts
> Her virgin-ear, where music loves to dwell:
> 'Tis malice now, 'tis wantonness of power
> To lash the laughing, labouring, singing throng.   (III: 141–6)

The slave presence consistently permits Grainger (and, we will discover, also Beckford) to achieve these complex double aims that are centrally defined in negotiation: here the georgic suppression of cries and denial of pain are selfish negotiations to purchase for Grainger that coveted moral status of being thought 'a good man', a desire expressed in his opening statement of purpose, and to make a genuflection to the higher value of aesthetic decorum (to avoid offending sensibilities). The slaves' broader social role in the poem's deeper political negotiations is to render their physical bodies for imprinting and display to underscore the genteel aspirations of the Creole masterclass.[25] Grainger compounds the absolute meaning of this negotiation for Creole culture by translating the use-value of some slaves' claims to privileged origins into enhanced worth for their masters and their masters' communities:

> Yet, planter, let humanity prevail.
> Perhaps thy Negro, in his native land,
> Possest large fertile plains, and slaves, and herds:
> Perhaps whene'er he deign'd to walk abroad
> The richest silks, from where the Indus rolls
> His limbs invested in their gorgeous pleats   (IV: 211–16)

Nor is this search to ratify human value confined to the human sphere. In the moral economy of georgic and colonial aesthetics the landscape occupies a place on a par with slaves. The natural life of St Christopher is extensively implicated in the poem's mythic constructions. Drawn from a wide variety of external forms, natural description in *The Sugar Cane* is collusive with Grainger's design for negotiating a stable balance of use and exchange values in the Creole imperium in the face of rising political and economic pressure on the West Indian interest. The selection of objects and the shaping of language to the arduous demands of this unfamiliar, hybridized environment produce visual metaphors whose import mirrors the ironic oscillations of the *neg* pole of the text's negotiation. A case in point is to be found in these lines of Grainger's nostalgia for the lost companionship of his London friends:

> O, were ye all here,
> O, were ye here; with him my Paeon's son!
> Long-known, of worth approv'd, thrice candid soul!
> How would your converse charm the lonely hour,
> Your converse where mild wisdom tempers mirth;
> And charity, the petulance of wit;
> How would your converse polish my rude lays,
> With what new noble images adorn?
> Thence should I scarce regret the banks of Thames,
> All as we sat beneath that sand-box shade   (III: 513–22)

The lines express the genuine, natural sense of isolation a man of letters might feel where geographical and cultural barriers have cut him off from the 'converse' of companionable souls; but the lament stays substantively at the deep, personal and subjective level. It does not suppress the creolized voice nor diminish the force of the native landscape (natural or constructed) to assert its value to his mind: a quick exchange of mental images in the succeeding lines illustrates the point:

> See, there, what mills, like giants raise their arms
> To quell the speeding gale! what smoke ascends
> From every boiling house! What structures rise,
> Neat though not lofty, pervious to the breeze;
> With galleries. Porches, or piazzas grac'd!
> Nor not delightful are those reed-built huts,
> On yonder hill, that front the rising Sun;
> With plantanes, with bananas bosom'd deep,
> That flutter in the wind   (III: 526–34)

Those early failures of self-confidence now behind him, and armed with the translated imperium of the cane's 'independency', he can consult the originary use-values of sandbox shade, bananas, and plantains. In fact, by Book II symbols of local difference (perhaps the most striking, the dramatic power and sublime fury of the hurricane, II: 270–86), furnish the novel signs the poem needs to inaugurate a new 'empire of the air'. This privileging in these natural descriptions of originary use-values immunizes the poem's intentionality from rationalist rigour because the apparent contradictions are subsumed in its defined negotiations and in georgic's tendency to fictionalize reality. In concert, these two formations affirm the landscape as its own sufficiency. The collusion of georgic and negotiation within the poem's symphonic structure holds the compelling Creole secular interests (the *neg*) at bay while maximizing an ethic of landscape values (the *otium*).[26]

Grainger expresses in architectural figures this potentiality of the landscape to invent a tropical Creole aesthetic. In a fitting and suggestive placement near the climactic lines of the poem, the palmetto, or royal palm, is made to function as the principal columnar structure in the Creole aesthetic. Classical and neoclassical models are invoked only to pronounce the institution of this ideal founded on the material 'sweete negotiation' of sugar and aesthetically on the protean facilities of georgic:

> But, chief of palms, and pride of Indian grove
> Thee, fair palmetto, should her song resound:
> What swelling columns form'd by Jones or Wren
> Or great Palladia, may with thee compare?   (IV: 522–5)

Grainger's premise that Creole desire and Creole cultural self-consciousness can be grounded in the self-validating positivism of St Christopher's landscape finds its highest personification in the figures of Montano (Book I) and two young lovers Junio and Theana (in Book II). Their placement within the first two books of the poem and the plotting of their respective histories as the climactic episodes of each book humanizes the heroic type signified in Grainger's ideal concept of Creole civilization.

This introduction of Montano in the formative stages of the poem as a paragon of European gentlemanhood, tested and tried by adversity, reiterates the point made earlier about the work as vehicle for its author's self-fashioning. Montano embodies and achieves all the main motivations of Grainger's personal desire. And Montano's record of individual action realizes both the desire of georgic for history and the rich complex values of the colonial *negotium*.

Driven to exile in St Christopher, Montano brings diligence and determined industry to exploiting and managing the resources of his New World estate; his munificence with his worldly goods wins him the respect of his neighbours; his paternal compassion earns him the love and obedience of his slaves (they are 'sturdy,' 'well-fed, well-cloth'd, all emulous to gain / Their master's smile, who treated them like men' [I: 609–11]). For the care he exercised in ordering the physical landscape around his property, Grainger adjudged him a 'friend to the woodland reign' (he planted tamarind groves, hedgerow-trees and cool cedars to shade the public way and to provide protection from the sun's burning rays for slave and stranger alike). The presence of such an exemplar of liberal social ideals and thoroughgoing public-spiritedness provided Grainger with the paradigm of Creole yeomanry. In the microcosm of Montano and his estate we see the vindication of the West Indian slavocracy, the revisioning of St Christopher into Grainger's ideal of a paradise regained from the negotiations of virtue and secular value. Montano is the perfect personification of the eighteenth-century ideal of the active and the retired life; St Christopher the perfect harmony of the busy plantation (prosperous and profitable: *neg*) and the sylvan retreat (leisure-promoting and recreative: *otium*). The mythic proportions Montano's figure achieves by poetic representation is an instructive gauge for measuring the progress achieved in the cultural discourse described by the present selection of texts. Georgic affords Grainger the luxury of retrospect to Rochefort's collusion and prospect to Lewis' more radical envisionings. The Montano narrative colludes in the illusion of amelioration, the image of cheerful slavery reflected in lines IV: 211–16, while confirming the master's timocratic desire. Prospectively it institutes an originary source for Lewis' idealism by imagining a symbolic political microcosm radically isolated from the larger hegemonies of immediate local and remote metropolitan control.[27]

A literalist interpretation of Montano's death early in the poem (at the end of Book I) could prompt a simplistic analogy with the impending collapse of the system he so honourably personified. This would certainly consist with subsequent history, but the coherent unity of Grainger's symphonic structure in its relation to a poetically constituted ideal suggests otherwise. Furthermore, within a georgic context, that history is exchanged for a palatable aestheticized construction. The figure of Montano sets the paradigm for Grainger's vision of a wise and virtuous Creole future, which is inherited by two equally worthy vessels of Creole virtue, the tragic romantic couple Junio and Theana, whose brief career parallels that of Romeo and Juliet. Their narrative need not concern us further except to draw certain inferences germane to our argument. In their death and Montano's the poem negotiates the opposed yet complementary values of secular historical continuity and transfiguration. They are succeeded in the symphonic pattern by images and intimations supporting this theme of Creole slavocratic culture mediated by a leadership of honour, benevolence and enlightenment. Georgic and the specific material sweets of colonial negotiation combine to validate the credibility of Grainger's assurance that the sugar isles afford diverse opportunities for balanced, civilized life, civic honour, political leadership, soldiering, and luxury.

Directed to absentee plantation owners and their wayward sons still seduced by the myth of the Grand Tour and other rituals promising status and personal fulfilment, the appeal induces them to exchange the frustrated pursuit of moribund dreams for distinguished roles in the pioneering work of evolving a new civilization:

> Say, is pre-eminence your partial aim? –
> Distinction courts you here; the senate calls.
> Here crouching slaves, attendant wait your nod:
> While there, unnoted, but for folly's garb,
> For Folly's jargon; your dull hours ye pass,
> Eclips'd by titles, and superior wealth.   (III: 580–5)

In this appeal and its implications we may observe a series of divergences that further intensify Grainger's rift with metropolitan identities, accentuate his departure from some aspects of the earlier publicists' use of display and emulation and foreshadow cultural construction patterns to unfold in the later ones.

While abundance of food to be had from sea and land is made one of his prominent selling points and a significant criterion of privilege for the average Creole, Grainger inscribes the publicity with considerably more deliberate control now, carefully muting the more garish features of lavish display observed in Ligon. Variety and abundance are now advertised not so much as lures to prospective settlers or as symbols for the Continental bourgeoisie's emulation, but more as the hard-won rewards of that constant labour that is the essence of georgic ideology, a sign of Creole virtue approved by a congenial Providence.[28]

How the creolizing dissensus negotiates his affections (and here dissensus imports an alienation, a splitting, or fracturing) still farther away from his traditional allegiances may be located in a sudden turn the poem makes in Book III to disavow the flawed logic of its initial assumption that cultural authority must be based on older historical consciousness. (This turn definitively separates him from the *premiers temps* topos of Rochefort.). This shift marks the beginning of a reversal that gives priority to West Indian nature.

By Book III Grainger's critique of that flawed logic places European nature rather near its point of exhaustion, as, from his viewpoint at mid-century, he perceived it to stand thoroughly 'methodiz'd,' 'pursued' 'through all her coyest ways' and 'secret mazes' (III: 625–6). By contrast West Indian nature, because still a novel idea to the European mind, stands fresh and abundant ('with savage loneliness, she reigns').

Also in Book III, a passage near the end illustrates Grainger's personal imaginative progress away from the lament 'O were ye all here', and affirms the maturity of his West Indian cultural ideal. As well, it explores a variety of negotiations in a single poetic construction: the use of herbs for medicines (a socially redeeming commodification?), and of the seas and caves for commercial mining, with both inextricably allied to the advancement of learning:

> Leave Europe; there through all her coyest ways,
>> Her secret mazes, Nature is pursued:
>> But here with savage loneliness, she reigns . . .
>> Heavens! what stupendous, what unnumber'd trees,
>> Stage above stage, in various number drest . . .
>> Heavens! What new shrubs, what herbs with useless bloom
>> Adorn its channel'd sides; and, in its caves
>> What sulphurs, ores, what earths and stones abound!
>> There let Philosophy conduct thy steps,
>> 'For nought is useless made:' with candid search
>> Examine all the properties of things;
>> Immense discoveries soon shall crown your toil,
>> Your time will soon repay . . .　　　　　　　　(III: 625 *passim*)

The impulse to display is still present but now it has been translated to higher purposes: West Indian nature is revisioned not primarily for economic exploitation but for enlightened aims broadly bracketed under the rubric of 'philosophy'.[29]

This vision of a reformed order could hardly stand immune to social and moral strictures, even if the aesthetic entailments of georgic would sustain it. No doubt, too, the intensifying political climate of dissent towards the trade and the institution of slavery must have engendered some of these liberalizing, if self-serving (to Creole elites), impulses. Slave revolts in neighbouring Nevis and Montserrat (1760) no doubt quickened the consciences to ameliora- tion. Thus, in the concluding movement of *The Sugar Cane*, about two hundred lines of Book IV are given over to meticulous prescription of measures for selecting, managing and protecting slave populations. The moral evil of slavery itself is acknowledged only within the un- threatening context of the visionary imagination. A totally free Creole order is countenanced only in the poet's subjective conscious- ness, not within the context of any explicit moral appeal.

> Oh, did the tender Muse possess the power,
> Which monarchs have, and monarchs oft abuse
> 'Twould be the fond ambition of her soul
> To quell tyrannic sway; knock off the chains
> Of heart debasing slavery; give to man
> Of every colour and of every clime,
> Freedom which stamps him image of his God.
> Then laws, Oppression's scourge, fair virtues prop,
> Offspring of wisdom, should impartial reign,
> To knit the whole in well accorded strife:
> Servants, not slaves; of choice, and not compell'd
> The Blacks should cultivate the cane-land isles.   (IV: 231–43)

This passage is synoptic in its relation to the complex levels on which negotiation facilitates the cultural desire of *The Sugar Cane*. The conditional voice it uses to code the power of Muse and monarch ('Oh, did the tender Muse' etc.) is a fit emblem of the extent to which the progressive creolization of Grainger's conscious- ness has produced a corresponding depletion in each privileged subject's imperium. By extension and categorical association, as shown earlier, imperium subsumes also the strong influence of Johnson and kindred literary interests. From this point to the end of the poem, all further references to these former authenticators are noticeably hemmed in by similar conditionalities or reduced to their immaterial form and perfunctoriness. The poem's title transcends its function as a marker of content and translates its references into the cultural capital Grainger negotiated from the phrase 'the imperial cane'. The *negotium* resides in the odd coupling of specific values; it marks in one locution dualism and simultaneity. *The Sugar Cane*, which began with its own diffident struggle to migrate and placate borrowed authority, closes in full command of its own imperium: a power wrested from that authority and appropriated to the uses of Creole autonomy. And, like Rochefort's *Histoire*, it rests secure in the essential oscillations of *negotium*, because it signs its imperium 'creole', tolerant of relativity, resistive to absolutizing.

But while Grainger succeeds in using these practices to mediate and aestheticize the reactionary pull of georgic, his legacy is substantially reversed by Janet Schaw, whose particularist objectives either efface or negate Creole idealism in order to reassert the priority of British value with a decidedly Scottish definition.

CHAPTER 4

Schaw: a 'saccharocracy' of virtue

We have seen how in Grainger the persistent oscillating dynamic of the *negotium* provides a model both for the divided allegiances of an author's mind and for the shape of cultural mythmaking produced by that mind. In *The Sugar Cane*, the shift and flux of the *negotium* discloses a persistent dilemma in colonialist discourse, a dilemma produced in the text as a struggle between two forms of cultural production. On the one side it illuminates the problem of desire for producing Creole authorship in the face of ideological contestations from metropolitan sources. On the other, it brings into sharp relief the interrogating power of coercive productions (the economies of sugar and slavery) to disrupt that desire.

Following the publication of *The Sugar Cane* by only a decade, Janet Schaw's inscription of her voyage and visit to the West Indies in the *Journal of a Lady of Quality* (written 1774–6)[1] illustrates how the essentialist reduction of authorship and colonial identity to specific narrow assumptions worked to arrest (albeit temporarily) and redefine the *negotium*.

Where Grainger explicitly courts the approval of a small but powerful literary establishment and the larger public audience it commanded, Schaw deliberately constricts those potential sources of criticism by her choice of literary form and her rigorous exclusivization of audience. Defined by form and manner as an epistolary journal, the text addresses its thoughts, reflections and observations to a single friend back in Scotland. Though the particularities of the journal and the always engaging intelligence and sensibility of the author would have held as much interest to her contemporaries as they offer value to present-day colonialist scholars, the *Journal* betrays no very strong evidence that its author designed them for broad public consumption. These differences in the choice and adaptation of literary form and in the definition of audience modify the shape and dynamics of the *negotium* in Janet Schaw.

This chapter will demonstrate how those formal and rhetorical constrictions enable Schaw to pursue a correspondingly reductionist critique of Creole identity, frequently to the extent of negation. Schaw's *Journal* stages a peculiar divergence from the evolving pattern of privileging Creole value; it subverts the vaunts and privileges of the texts on either side of it, substituting in their place an older myth of British social virtue and class entitlement (articulated with a decided bias for Scottish preferment).

Indeed, in the *Journal* this ideal destabilizes the self-conscious pretensions of creolization, especially those rooted in and identified with local sources of value and order. In their place the journal theorizes a Scottish essentialism as the verifying criterion of culture in the colonies the author visits. This sharply contrasting critique exploits the *negotium*'s adaptability while subverting its terms of order to replace the vision of Creole cultural evolution with an older normative ethos that is identifiably and defiantly British with a decidedly Scottish inflection.

Schaw's patriotism and her Scottish consciousness are widely evidenced throughout the journal and that evidence will form the basis for my emphasis on her ethnic particularism. However, these positions are necesarily complicated by the constitutional relationship of Scotland to England – Union 1707 – and Schaw's avowed loyalist allegiances. The *Journal* pronounces a widely acknowledged tension between Englishness and Scottishness which must be assumed, finally, to mediate her ideology.[2] Schaw effectively relegates sugar, slaves and creolization to values far subordinate to those ascribed them by any other author in this study.

Those distinctions argue for her strategic location in the historical and conceptual pattern of this book and therefore merit expansion. When she is placed in a deliberate comparative relationship to the other authors of this study, some interesting patterns emerge. As the only woman within the group, the sense of control she commands in the face of the emergent and the unfamiliar establishes her as a self-confident subject, keenly aware of her social place and intellectual talent. At the same time, the uniquely feminine sensibility and perceptiveness she brings to the assessment of character and definition of value qualify her as an important mediating factor in the overall conceptual structure of this book.

Ligon, we will recall, was preoccupied not only with themes of
individual enterprise (his own material prospects, his patrons' and
their close associates') but also uniquely with valorizing the identity
of settlement and settler to sceptical metropolitan detractors. Schaw
enters the colonial arena a century and a quarter later without any
discernible personal economic interest and destined to stay for only
some five weeks. That anxiety over fashioning a new self from a
divided consciousness was, therefore, not an urgent issue for her.
Rochefort emerged as the consummate 'negotiator', a vigorous
promoter of French national interests and imperialist aims, the adept
exponent of a cultural politics that posited the compatibility of
indigenous mores, creolizng processes and established traditional
values. The persistence of these implicit tensions leaves Grainger's
work always ambivalently torn between his colonial and metropolitan allegiances. After Rochefort and Grainger, Schaw is the third
author with an important relationship to the colony of St Christopher (St Kitts). She shares with Rochefort an enthusiasm for the
island's flora and fauna, both as alimentary and aesthetic sources.
With Grainger she shares Scottish nationality, though she assigns
that identity greater formative value in her vision of colonial order
than he does. By pursuing a distinctly social critique of actions,
forms and relationships she observes (without any pronounced
interest in the more public matters of economy and politics), she
concerns herself uniquely with the projection of family and ethnicity,
the value of the connections that flow from them, and the social
capital these return to strengthen an elite's public visibilty.

These values are projected in the *Journal* within closely drawn
circles centred on the ship, the plantation home, meals, visits,
churchgoings and other forms of convivium. Thus Schaw inserts
into the textual economy of creolization the primacy of her own
subjectivity, without troubling herself overmuch with the weightier
themes of empire, governance, slavery or the sugar trade. In so far as
she seems driven to supererogate Scottish identity as a source for
conferring moral value and social quality on colonial life, she
reproduces the type of Rochefort's public nationalist impulses for
her own privately defined purposes. In so far as these stances model
an imaginative desire to reconfigure the social–cultural identity of
power within the colonial polity, she serves as a fulcrum for broad
British desire and a counterweight to Rochefort's Gallic nationa-
lism(we shall have occasion to remark her undisguised francophobia

in a later reference). This embodying of an ethnic particularism within a broad British imperialist design codes her authorial subjectivity, in Simon Gikandi's formulation, as a 'conduit' for synthesizing and legitimating that design. 'Thus, to be Scottish in the service of colonialism was to belong to a larger, more compelling and authoritative narrative, one made possible by the imperial mission.'[3]

Because she so deftly contains her critique of cultural order within the intimate spheres coded above as 'closely drawn narrative circles' her journal fictionalizes an apolitical stance with respect to the order of things in the West Indies, thus appearing prospectively to place her at odds with Beckford, who assumes the public role of Creole publicist and pro-slavery apologist in defence of his private economic interests in slave plantations.[4] Her kinship with Lewis resides in some shared features of temperament and cognitive attitudes: both exemplified strong opinions, strongly enunciated; both kept journals, a form that facilitates self-revelation and places high privilege on the prerogatives of private judgement and subjective intelligence. But Schaw differs from Lewis by her immersion in and relish for the world of aristocratic privilege. Her interest is consumed by the perquisites and appurtenances of such privilege, while he distances himself from the other slave-owners, alienating them by his liberal views and reformist tendencies. While she shows little interest in the slaves, he finds them human creatures of bewildering complexity and endless fascination.

A biographical sketch of Schaw with some reference to the social and intellectual forces that animate her thought will provide some context for the origins of her attitudes and their informing ideologies.[5] Related on her mother's side to the renowned Sir Walter Scott, Janet Schaw was born, as nearly as can presently be estimated, between 1739 and 1744. She almost certainly spent most of her life between the Edinburgh suburb of Lauriston and other addresses within the city itself. Though we know little about the actual conditions of her education, it is clear from the standard of her writing that she was well schooled, from her learned allusions that she was widely read, and from her skill in observation that her formation must have neglected neither the phenomena of mundane life nor the higher values of the intellectual and the aesthetic. The incidence of learned allusions in her writing places it in favourable comparison with some of the most literate of her day. (Among authors mentioned are David, Milton (191), Shakespeare (191), Lord Kames, and Ossian (119.) A single woman all her life, she travelled to the West Indies and North Carolina (1774–5) and to Portugal (from the autumn of 1775 to the winter of 1776). On her return to Scotland, she is thought to have lived in Edinburgh at least until 1779, after which date the remaining record of her life is difficult to verify.[6]

Her parents, Anne and Gideon Schaw, were landowners of substance, with a 14-acre farm in Lauriston.[7] Gideon Schaw served as an important functionary at Perth and Edinburgh in the regulation and collection of customs duties on tobacco imported from the Americas.[8] Her two brothers sought their fortune and success in the New World. Alexander, the younger, a member of the travelling party described in the *Journal*, followed in his father's footsteps, and gained an apointment as a customs official in St Christopher.[9] He was to attain an even more lucrative post as Paymaster to the Board of Ordnance in Dublin early in the nineteenth century.[10] Robert Schaw, the elder brother, emigrated to America, where he became a successful partner in a Wilmington, North Carolina, merchant firm in the 1760s. He was later to attain the rank of colonel in the revolutionary forces in 1775. Also in her travelling party were three children, Fanny, John Jr., and William Gordon Rutherfurd whose father, John Rutherfurd, was the nephew of Anne Schaw. Rutherfurd married the widow of a governor of North Carolina and inherited through her and these children notable wealth and property. In her possession as she entered Antigua, Schaw was carrying letters of introduction to the governor-general from one of the chief luminaries of eighteenth-century British jurisprudence, Lord Mansfield.[11]

Janet Schaw came to maturity in the Edinburgh of the Scottish Enlightenment. It would be instructive to discover from future research what her personal contacts with the great figures of that intellectual connection might have been, but it is not difficult to infer the relationship of her ideas to those that were the common topics of discourse in some of the homes of persons of quality, and in the academies and places of public discourse in her time.[12] Schaw's implicit and expressed notions of quality as a metaphor for reimagining the ordering values of Creole society may be conclusively recuperated from a broad domain of Scottish Enlightenment ideas. The previously mentioned tension of English/Scottish identity, so definitive to her ideal of the ruling plantation ethos, finds an expedient resolution in Lord Kames' validation of the Scots' claim to 'shared Britishness', and in the enabling legitimacy he ascribes to property. Schaw pointedly remarks the irony that Fanny should be reading that author's *Elements of Criticism* to strengthen her composure when the storm breaks out.[13] The ability to rationalize the dissonance between the idea of a ruling elite identified with superior social rank and moral virtue and simultaneously identified with the corrupting effects of slavery is traceable to disparate readings of Adam Smith.[14] While the generic basis for her belief in the natural inferiority of certain races, the proper subordination of the lower classes and their alleged greater tolerance for pain and other forms of deprivation can be found in a wide assortment of authoritative sources, her specific attitude to African slaves in Antigua and St Kitts resonates in David Hume's palpable revulsion to African nature.[15] The easy leap from prescriptive inferiority and radical inequality to ethnic or cultural particularism is another aspect of her ideology that has broad buttresses even among enlightened thinkers.[16] There were in Schaw's Scotland so many social controls for what Bruce Lenman calls the 'inculcation of deference' it is not surprising to find within her own national intellectual tradition key legitimating doctrines for analogous colonial conditions.[17]

The Scott bloodline, her brimming pride in her brothers' ambitions and successes, her ties to colonial wealth and power in the Rutherfurd and other well-placed connections both in Scotland and in the New World – all these Janet Schaw wears with a self-consciousness that rings clear in the reference to rank encoded in the titular 'lady of quality'. Imbued with a stock of ideas authorized by some of the best minds of her age, Schaw models certain implicit assumptions about her entitlements to judge, value and negotiate which we shall see in the forthcoming analysis of her colonial experiences. How that ideal of quality assumes conceptual importance for this book will be demonstrated as the chapter traces its development from a solipsistic identification with herself into a distinctive criterion of value for her class. Her ideal of quality redeems the image of colonial society, focusing it on a select circle of well-placed Scottish friends and connections in the West Indies.

Though the *Journal* contains the record of Schaw's travels during the years from 1774 to 1776, it would be nearly another century and a half before modern scholars discovered, edited and published it for wider readership. The material is arranged in a four-part structure, each part a chapter covering the successive stages of Schaw's travels, the first the voyage to the West Indies, the second her visit to Antigua and St Christopher, the third her visit to North Carolina, the fourth her return voyage to Scotland with a stopover in Portugal. That sequencing traces the linear progression of the author in time and space. It also functions, in interesting metaphoric ways, to produce an outward visible image of the inward shape and pattern of meaning which the *negotium* of creolization takes on as it is subjected to Schaw's purposeful scrutiny in two West Indian localities. The considerable length of the voyage narrative not only corresponds to the comparatively long (seven weeks) and perilous trans-Atlantic crossing, but also furnishes the writer with materials for a critique of those discontents of late eighteenth-century Scottish life (poverty, tyranny, agrarian crisis) that fuelled emigration and problematized her vision of colonial quality.

Amounting to nearly one-fourth of the journal, this narrative duration fulfils a significant two-fold function, generic and structural. The perils of storm, food scarcity, class and race discrimination – all experienced in the first chapter – situate the text within the larger historical framework of narrative genres representing travel, discovery, and expansion (national and individual). As a structural factor, the voyage prefigures larger social, moral and ideological themes, particularly as it brings Schaw into close confinement with servants, displaced lower-class emigrants, and an exploited, abusive ship's crew, all conditions which elicit from the author critical attitudes about class and cultural desire. Displacement, political and economic oppression, slavery and indenture, class and cultural identity – all these themes that are typically deployed on colonized terra firma and are such an integral part of the complex process defined as creolization, are foregrounded (within the narrative microcosm of the *Jamaica Packet*) well in advance of Schaw's landing in the West Indies. These generic and structural relationships will be developed further on in this chapter.

The form of Schaw's text has already been identified as an epistolary journal, and though each part of that composite is familiar enough to eighteenth-century letters, the composite merits some comment and qualification. The writer of these dispatches addresses herself to an unnamed (presumably female) recipient back in Scotland, though the journal contains no responses from that addressee. The *Journal* portrays that reader as an intimate and a social equal, sharing with the writer similar tastes and sensibilities, assumed to possess enlightened interests and intelligent understanding. These assumptions are set out in Schaw's delineation of her working plan for the journal:

I propose writing you every day, but you must not expect a regular Journal. I will not fail to write whatever can amuse myself; and whether you find it entertaining or not, I know you will not refuse it a reading, as every subject will be guided by my own immediate feelings. My opinions and descriptions will depend on the health and the humour of the Moment, in which I write; from which cause my Sentiments will often appear to differ on the same subject. (20)

Schaw addresses her reader directly, consulting her affections, professing her own sentiments of love, together with her abiding regard for the special bonds that tied them together in friendship and cultural identity, reaffirming the priceless values of hearth and home. In this respect, her journal differs also from Lewis', where the implied audience is either the very writing, observing self, or a wider public of likeminded aesthetes and readers sympathetic to liberal ideas. In another marked divergence from the expectations raised by the label 'epistolary', this journal is not ordered as a volume of many individual letters or regularly dated entries; it is composed rather of continuous observations and discourses written at different times, and yet held together by the coherent purposes and good sense of the author. Here and there one encounters some passages that were obviously 'written to the moment', as, for example, Schaw's account of the rites of passage observed when the ship crossed the Tropic of Cancer(69–72), or the chapter relating the last part of the voyage, in which she describes the sighting of land (Antigua) and the dropping of the anchor.[18]

When read in its relation to the other texts of this study, the *Journal*'s characteristic contraction of the audience is well suited to the ideal of social and cultural exclusivism Schaw pursues. She is even more extreme in her emphasis on social selection than Rochefort; the form negotiates away the sources of division and ambivalence so explicitly acknowledged in Grainger and so deliberately masked by aesthetic devices in Beckford. In Schaw the journal offers precisely the kind of private form in which the dichotomies of the *negotium* can be contained: it affords her adequate cover to rationalize the coexistence in the West Indies of contradictions like social inequality, brutality, and slavery (*neg*), alongside benevolent paternalism, genteel elegance, and sumptuary excess (*otium*). It provides her with a necessary insulation from the insistent contestations of more public discourses like Rochefort's *premiers temps* and Grainger's georgic.

Nor are these themes, or the strategies linked to them, restricted to the conventional creolized arena of plantation colonies dominated by an affluent and powerful white ruling class and supported by a large population of black slaves. The conditions outlined below illustrate the early appearance of those themes and strategies in the narrative. Thus prefigured, they furnish a compelling motive for Schaw to set an ideological agenda predicated on her own social identity and cultural values, and extrapolated later to a well-defined visible class in West Indian plantation society. Indeed, as was indicated earlier, the voyage narrative of chapter one prefigures and anticipates these relationships, serving as a pre-text to the central chapters set in Antigua and St Christopher.

Included in her travelling party are the Schaws' two servants, Mrs Mary Miller (Abigail), Janet's maid, a native Scotswoman; and Robert, Alexander Schaw's manservant, an East Indian. While Abigail is always referred to by the more formal title of 'Mrs.' Robert's cultural identity is virtually effaced by this adopted name with not even an apologetic recording of his true name. For both servants, the point of their social subordination is strongly accentuated: in Robert's case particular attention is drawn to the idiosyncrasies of his non-native English by direct quotations which function as allusive markers for natural class and race inferiority. For both servants that social distinction is reinforced by other references to their domestic functions and personal manners.

The main body of Schaw's fellow passengers is composed of Scottish emigrants driven from their homesteads by heartless landowners.[19] The ship's owner and the ship's captain reproduce that pattern of abuse and victimization on both these hapless figures and on the crew. The passengers are cold and wet most of the time, their physical accommodations straitened by the combined chicaneries of owner and captain. As if these were not sufficient adversities, the ship is assailed by two violent storms, one lasting for some ten days of the long Atlantic crossing. These natural disorders exacerbated the already incommodious living conditions; billows flooded the cabins and destroyed food, thus reducing both high and low ranks to a common lot of deprivation and misery.

The plight and inferior status of the emigrant passengers make

them irresistible sources of narrative interest for Schaw, and that
interest consistently serves to elicit and promote her theory of class
and society. Historically these people formed part of that human
wave known as the highland emigration, landholders evicted from
their homesteads by proprietors bent on increasing their profits by
using the lands for other economic purposes.[20] Like the slaves of the
African trade, they had been smuggled aboard the ship and confined
in hatches below deck. Entirely unaware of this trickery, Schaw had
assumed the ship to have been reserved for the exclusive charter of
her family group:

I saw the deck covered with people of all ages, from three weeks old to
three score, men, women, children and suckling infants. For some time I
was unable to credit my senses, it appeared a scene raised by the power of
Magic to bring such a crowd together in the middle of the Sea, when I
believed there was not a soul aboard but the ship's crew and our own
family. Never did my eyes behold so wretched, so disgusting a sight. They
looked like a cargo of Dean Swift's Yahoos newly caught. (28)

Schaw's reaction of shock ('I was unable to credit my senses') can be
attributed to the shipowner's unscrupulous abrogation of a common
contractual agreement. But further intensifying sensations exceed
that motive. They introduce class sensibilities and anxieties about
the threat of social contamination ('so disgusting a sight' and 'a
cargo of Dean Swift's Yahoos') and move her concern closer to the
stock discourses on the sight of the black slave body, notably in its
relationship to producing sugar, but generally in its proximity to
whiteness in Creole contexts. The immediate recoil from this threat
to the refuge of writing validates my earlier claim that her journal
serves as an insulation (*otium*), in this case from the *neg* of perceived
subhuman contact: 'As I am resolved no more to encounter those
wretched human beings, I will have the more time to write.' The
passage continues to raise Swiftian animalistic images of fear and
loathing, calling into question the biological and moral equality of
these passengers:

Indeed you never beheld anything like them. They were fully as sensible of
the motion of the Vessel as we were, and sickness works more ways than
one, so that the smell which came from the hole, where they had been
confined, was sufficient to raise a plague aboard. I am besides not a little
afraid they may bestow upon me some of their live-stock [presumably body
lice], for I make no doubt they have brought thousands alongst with them.

Partly to her credit, it must be acknowledged that she is mollified by the warm, 'tender sensations' and 'sweet remembrance' stirred in these emigrants as they catch a last fleeting glimpse of their native home, the Orkney Islands (33): 'oh! had you seen them their hands clasped in silent and unutterable anguish, their streaming eyes raised to heaven in mute ejaculations, calling down blessings and pouring the last benedictions of a broken heart on the dear soil that gave them being . . .' (34). This description bears a striking analogy to a recurrent topos in slave narratives.[21] By this act of transgressive slippage, the lower-class Scottish refugees are effectively equated with the African slaves, already initiated into a paradigm of the social order that awaited them in the colonies. (When their money ran out half way through the voyage, they were obliged to indenture themselves to the captain in return for food and lodging [54–5].)[22]

At the same time, Schaw inscribes her own text into that larger narrative by which the creole *negotium* was initiated in Ligon. Her sympathy is easily recognizable as an expression of fashionable sentiment common among certain readers and writers of the late eighteenth century, but the authenticity of the sentiment can be gauged from the way she holds herself at a safe remove from the final meaning and profundity of these emotions by insisting that the prospect before them was '*their native* land', a place of '*rude, wild rocks*' (emphases mine) and snow-covered mountains. Moreover, the true motives of her concern are exposed and their integrity further subverted by her explicit speculations about the depleting effect these forcible evictions and large-scale depopulations would have on the capacity of the metropole to recruit soldiers for the gathering political upheavals in America. We will see a similar detachment from personal emotion in Schaw when she describes the use and effect of the whip on the slaves in St Christopher.

In still more dramatic ways life on board this ship, conceived in Schaw's mind as the private conveyance of a genteel family, fore-shadowed and reproduced some of the more horrific scenes of the Atlantic slave trade and plantations. In these examples the perpe-trators were the ship's owner and the ship's captain. On the day of the ship's departure, a black slave named Ovid (Schaw calls him 'our [ship-] owner's poor Devil') was forcibly dragged aboard (22–3) and bound in irons. About a week later, as they stopped to take on supplies at Fair Isle in Scotland, the captain and other crew members stripped and bound one islander to the ship's mast while holding other islanders prisoner below deck (41–2). This arbitrary abuse was the captain's attempt to avenge himself of a theft he had suffered allegedly at their hands on an earlier trip. Schaw depicts these natives as rude in looks, manners and dress, and 'speaking a bad sort of English' (38–39). Emphasizing those attributes codes the islanders on a social parity with persons of lower social class in the *Journal*. Schaw's sympathy is engaged only to validate and ennoble her brother's resolute intervention on their behalf. And, in a subsequent episode, she emphatically reflects that nobility on herself by adverting to her own compassion in offering a few hartshorn drops to a young emigrant woman who had miscarried under the stress of stormy seas (50). As in the case of the weeping emigrants, the suffering objects here are humanized by the social prerogative of a Schaw, a kind of *noblesse oblige* that redeems poor wretches from torture but, even more essential to Schaw's social ideology, it also underlines the Schaw class distinction and foreshadows the criteria her journal will imply for exerting political influence in the colonies.

With the ship now transformed into a liminal arena permissive to blatant forms of fraud, abuse and tyranny, the crossing functions to test Schaw's tolerance for extreme patterns of behaviour that may be engendered in minds released from the normal constraints of civilized life, in effect to confront her with an ironic foretaste of the colonized environment on which her desire for idealized culture will eventually become cathected. As the ship crossed the Tropic of Cancer she was 'entertained' by certain traditional rituals incidental to that stage of the Atlantic voyage. Passengers are subjected to head-shaving, drenchings, and extortion on pain of being hoisted up the ship's mast and hurled from thence into the sea (70–1). Schaw's brother again intervenes with a response that once more uses moral indignation and outraged sensibility as powerful markers for social intelligence and cultural superiority. Assuming it to be his civilized obligation to restore social harmony, he reprimands the captain, and dispenses his own money to redeem the emigrants' confiscated clothes (72): Schaw records the episode in these terms: 'I never in my life saw my brother in such a passion; he swore solemnly, that the moment he got to land, he would raise a prosecution against the Cap[tain] who pleaded it was the custom, and only intended as a little drink money to the sailors. If that is the case, replied my brother, let them give up their cloths, and they shall be satisfied' (Alex in effect paid for their grog [72]).

That episode is pivotal to this chapter's thesis in several ways. It functions as the climactic scene with which the *Journal* inscribes the Schaw authority to project the weight of family, class and nationality on the conduct of life around them. It serves as the prologue to the next and main assay of cultural politics through which the meaning of Schaw's visit to Antigua and St Christopher will be negotiated. In attempting to fix family, class and nationality as stable sources of identity, Schaw was in effect redefining the criteria by which these plantation societies could attain cultural value in her eyes and in the eyes of her exclusive audience. The force and effects of difference that must normally be addressed or reconciled in these texts are thus, in Schaw, negotiated away by these three proffers so uniquely centered in her own person and subjectivity. Just as her brother asserted his superior self and presence to repudiate the ugly face of incivility, abuse and oppression, so she will, by specific revisionings of certain factors (until now indivisible from Creole thematics), revalue those thematics by some combination of those three presumptively higher values.

This revaluation is pursued by inverting the narrative emphases given to sugar and slaves, and their role in producing the ethos of creolization, and supplanting them by her essentialist myth of Scottish quality. Schaw's journal issues a philosophical challenge to the concept and constitution of the *negotium*. She imagines a highly civilized enclave of transplants, blissfully abstracted from that tainted nexus of sugar and slaves (*negs*), inoculated from the moral and cultural mutations of Creole experience, preserving their intrinsic virtue by a myth of Scottish national identity. Where in Ligon, the *negotium* is explicitly formulated with sugar and slaves at one pole, and with the cultural and material value that could be produced from them at the other, in Schaw the paradigm is revised to raise the profile of social value. Indeed, it is social value that dominates her discourse, while economic motives, despite their priority in the colonial context, are fictively suppressed, so that the themes and occasions of difference (slaves and slavery, sugar cane and sugar production) are rendered merely subservient or are altogether effaced from the discourse.

The earliest manifestation of this implicit revisionism is to be found in Schaw's assessment of Antigua's natural beauty. She wrestles to keep her grip on reality in the face of the colony's exotic differences. The openness of the houses ('Nobody here is ashamed of what they are doing, for all the parlours are directly off the street,

and doors and windows constantly open'), the comparative inform-
ality of social life there ('I own it appears droll to have people come
and chat in at the windows, while we are at supper, but if they like
the party, they just walk in, take a chair, and sit down' [85]), or the
milking of a goat at the breakfast table (86) all force her to
acknowledge differences that destabilize her sense of normal order.
However, all these tokens of the exotic and the unfamiliar are
curiously negotiated away by the colonizing impulses of her imagination. Her remote positioning, offshore, aboard a ship about to drop
anchor does not deter the appropriative tendencies of the colonialist's gaze. Antigua's landscape is immediately assimilated and
domesticated: 'We had the island on both sides of us, yet its beauties
were different, the one was hills, dales and groves, and not a tree,
plant or shrub I had ever seen before; the ground is vastly uneven,
but not very high; the sugar canes cover the hills almost to the top,
and bear a resemblance in colour at least to a rich field of green
wheat . . .' With only modest apology, she argues herself out of any
residual diffidence the comparison might raise: 'Will you not smile, if
after this description, I add that its principal beauty to me is the
resemblance it has to Scotland, yes, to Scotland, and not only to
Scotland in general, but to the Highlands in particular' (74). The
political arrangements of union having located Scotland within the
core of empire, this initiating gesture presages the character of
cultural discourse to be evolved from this place and public. Read in
the light of the vital role Scots Highlanders played in the defence of
empire, notably in the American Revolution, the discursive figures of
assimilation and appropriation take on even greater point here.[23]

For all its centrality to the enterprises of expanding empire, trade
and bourgeois/Creole consciousness, sugar does not enjoy major
discursive privilege in Schaw's journal.[24] Her ideology of social
value, primordially grounded in nationally defined cultural norms,
precludes that earlier established narrative priority. Naturally, the
plant's ubiquitousness and the extent to which its production
engrossed human energy and natural resources exercise an inescap-
able power on her physical senses and on her imagination. These
features earn scattered references.

Sugar's virtually total permeation of daily life struck her in a very
dramatic way in one of those shipboard scenes that so insistently
intimates colonial realities. In the turmoil and disarray of the second
storm at sea, the author suffered the most inglorious affront to her

dignity when a barrel of molasses capsizes over her (52). Then later, on her arrival in Antigua, sugar figured once more with irresistible prominent as an object in the hospitality extended to her by local hosts. A tour through the canefields afforded her enough authority to pronounce the produce then standing a 'good crop.' But a combination of calculated denial strategies and merely passing interest for the subject informed her decision to assign the writing of a full chapter to another party. That chapter was mysteriously lost from the *Journal*'s final contents.

By these diverse vagaries sugar is demoted from the journal's primary narrative preoccupation. In Ligon and Grainger its mythic valuation was always finally something of an idiosyncrasy. In their texts, it commands the place of distinctive, autonomous moral agency in the project of displaying Creole culture. In Schaw, that idiosyncrasy is recuperated to the authorial identity itself, to privilege her own superior sense, intelligence and sensibility above the priority such factors as landscape and natural vegetation enjoyed. Those prior associations with mystical essence, its rhetorical implication in the very fate of civilization (both hyperbolically fantastic), are now displaced by significant identifications with those (*neg*) forces that were subverting the Creole idea.

Three salient instances that illustrate this inversion of sugar's value are to be found in significant coincidence with negative consumption and exhaustion. In each instance sugar is signified as a source of exhaustion and enervation. The first occurs during the Antigua visit, in the middle of a lavish Sunday dinner scene. In one of those familiar catalogues of Creole publicity Schaw lists 'Guine[a] fowl, Turkey, Pigeons, Mutton, fricassees of different kinds intermixed with the finest Vegetables in the world, as also pickles of everything the Island produces' (96). Two very respectable planters of the island, Martin and Halliday, were among the company. Against this backdrop of opulence and repletion, the demise of sugar is darkly reflected as Schaw notices that cattle-rearing is beginning to displace sugar cane on upland plantations that 'have begun to wear out from the constant crops of sugar that have been taken from them'. The second, referring to St Christopher, is another allusion to the all-consuming appetite of the sugar cane in the colonies, but is partly erased because positioned within a conventional landscape topos: 'The whole island is a garden divided into different parterres. There is however a great want of shade; as everywhere is under sugar' (130). And the final reference implicates the mercantilist strictures that characterized the trading relationship between Britain and her colonies, a sore indignity to the autonomous aspirations of the Creole economic and political elites: 'They drink only green Tea, and that remarkably fine; their Coffee and chocolate too are uncommonly good; their sugar is monstrously dear, never under three shillings per pound. At this, you will not wonder when you are told, they use none but what returns from England double refined, and has gone thro' all the duties' (99).

These oblique modes of representing the most lucrative of British West Indian productions give point to the present argument that Schaw's *Journal* is distinctly implicated in a revisionist project whose objective is to reaffirm the interests and idealize the values of a colonial ruling class at a crucial moment in the history of sugar plantation economies.

Like sugar, slaves and slavery are equally under-represented in the thematic analysis of Schaw's *Journal*. And when these subjects appear in the narrative, their true proportions are distorted by heavy-handed absolutizing to one extreme or other of the *negotium*. In either case the distortions serve to rationalize the validity of Schaw's myth of Scottish cultural exclusivism even as they elide the inherent contradictions of that idealism by narratively subverting the factors that constituted the Creole ethos.

Schaw destabilizes the human identity, social place and political relationship of the slaves to their white overlords by a variety of subjective constructions. Her first encounter with slaves comes early in the Antigua letters, and is inscribed with the virulent candour of those same images of animalism and savagery that characterized her class response to the hapless emigrants. The very first page of the Antigua and St Christopher chapter documenting the events of her first minutes on land identify slaves with animals by drawing on that very pattern of assimilation evoked on shipboard: 'Just as we got into the lane, a number of pigs run out at a door, and after them a parcel of monkeys. This not a little surprized me, but I found what I took for monkeys were negro children, naked as they were born' (78). That this imagery should have issued so spontaneously from her mind not only attests to the potency of widely retailed racial stereotyping, but also dramatically symbolizes the narrow construction of human order essential to her ideal of a slavocracy of virtue. To accommodate this kind of otherness, the criteria must be rigidly prescribed; African slaves must be abased to an equality with beasts (not only were they monkeys; they appeared in close concourse with pigs!) and, as such, they are proscribed from the natural condition of humans.

As we have shown in preceding illustrations, the predication of cultural superiority on the claims of a myth of moral virtue and social purity invariably coexists in an inextricable relationship with the very sources that produce social anxiety about corruption and contamination. That paradox materializes for Schaw immediately after this incident when a black slave girl welcomes her with a glass of sangarie (= sangria, a drink made of Madeira wine, water, sugar and lime juice). On this occasion the black presence passes without comment; the beverage is pronounced to be a 'most refreshing drink', and the clear, sharp tension between this slave's role here and the simian imagery eight pages earlier is masked by Schaw's convenient shift to compliment the innkeeper's gracious manners, and the exceptional character of her deceased husband (a Scot). The hostess requites those compliments with equally respectful reference to the Schaws' Scottish provenance. In a later description that places a slave in close proximity to the drinking water of white people, Schaw particularizes the scrupulous measures taken to preserve the separation of orders: slave from free, impure from pure: 'It is presented to you in a Cocoa nut shell ornamented with silver at the end of a hickory handle. This is lest the breath of the Servant who presents it should contaminate its purity' (111).

This anxiety about social purity is revisited in remarks on the widespread evidence of interracial sexual relations. Miscegenation clearly impeaches her mythic desire, but she diverts this cognitive dilemma to serve her own thesis correlating moral capacity with social class. She imputes the cause of such relations to an especially sexually aggressive category ('wenches'), one coded with biological inferiority ('a spurious and degenerate breed') (112).

This theory of biological determinism is further invoked to mitigate the brutal practice of whipping and other forms of torture inflicted on the slave body. The journal's portrait of a work gang is the clearest enunciation of Schaw's relation to eighteenth-century race theory:

They are naked, male and female, down to the girdle, and you constantly observe where the application has been made. But however dreadful this must appear to a humane European, I will do the Creoles justice to say, they would be as averse to it as we are, could it be avoided, which has often been tried to no purpose. When one comes to be better acquainted with the nature of the Negroes, the horrour of it must wear off. It is the suffering of the human mind that constitutes the greatest misery of punishment, but with them it is merely corporeal. As to the brutes it inflicts no wound on their mind, whose Natures seem to bear it, and whose sufferings are not attended with shame or pain beyond the present moment. (127)

In an age when a proportionate endowment of sense and sensibility was increasingly taken to be the measure of individual value and consequence, it is significant that Schaw's assessments here place blacks outside the notice of the civilized systems of value. In effect, it renders them both sentiently and socially dead and therefore not deserving of enlightened moral sympathy or defence.[25] Consigned to the category of the socially dead, they are properly excluded from civil and political status.[26] Denied the fundamental human trait of sentience, they are reassigned to a category that is at once apathetic (lacking in or incapable of feeling) and asocial (falling outside legitimate human categories).[27]

Central statements in Schaw's forays into an ethnography of morality and purity, these speculative leaps complete the circuit of social taxonomies begun with the emigrants. Raising the spectre of the Yahoos there and of brutes here, she rules lower-class white emigrants and black slaves out of the morality–purity myth which naturalizes her system of cultural exclusivism.

This construction identifies Schaw's opinions with some very clearly determined ideologies. My postulation of a system here is fortified by Charles H. Hinnant's strong assertions that the classic eighteenth-century preoccupations with these themes in Swift's *Gulliver's Travels* are related to the construction of a conceptual scheme that desires to exclude 'the anarchic implications of dirt' and other 'dangers' of the natural world as threats to order.[28] The near dogmatic certainty with which the African relation to mind is here negated echoes David Hume's famous position.

Thus Schaw's social ideology is legitimized by its inferential identification with the moral antithesis of the Yahoos and by its allusive relations to the established authority of a Scottish Enlightenment mind: both inference and allusion combine to invent authority for the surrogacy role of Scotland in British imperial designs.[29]

All these ideas propel the journal's pendulum towards the negative pole. At the opposite pole of the *negotium*, the more desirable (to plantation interests) images of slaves draw from that very serviceable fund of European mythology about Africans: primitivism. Ligon tapped it to validate his conceit that slaves possessed an infantile, compliant nature, completely devoid of the will to resist or to desire freedom, their happiness the benevolent gift of liberal-minded masters.[30] Grainger invoked it in his portrait of the paternalistic Montano. Now, at a moment of growing political instability from rising anti-slavery agitation and anti-colonial sentiment, Schaw appropriates the mythology to imagine political continuity for the select but ominously threatened ruling families of her own private myth. The soul-preserving adaptive capacity of the slaves is construed to the credit of the master class. The good nature, health, and contentment of the slaves redound to the credit of propertied virtue. Cheerful workers in the fields, fecund females at home (no less than fifty-two were then pregnant), 'well fed, well supported, [they] appear the subjects of a good prince, not the slaves of a planter' (104).

Those factors that seem truly antithetical (*neg*) to an aristocratic republic are negotiated as differences to be excluded from the journal's construction of a meaningful social sphere, or they are made paradoxically to emphasize excellence in Schaw's idealized paragons of quality. In the quotation above, all the Creole connotations are negated ('slaves of a planter'); the masters in the immediate reference, all eminent Scots, become the type of the 'good prince', elevated to a higher order of merit.

This magnification of the slave owners' beneficence and mitigation of slavery's hardships prepares us for the elevation of the Scots plantocracy in Antigua and St Christopher to the status of cultural exemplars. Because it is in the nature of such myth-making to mask and occlude, the aesthetic of the picturesque rises to functional preeminence in the *Journal*. The conceptual design of this chapter does not require extensive accounting for the effects of the picturesque in Schaw, but they will be given brief acknowledgement here and fuller treatment in the Beckford chapter, where they reach full ideological significance.[31]

The aesthetic language of the picturesque enables Schaw to mask the social injustice of the emigrants' plight by transfiguring them from frightened huddled families into an idea of a 'group of sorrow'. Similarly, the picturesque is invoked to occlude the threat-and-fear-fraught undercurrents of plantation Christmas festivities: the slaves are sanitized into an image of 'joyful troops – one of the most beautiful sights I ever saw' (107–8). Here art is used to mask reality, to abstract the slaves into a 'group of sorrow' (35), so displacing emotions as to mute their pain, so pictorializing the landscape of their experience as to nullify the political causes that determined their condition. In effect the picturesque is used here to translate both emigrants and slaves into one of those expressions Gikandi identifies with the 'greater imperial narrative' whose function is to ensure the uneven 'encodement' of identities and to 'secure British [in Schaw's case coded as Scots] identity in the service of empire'.[32]

These themes and images, then, exemplify the essence of Schaw's social ideology. They lay down the ground rules by which her project of inventing a myth of cultural and political pre-eminence for fellow Scots could be established.

The foregoing exploration of Schaw's attitudes to the two central themes of colonialist literature in the eighteenth-century West Indies reveals her posture within that practice as one which, like the *negotium*, figures a dualistic conceit. While on the one hand the ineluctable forces of nature (the storms), history (the gathering clouds of revolt and abolition) and the irrepressibility of cultural process (creolization) compel her discursive attention, on the other she resists or occludes those forces by ideologically motivated strategies of subordination, wilful selection or revision, all of these collectively intended to invent the higher subjective ideal of Scottish cultural leadership.

Perhaps the most striking singularity of the *Journal*, the critical property that distinguishes it from the other texts, is the degree to which it sustains its focus on the human social sphere of whites in Antigua and St Christopher. Where the intense social preoccupations of the other texts revolve around the exotic manners and mores of indigenous island peoples and African slaves, Schaw turns a steadfast gaze on the families, hereditary connections, daily lives and continuity of national manners and traditions that marked those whites as being unalterably British/Scottish in her eyes. Gikandi assesses this insistence on continuity as 'a desire for an all encompassing imperial identity', a particular expression of the Scottish subject's wish to inscribe itself into the larger British imperial narrative.[33]

We have already sketched briefly the social and economic conditions that brought waves of Scottish immigrants into the colonies in the eighteenth century. Janet Schaw had particular family and social connections already settled or about to settle in the colonies. Some of these in each category were prominent persons in the plantocratic, political and professional hierarchies of America and the West Indies. Here it is useful to outline certain characteristics of population composition and class shifts over time that will suggest some rationale for Schaw's insistent claims for social superiority among the Scottish element of Antigua's and St Christopher's white elites.

The white population of the British West Indian colonies was predominantly English. At the time of Schaw's visit, there were some 2,590 whites in Antigua and 1,900 whites in St Christopher.[34] The numbers of slaves and free stood at characteristically higher dispro-portions: 37,808 in Antigua and 23,462 in St Christopher. It is difficult to establish precise figures for the total number of Scottish residents in these two islands. The fragmentary statistics for Scots immigrants entering these two colonies as a result of eviction or transportation are valuable, but they clearly do not tell the whole story.[35] It is all the more instructive therefore that Schaw manages to narrow the focus of her ideological lens to accentuate the Scots presence, power and influence. This deliberate selection propels her circle of family, friends, and social equals (real and desired) into the limelight of cultural eminence to embody and project that challenge to prevailing Creole assumptions. Elsa Goveia's distinguished, foun-dational study on population features in the eighteenth-century Leewards partly illuminates the social basis for Schaw's optimism.[36]

In the eighteenth century, the islands in question were dominated by a small rank of very wealthy absentee proprietors, merchants and professional men. Next in importance (and first among resident elites) was a white upper class consisting of resident planters, governors, professional men, civil and military officials, merchants, traders and other administrators. Their identity was marked by independent-mindedness, solidarity and racial pride.[37] In their quest for economic security, they embodied an ethic of enterprise and industry that earned them success. By their practice of relative equality within the ranks, they facilitated the upward mobility of poor whites who had improved their economic standing by initiative and resourcefulness. Although this latter group is hardly noticed in Schaw's exclusivist ideology, Goveia and other important eighteenth-century sources accord greater weight to their presence and value in the colonies' economies. Pinckard vividly depicts a class of poorer whites, 'men of meagre figure, half dissolved in perspiration, and exhausted almost to shadows . . . mostly, among the clerks, the book-keepers and those orders of white people below the managers – those who are employed in active and busy occupation, and have but little time to devote to indolence and the luxuries of the table'.[38] By documenting the broader social diversity of white populations, Pinckard's account categorically impugns Schaw's idealism.

While the evidence of formal history corroborates Schaw's little-disguised chauvinism for the Scots and their significant command of political visibility and cultural influence in Antigua and St Christopher, that same evidence strongly insists that not all Scots there were of rarefied social provenance. Schaw conveniently ignores or was not there long enough to inquire diligently into the true antecedents of those numerous artisans who had elevated themselves to ownership of property and slaves, or of young overseers who had become managers, a cohort John Luffman describes as 'generally poor Scotch lads, who, by their assiduity and industry, frequently become masters of plantations, to which they came out as indentured servants'.[39]

This kind of social heterogeneity, then, must of necessity mediate our understanding of the *Journal* as an instrument of determinate cultural idealism. It served Schaw's purposes well to reify the Scots element into an idea that was durable enough to embody that idealism and inoculate the colonial body political against its negations. That claim of Scottish priority (derived from social quality and material worth) provides her with a kind of tribal security that allows her to finesse the potential questions of private identification with an increasingly despised colonial elite. The journal form refigures the meaning of her reunion into a harmonization of the sundered parts of a fictive self. The visit is transformed into an occasion for symbolic self-discovery: 'Here was a whole company of Scotch people, our language, our manners, our circle of friends and acquaintances' (p. 81).

Obviously, this imagination of a Scottish republic of virtue, enduring intact and untouched by the decay of history, collides with powerful sources of mediation from economic decline, moral decadence and social unrest. The *Journal* degrades the value of these sources by its distinctly occlusive positionings, but they are not entirely erased from Schaw's consciousness. Indeed, she voices her own private ambivalence about the social risks of her westward journey and about emigration as a whole. The ensuing critique of her cultural project will therefore be understood to assume those qualifications and should be located in an oppositional relationship to the competing values of creolization.

The objective of Schaw's project of social engineering is to downgrade creolized and creolizing effects in favour of a Scottish myth, but the reality of her actions and engagements works to compromise the integrity and consistency of that myth. In fact she uses the terms 'Creole' only about three times, and two of those are in negative contexts: Creoles beat slaves (127); a vigorous two-mile uphill walk would not be an exercise likely to animate a Creole (125). It is to the ethical complex of creolization that she alludes in her expressed desire to inoculate herself against the storied bland-ishments of the 'western world' as she casts her last glances at Scotland: 'Adieu, then, thou dear, loved native land. In vain I am told of finer Climates, or of richer soils, none will ever equal Scotland in my estimation. And in the midst of all the luxuries of the western world, I will envy the Cottager in his snow-surrounded hamlet' (42). Whispered near the outset of the voyage, these words figure more the nervous anxiety of a self-conscious traveller than the fixed resolve of a pious heart. Once she is landed in the West Indies, one does not hear this elegiac strain in Schaw's journalistic voice again.

In another critical obloquy against the common practices of Creole culture, Schaw deprecated the plight of children who were born in the colonies and sent to England (and Scotland, in the case of the Rutherfurd children) to be educated, and then repatriated to the colonies. Her empathy for the long estrangement and broken friendships that shaped these children's experiences inscribed her critique of a peculiar Creole bourgeois dilemma identified in the preceding chapter. Where Grainger transforms his returning Junio into a mythic hero whose dual identity would fit him well for enlightened leadership and reform, Schaw keeps her subjects frozen in the quality of 'banished exiles'.

Those emotions notwithstanding, Creole comforts are quickly promoted from allurements to be renounced to yardsticks of social quality. The level of affluence possible in the West Indies suggests ideas of equivalence with England. Her first dinner at Mr Halliday's is a metaphor for gastronomic excess. With courses laid out in three rows, six dishes to a row, and thirty-two different kinds of fruit to choose from, she cannot resist the observation that in England such entertainment 'might figure away in a newspaper, had it been given by a Lord Mayor, or the first Duke in the kingdom' (95). Schaw's personal creolization progresses rapidly. A homebred aversion to turtle turns into a fondness; a native frugality is exchanged for full-bodied indulgence: 'When I first came here I could not bear to see so much of a pineapple thrown away. They cut off a deep pairing, then cut out the firm part of the heart, which takes away not much less than half of the apple. But only observe how easy it is to become extravagant. I can now feel if the least bit of rind remains; and as to the heart, heavens! Who could eat the nasty heart of pine apple' (98).

Schaw formulates a critique that situates luxury squarely within the logic of nature and therefore beyond censure: 'Why should we blame these people for their luxury? Since nature holds out her lap, filled with everything that in her power to bestow, it were sinful in them not be luxurious' (95). Thus where the *Journal* engages those forms and behaviours that were the common targets of Creole detractors, it manages to invert the conventional moral order on which those detractors stood.

In some rather more profound ways the *Journal* reveals its definitive ideological bias. Its programmatic motives as a whole produce the author's visit to the West Indies as a challenge to the intrinsic nature of Creole society. Those motives work to disrupt the pattern of creolization by inserting certain deliberate culturally weighted choices that swing the pendulum towards her idea of Scottish essentialism. At the dinner table she openly flouts the feminine custom of Antigua by drinking wine (80); contrary to their practice, too, she refuses to cover herself with thick layers of clothing as a protection from the tropical rays of the sun, authenticating this with the apology: 'As to your humble servant, I have always set my face to the weather; wherever I have been. I hope you have no quarrel with brown beauty' (p. 115). The image is fraught with the definitive tensions of emigration and assimilation. It interposes a Scotswoman's own subjective authority to that of Creole custom. It projects a self who is confident in her own individual authority, an authority won from the rigours of Northern winters and projected in the very image of hardihood. Liz Bohls reads this image as a dissociation from female Scottish anxiety about immersion or total acculturation.[40] I would extend and explore that further to reinforce my argument here. This dramatic depiction of the head pointed firmly into the elements figures the dramatic inscription a strongly inflected Scottish consciousness into the discourse and politics of empire (see Schaw 64–65). In this positioning Schaw is opposing the presumed immune factors of her own identity to the negative mutability of creolization (West Indian climate, and the effeteness that flowed from soft, overprotected indolence), a narrow reductive definition of those allurements referred to earlier.[41]

Instituted in the *Journal* by the sheer force of iteration and encomium, the notion of Scottish excellence is made axiomatic by naturalizing the subjects' relation to power, wealth and patriotism, a relation inferentially argued by the claims of unimpeachable social manners and moral probity. While the Scots' dominance in the principal spheres of public action and social visibility offered ample opportunities for them to vindicate those claims, the key criterion by which their social worth is measured is their disposition to honour the values of family and nationality. As a signifier of meaningful cultural value, this criterion idealizes the notion that a Scottish colonial's demonstrated commitment to close-knit ties of kinship and nationality could neutralize the anxiety inducing taints of Creole identity.

Though the particularities of climate, topography, sugar and slaves are hard to erase, Schaw's feminine sensibility deflects reader interest away from these creolizing constituents to factors that are by definition more resistant to colonial change, more susceptible of assimilation to or penetration by British/Scottish cultural forces. Through Schaw's deliberate strategies of emphasis, selection and suppression, objects and actions are assigned value in the degree of their capacity to raise in herself and in her audience those sentiments that ratify 'quality', a metaphor for class.

For Schaw the most robust defiance to creolization is revealed in the colonial continuities of British cultural form. The author is reassured to find such forms preserved in the rules governing social access: she makes emphatic reference to the obligatory presentation of letters of introduction to Mrs Mackinon (p. 89), to the rules governing women's movement in public places ('No woman ever goes without a gentleman to attend her [and] in carriages drawn by English horses . . . a needless piece of expense; as they have strong horses from New England' (87), to the regular timely commerce of style: 'They have the fashions every six weeks from London' (p. 115). In Antigua the capacious, fine plantation home of Dr John Dunbar, 'The Eleanora', reproduces in her judgement ideas of social style and value correlative to the British country-house tradition. Situated in one of the most desirable locations in St Johns, it unites within itself charm, novelty and architectural elegance. Clearly enchanted with its physical appointments and its enviable 'prospect' of a varied landscape, Schaw finds it 'impossible to conceive so much beauty and riches under the eye in one moment.' In St Christopher 'The Olivees', the plantation seat of William Leslie Hamilton and Lady Isabella Hamilton, assumes congruent meaning in her cultural project. A great hall, from 50 to 60 feet long, with a prospect of the sea and shipping, and drawing-rooms and bedrooms furnished in 'English taste' are all proudly advanced to support the popular consensus she endorses in the words: 'this is esteemed the finest house on any of the islands' (124). Both properties attain cultural merit by the private terms of Schaw's approval and the public terms of eighteenth-century British aesthetic language. The Anglican liturgy she witnessed at her first church service in Antigua trans-planted faithfully the form observed at the metropole (though that fidelity struck her Presbyterian instincts as being cold and soulless) (93–4). The interior appointments of the church observed the proper decorums and these were fittingly reproduced in the protocols denoting rank and status:

The seat for the Governor General is noble and magnificent, covered with crimson velvet; the drapery round it edged with deep gold fringe; the Crown Cyphers and emblems of his office embossed and very rich. Below this is the seat for the Counsellors equally fine and ornamented, but what pleased me more than all I saw was a great number of Negroes who occupied the Area, and went thro' the Service with seriousness and devotion. (94)

This dichotomy between the tepidness of Schaw's private attitude to religion and her gratified underscoring of the worshipping slaves' devotion mirrors the dichotomy that will manifest itself in the ensuing critique of her social portraiture. There that sharp division continues to be rationalized on the basis of property, its attendant privileges and elitist mystiques for which Schaw would have found express philosophical grounding in Ferguson and Hume.[42]

Though her visits and contacts are not restricted to them, she accords the highest profile to a selection of families whose names attest to their unmistakable Scots ethnicity. In the history of the two colonies, the Martins, the Hamiltons, the Dunbars, the Hallidays, the Mackinnens and the Duncans all figure prominently in the roles of governors, military, officials, planters, merchants, traders, civil and other categories of administrators. Walter Hamilton was a governor of the Leeward Islands in the early part of the century.[43] The editors identify John Halliday, the customs collector, assemblyman and owner of seven plantations as derived from old covenanting stock who figured in the history of Scotland since the sixteenth century.[44] Members of these families earn distinguished profiles in the *Journal*.

Even figures noticed in the briefest, glancing sketches manage to advance the myth of cultural eminence. Mr Freeman, an Antiguan councilman, gets the accolade of 'a gentleman remarkable for his learning, no stranger to the Polite Arts', and Dr Patrick Malcolm, sometime surgeon of the same island, a relative of the Rutherfurd children, is highly commended for his generosity and affection (103).

The list is longer, but two further distinctive portraits will suffice because they are culturally paradigmatic and therefore definitive of our present thesis. Held up as the cream of this Scottish colonial aristocracy Colonel Samuel Martin, representing the plantocrats, and William Leslie Hamilton, representing the professional class, are clear cultural icons. These two eminent figures are paragons in Schaw's ideal of colonial manhood.

A planter of wide repute in the West Indies ('loved and revered father of Antigua'), Colonel Martin is depicted as a benevolent patriarch, an enlightened master of slaves ('a kind and beneficent Master, not a harsh and unreasonable Tyrant') (104), so enlightened he allowed none but freed servants within his private domestic sphere.[45] In pointed differentiation from the stereotype of the sybaritic Creole, Schaw commends his wise use of riches, and elevates his bond to the land (he foreswore absenteeism) into a well-known neoclassical paradigm of virtue. His identification with the very best impulses of his nation and class is assigned high value in the historical culture of the island and region. Schaw's ideological objectives aside, Martin enjoys a deservedly wide reputation for formulating new ideas to improve agricultural methods (especially aimed at diversifying Antigua's economy from monocrop sugar) and implementing experiments to reform general plantation practice.[46] This sets his figure off in sharp contrast to stock images of self-absorbed, hedonistic Creole elites. In Schaw's social encounter with him he emerges as the epitome of wise experience, the soul of gentility and graciousness. His compliments addressed to her and Fanny Rutherfurd are accented with gallantry: 'You must not leave me', said he taking both our hands in his, 'everything in my power shall be subservient to your happiness; my age leaves no fear of reputation' (106). Her journal leaves the meaning of this speech elegantly ambiguous, but in context it reads suspiciously like a marriage proposal.

Schaw's idealization of Martin is proportionate to his objective standing in colonial history. He embodies certain key redemptive symbols in the apologetic representation of slave society's social institutions. His paternalism accommodates itself suitably to romantic assimilations of West Indian slavery to European feudalism. It functioned also as a familiar strategy for instituting a fictive kinship that secures control and social order.[47]

If Martin represented to her a Scottish paragon of those rarer virtues (wisdom, prudence, generosity) consistent with a man of some eighty-five years, in Hamilton she saw the supremest image of masculine beauty, sexual appeal and professional success. ('He is about twenty six or twenty seven, tall and elegantly made; his shape uncommonly easy, his complexion dark brown-nut, his eyes dark and penetrating, yet soft, his manners at once genteel and manly . . .' 123). The clearest signal of his literal and metaphoric value to Schaw's project resides in that subtle understatement she attaches to her praise of his business and professional ethics: 'Far from giving way to pleasure and indolence, he applies [it] with avidity to business.' In the words 'pleasure and indolence' she raises and lays to rest in a single gesture those two old spectres of Creole decadence (*neg*); in the words 'avidity and business' she signs Hamilton with two distinctive marks of a late eighteenth-century man of affairs, a new definition for *otium* in Schaw's reinvented cultural conception.

Though Schaw's ideal of Scottish colonial culture is decidedly male-gendered, she proposes the privileged women of Antigua and St Christopher as fitting complements to this ideal, eminently suited to fulfil their roles in this mythic polity. What she most admires in them is their reserve, their virtuous manners, the care they take of their reputations ('while the men are gay, luxurious and amorous, the women are modest, genteel reserved and temperate') and 'in general the most amiable creatures in the world, and either I have been remarkably fortunate in my acquaintance, or they are more than commonly sensible, even those who have never been off the Island are amazingly intelligent and able to converse with you on any subject. They make excellent wives, fond attentive mothers and the best house wives I have ever met' (113).[48]

If they may be accounted so, she makes only two conceivably unfavourable reflections on the behaviour of colonial females, one in reference to their insistence on covering themselves against the effects of the hot tropical sun ('From childhood they never suffer the sun to have a peep at them, and to prevent him are covered with masks and bonnets'), the other on their steadfast abstinence from wine at meals. But though Schaw pointedly demurs both habits, even these manners obliquely and ironically further her objective of distinguishing the cultural quality of Scots colonials from the ethics of common Creoles. Blocking out the rays of the broiling sun kept their skins white and close to purity. The language used to reference the sun's action ('peep at them') is a term of voyeurism, and the referents for the women's actions ('prevent' and 'covered', 'masks and bonnets') all raise conventional ideas of female sexual tension, particularly the feminine role as both protector of her own virtue and as moral restraint on male lust. Their abstention from wine bespeaks modesty and feminine virtue. Each one of these practices stands in a highly visible contradistinction to widely retailed negative stereotypes that associate Creoles' exposure to the sun with an excess of temperamental heat and carnal ardour.

Fitting consort to her excellent husband, Lady Isabella Hamilton stands unparalleled among the women of Schaw's journal. A friend of long standing whom she had not seen for four years, Bell, as she was affectionatley known, embodied the highest attributes of feminine grace and beauty. Her perfect manners and social charm suffuse the great hall in which she receives Schaw; she presides over this virtual palatial dwelling like a regal idea, fittingly attended by a 5-year-old mulatto girl ('brown beauty to show off white') (123–4).

This woman, her husband and Colonel Martin occupy the centrepieces of Schaw's individual characterization. The individual personal value of each translates into a collective social worthiness for the class Schaw raises to cultural essence by the mythic proportions of her journal's idealizing discourse. In them she restores to British (Scottish) patrimony those virtues Grainger had negotiated away to a benevolence identified as uniquely Creole. A similar posture would persist in Schaw's attitude as she confronted in America some of those dissonances she glossed over in Antigua and St Christopher. Though her commitment to continued British hegemony would remain undivided, she would witness in North Carolina the destabilizing effects of the American Revolution on that hegemony. The West Indian colonies would experience the challenge of that historical event in similar ways. In the next chapter, we will see how William Beckford, one of Schaw's literary successors, used those effects as a major spur in his pursuit of a reactionary aesthetic with which to stabilise faltering Creole political and cultural power.

CHAPTER 5

Beckford: the aesthetics of negotiation

Not to be confused with his more wealthy and famous cousin, the author of *Vathek*, the William Beckford (*d.* 1799) of this study is listed in the *Dictionary of National Biography* (*DNB*) as an historian. That source credits him with the authorship of a history of France and also documents his slightly earlier (1788) work on slavery, *Remarks on the Situation of Negroes in Jamaica*. From his own account, Beckford must have arrived in Jamaica in 1764, the year Grainger's *The Sugar Cane* was published. The historian spent thirteen years in Jamaica. On his return to London in 1777 he was arrested and imprisoned for debt, circumstances entirely ignored in the *DNB* entry, but which, from his several aggrieved allusions to personal financial insolvency and loss of personal freedom, may be assumed to have given significant impulse to the writing of the *Descriptive Account*. The book itself was actually written from his place of confinement in the Fleet Prison.

A substantial work (more than 800 pages) in two volumes, the *Descriptive Account* proposes on its title-page to offer a treatise on the cultivation of the sugar cane, as well as to address the consequences to the West Indian slave economies (Jamaica was Beckford's chief interest) of abolition and emancipation. Beckford ably fulfils these promises, though never confining himself either to the strict objective methods presupposed by the first or the rigorous rhetorical criteria implied in the second theme. Indeed, he discloses in his extended title his clear stylistic intentions and aesthetic interests in describing the sugar cane by adding the qualifier 'chiefly considered in a picturesque point of view', and then interspersing his procedures throughout the book with repeated self-conscious references to georgic and picturesque modalities.

As presaged in these remarks, the progress of the text is unencumbered by any strict notions of narrative control or of linear, logical sequence: the factual is persistently interrupted by a compulsive aestheticism, the historical by compulsive retreats to nostalgia, and the objective by the irrepressible mimicry of desire. To the extent that these finely interwoven threads of thought and feeling can be separated from one another, the basic structure of the text may be represented as follows. Volume I depicts the particularities of Jamaica's physical landscape (soil, climate, vegetation, landforms). Volume I places considerable emphasis on the various skills and material resources required for successful sugar-cane cultivation, while casting timely and favourable reflections on the planter class. The full amplitude of 'sweete negotiation' is displayed in the volume's constant oscillations: digressions from the slaves, their songs and their dances to the pleasures of ease and retirement, from a broad dissertation on national characters, to a philosophical speculation on the origin and progress of music. The volume closes on a note accentuating the categorical ambivalence of its larger constructive framework: it shifts warily between the *neg* of an indirect commentary on the gathering clouds of political and social change in the colonies, and the *otium* of Beckford's own optimism that the slavocrats' benevolence could arrest the threat of violent cataclysm. Volume II provides a more sustained discussion of cane cultivation, the processes of sugar manufacture and the state of the trade. Slave life receives a heavy overlay of sentiment and denial; the image of the slave masters is heavily retouched to personify favourably the most persuasive arguments against emancipation. Anti-slavery propaganda comes under intense scrutiny and refutation in set-pieces aimed at debunking its frightening charges (both volumes contain detailed bookkeeping tables and other financial information pertinent to plantation management). Volume II ends with Beckford reaffirming his support for the retention of slavery on the grounds of economic necessity and social stability. Certain closing remarks allude to his return to England, his arrest and subsequent imprisonment for debt.

Beckford held out the thematic, structural and stylistic features of his narrative as tangible proofs that the material and aesthetic constituents for producing a picturesque civilization were already in place and that he, as a Creole publicist, personified those proofs. The text fulfils its overt didactic purposes of depicting landscape, life and action with great detail, colour and imagination. The high incidence of natural description transcends its value as local colour when

particular conditions of Jamaican physical nature are produced as
'awful and sublime views', with one pre-eminent event being the
narrative record of the tropical hurricane he witnessed in 1780. These
evocations of beauty and terror function in the aesthetic structures of
the picturesque and the sublime, but they also construct the powerful
metaphors of threat and violent cataclysm that clearly dominated
Beckford's consciousness as anti-slavery strengthened its political and
intellectual forces in the final decades of the eighteenth century.

In the 26-year passage between the publication of Grainger's *Sugar
Cane* and Beckford's *Descriptive Account*, much had transpired to
change the personal perspectives of Creole author-publicists and to
affect the ways the cultural practices of *negotium* were deployed in
their texts. By Beckford's dates, the creolizing text, as an interest-
driven instrumentality, had refined its forms and solidified its
structures. The shape of Creole discourse had by now become
inured to questions of cultural credibility and moral rectitude. But
where, in its earlier exemplary documents, the creolizing text's most
urgent enterprise was to mediate the effects of cultural crisis
originating at the centre by seeking resolution in the abundant
resources of the colonial margins, in Beckford's text the focus of
crisis becomes sharply inverted: rapidly developing political and
economic events translate the scene of crisis to the colonies, thereby
destabilizing the idea of a Creole cultural imperium, only recently
and all-too-tentatively articulated in Grainger. The functional capacity of the *negotium* is stretched to the farther limits of its acknowledged elasticity to image this proximate crisis. It strains continually
to imagine sources of cultural survival in the combined energies of
the old imperium recuperated as conventional aesthetic practices
with implicit political and ideological values. With the appearance of
the *Descriptive Account*, the impetus in textualizing Creole legitimacy
passes from profound anxiety about stabilizing the ideal relationship
between metropole and colony to narrativizing a very determined
politics of reaction mediated through aesthetics and ideology.[1]

As defined by the reach of its desire at the end of the poem,
Grainger's poetic imagination assumes a liberalizing posture before
the unfolding scene of political change. *The Sugar Cane*'s closing lines
reveal that imagination contemplating some practicable accord
between the progressive principles of Louis XIV's slavery reforms
(embodied in the Code Noir), and his own creative negotiation (an
appropriation really) of the old imperium to implement a Creole –

based reform solution – his plan for repatriating enlightened absentees and elevating black slaves to the status of servants. Where Grainger's colonial allegiances are mediated by the restraining influences of his anti-slavery friends, and his georgic formalism is mitigated by the comic irony of associating the Muse with rats, Beckford's sympathies remain faithfully wedded to pro-slavery interests, his personal humour constrained by self-pity, the powers of his imagination ceaselessly colonized by traditionalist modes of thought and reactionary aesthetics. Grainger's fleeting sense of an imperium wrested away from its prescriptive holders and placed at the prudent disposal of a reformed Creole cultural elite is here (in the *Descriptive Account*) steadfastly subverted by the structural interplay (oscillations) of specific aesthetic choices. What Beckford appropriates from the legacy of 'sweete negotiation' is its potential to adapt and subsume kindred forms and practices into itself to meet specific cultural contingencies. Seen in a successor relationship to *The Sugar Cane*, the *Descriptive Account* assimilates georgic's 'protean discursive form',[2] mutating and shading its looser, more inclusive capabilities into the aesthetics of the picturesque, extending the resultant hybrid perilously into the transgressive space of the sublime. Witnessed in earlier texts, this process of generic linkage and interpenetration is replicated in Beckford in formal practices and constructions apposite to his style and temperament, but also strategically suited to the politico-cultural objectives of his book. The *negotium*, so definitively linked to sugar's economic power and cultural promise, must now intuit a relationship to the traditional agents of cultural power far more combative than Grainger's moderate compromises. 'Sweete negotiation' must in fact engage the intenser connotations of the Creole 'dissensus' to confect an aesthetics of crisis. It must defamiliarize the *translatio* (translated in Grainger) to the aesthetic practices mentioned above and, in the exigent abolitionist climate of the 1790s, imagine slavocratic autonomy by an aesthetic transmutation of the old imperium into an image of a new Creole imperium.[3] In underlining linkages and continuities, it is convenient to prefigure here a number of other themes that establish and strengthen the comparative relationships between Beckford's work and the foregoing texts of the present study. Coming rather late in the day for the historical process of colonization in the West Indies, anxieties about the displacement consequences of colonizing still weigh heavily on that author's mind. Indeed, it is powerful testimony to the durability of the displacement theme that the memory and mythic force of the islands' indigenous, as well as the guilt associated with African deracination, penetrate and disrupt the will to assert a purportedly pure and uncontested Creole cultural imperium. Themselves closely implicated in that history of African loss and erasure, mills and boiling houses stage a determined recrudescence on the narrative scene. Their reappearance in Beckford stands as a sharp structural reminder of the role they played either as proxies in Ligon or of their relatively diminished profile in Rochefort and Grainger. The powerful imagery of their physical mass and the aesthetic use of their noise to mute human pain underscore this text's profound sense of translated crisis. In the *Descriptive Account* they figure, along with the other two elements, as structural constants implicated in the search to fix and control the definition of Creole cultural identity, conduits for inserting Creole desires and anxieties into the changing narrative of *imperium*.

Previous allusions to a moment of crisis which conditioned the procedures Beckford used to manipulate his text's structural and thematic arrangements can now be explicitly defined from evolving historical events and rationalized with reference to pertinent cultural criticism, supported by internal evidence from the *Descriptive Account*. These sources offer solid buttresses for this chapter's argument that the book pursues concrete, interest-driven cultural objectives occasioned by unfolding historical developments and that its constituents crystallize into a poetics of reaction.[4]

As with most historical change, roots and causes resist simplistic resolutions. There is almost as much diversity in the enumerated causes of the crisis as there is trouble in fixing its onset. Some historians date planter decline from as early as 1763 (increasing taxes and duties, stiffer French competition); others place the onset of waning power closer to the decade of the 1820s when anti-slavery opposition bit hardest through systematic evidence-gathering, petition drives and the parliamentary campaign. Politically, three complex sources can be adduced as tributaries to the sense of crisis that is reflected in the *Descriptive Account*. The American Revolution, slave revolts in the colonies and the metropole-based abolition campaign figured prominently among Creole fears about a destabilizing social order. And no wonder: each of these developments is given a high assessed value in the historical scholarship on the causes of slavocratic decline.

The Revolution itself wrought severe economic hardships on West Indian plantation economies. By the terms of the Prohibitory Act of 1776 trade between the mainland American and the West Indian colonies was interdicted. Voicing the consternation that gripped other West Indian property-owners in 1777 John Pinney, a Nevis planter, wrote: 'What will become of us? The unhappy contest with America united with our internal distressed situation is truly alarming and will, I am afraid, cause the ruin of every individual.'[5]

Shortages of foodstuffs and other vital supplies resulted in starvation and higher prices. For Jamaica, it is estimated that between 1780 and 1787 some 15,000 slaves died as a result of the first effect[6], and price rises, ranging from a low of 35 per cent to a high of over 600 per cent, resulted from the second.[7] Carrington estimates that the Revolution dealt a 'severe psychological blow', to the slavocracy's morale: 'The revolution broke the spirit of the planters. They lost the resilience so characteristic of eighteenth-century planters, who were noted for continued sugar production despite the dangers to themselves and their families, and the hardships caused by slave rebellions, wars, droughts, and hurricanes.'[8]

In further exacerbation of these adversities, political eruptions on other islands certainly fuelled fear and tension in the masters and rebellious tendencies in the slaves. Close to Beckford's home in the parish of Hanover, a dangerous slave plot was discovered in July 1776.[9] Described by Michael Craton as 'the first Afro-Caribbean slave plot', this conspiracy holds strategic import for the diachronic evolution of the present *negotium* and its synchronic modification in Beckford. The participants were identified as a 'creole elite' of drivers, craftsmen, and domestics.[10] While Beckford's poetics of reaction holds fast to a conservative vision of power reserved for traditional elites, Craton documents a tendency that suggests a decisive redefinition of the markers for Creole identity. Of this growing willingness on the part of these subordinate classes to side with the imperial forces in defence of their islands, Craton writes:

Creole slaves as well as free blacks even seemed to have had a nascent sense that by serving in the forces they were helping to protect their homeland. With the process of creolization, a number of Afro-Caribbean slaves felt they belonged to their islands of residence just as much as – or even more than – their Creole masters.[11]

The bloody slave revolts in San Domingue (1791–2) that led ultimately to the formation of the Haitian Republic in 1804 intensified rumours and fears of slave conspiracy in Jamaica.[12] This nascent self-consciousness throws a revealing light on Beckford's compulsion to mute and efface inconvenient narrative elements; the identifier 'Creole' can no longer be taken as an exclusive marker for whites. The term has assumed a diffuse referentiality; its pretensions, desires and anxieties now devolved to a wider residency.

The history of abolition and emancipation has been so well served by numerous works of first-rate scholarship that it would be superfluous to replough the ground here. However, in addition to the sketch outlined in the Introduction, some specific factors can be identified which engender certain responses, expressed or alluded to, in Beckford's *Descriptive Account*.

Slave-produced sugar became the target of a nationwide boycott mounted by the London Abolition Committee in 1791. Thomas Clarkson claimed that some 300,000 families were involved in the boycott. Seymour Drescher calls this 'not at all an unreasonable estimate'.[13] Interesting as an example of the effective organizing strategies of abolitionist politicians, the boycott galvanized the rhetorical skills of some of Britain's most astute publicists and gifted writers. Figures from these two cohorts, as well as others, joined forces to launch this phase of the anti-slavery struggle. William Fox, distinguished philanthropist and associate of William Wilberforce, set a publishing record (50,000 copies in four months) for the time with the circulation of his *Address to the People of Great Britain on the Utility of Refraining from the Use of West Indian Sugar and Rum* (1791). His shocking identification of sugar consumption with cannibalism ('with every pound of sugar we may be considered as consuming two ounces of human flesh', he wrote) canonized a pattern of imagery that was to be widely reproduced by other authors. The once mystical body of sugar was hereafter, on the authority of abolitionist writings by Samuel Taylor Coleridge, Robert Southey and Mary Wollstonecraft (among others), shamefully demystified as containing the blood, sweat, tears and other assorted bodily secretions of slaves.[14] The metaphors of the degraded slave body, the myth of purity and its antithetical preoccupations of pollution and corruption were all pressed into service for this propaganda offensive. If the rhetoric was clearly overblown, and the imagery deliberately selected to produce revulsion and disgust, the two combined to produce a weapon that would take direct aim at the culturally exclusive desires of pro-slavery writers like Schaw and Beckford. Indeed, this powerful discursive weaponry would strike at the very survival of the 'sweete negotiation' ideal itself.

Situated in a wider domain of theoretical discourse on the consequences of empire but clearly definable as one of the categorical interlocutors of Beckford's apologies for the Creole imperium are those theorists whose attitude. Anthony Pagden succinctly and reductively fixes in his formulation: 'how to sustain certain kinds of cultural value over time'. This of course was the identical, concurrent question that Beckford and other pro-colonial publicists were struggling with. Those very practices that so instituted bourgeois emulative displays as symbolic sources of value and power for the colonial elites were now being contested as sources of exhaustion and enervation for the national character. Once the confident predicates of the empire's growth and expansion, those values and practices were now being reviled as images of that 'contagion which afflicted all peoples who had achieved a degree of military, social and technological success'.[15] By 1800 enlightened opinion was now convinced that unchecked expansion would be a deleterious 'threat to the stability and prosperity of the metropolis' because 'they had shown that every immigrant comunity no matter what its cultural origins or the degree of self rule it is able to exercise, will one day come to demand economic self-sufficiency and political autonomy'.[16] Now in the imaginative domain of the *Descriptive Account*, these fears were materializing as a 'sweete negotiation' to alienate the metropolitan imperium.[17]

Returning to the internal evidence of the *Descriptive Account*, we can inquire to what extent Beckford constructs a conscious polemical response to these critiques which so traduced the Creole ethos. The sense of cultural crisis engendered by this broad configuration of ideological discourses just described manifests itself in continuities with the foregoing texts and in other forms peculiar to Beckford's individual and public consciousness. With respect to the first, the poetics of reaction in the *Descriptive Account* constitutes itself from that familiar paradigm of cultural values established in Ligon. Beckford recuperates images of the Caribbean indigenous, the originary myths of purity and virtuous struggle, and the very palpable forms of the machinery of sugar manufacture as signs of cultural desire. Each of these has been shown to engender its own sense of crisis, to provide puissant weight to one pole or other of the *negotium*. The historical emergencies surrounding the composition and publication of the *Descriptive Account* increase their weight for its author and reinforce their significance for the present argument.

Where Grainger had entirely effaced them from the represented scene of St Christopher, Beckford resurrects the Indians in memory, though not in person, for reasons which betray quasi-mental panic and indisputable guilt. The reappearance is staged in a context characteristic of his complex narrative aesthetics and in his typical digressive style: his painterly narrative impulses trigger a train of associations that digress from a scene of slaves entering a cave to the descriptive values of the cave itself; these in turn occasion reflections on his personal loss of liberty which are then succeeded by an evocation of the lost history of the aboriginal inhabitants of Jamaica buried in those caves by the Spaniards' treachery. Assessing the discontinuous mental processes that produced these ideas, he writes that such ideas as may be 'cherished' in 'subterraneous abodes . . . may conduct us from fear to pleasure, and from silence to the investigation of sound, and from incorporeal darkness unto cheerfulness and light' (I: 240). *Neg* and *otium* are dramatically reproduced in this narrative episode as they are in a later return to its haunting power: 'There are many people who believe that these caves have been the inhuman depositaries of the skeletons of those original and wretched inhabitants whom the cruel policy of the Spaniards hunted down, and who, in the course of a very inconsiderable number of years, were exterminated, and became totally, and as it were at once, extinct. An instance of human destruction that cannot be exceeded in the bloody histories of any age or country!' (I: 248). The ironies of equating his own adversities to the enormity of racial extermination for the Indians, without any corresponding reference to the plight of the African slaves, are glaring enough. But the highly denunciatory language of censure against Spanish cruelty and the unfavourable comparison of the Spanish with the English identify his production with the culturally and politically motivated larger discourse of the 'black legend'.[18] This resurrection of that old narrative serves the calculated purposes of differentiating the British imperium from the tainted history of a maligned rival. At the same time, it deflects to Beckford's primary public a desirable share of the righteous purity that was formerly the exclusive preserve of the British imperium.

We have previously remarked the recurring coincidence of these representations of Indians and Indian history with the theme of purity and this last, in its turn, with the culture-validating procedures of *premiers temps*. We shall return to this theme later on in the context of the sublime, but here the connection can be posited that such an aesthetic and moral identification with the purity of originary myth purchases a salutary talisman against those assailants of the very founding philosophies of empire. But the belated timing of the attack suggests a motive narrowly dedicated to Creole class interests and situates its function well within the present critique of crisis. Unwittingly, though, this manipulation of history backfires and plays right into the hands of adversaries like the abolitionists and anti-saccharites, whose strictures against the Creole imperium were replete with spilled blood and mutilated bodies, imagery that served to construct this Creole domain in the minds of detractors as the undeniable definition of taint and degeneracy.

Nor is the book's witness to this crisis encoded merely in such masked, oblique structures. Beckford owns the climate of uncertainty in which the colony presently stood, tellingly linking its indeterminate fate with his personal debt crisis. In volume II he justifies a lengthy digression on debt laws and the cruelty and harshness of creditors on the grounds of the 'uncertain situation in which the West Indian islands at present stand' (II: 279). In this very digressive and thematically congested environment the resources of the *negotium* are called upon to affirm cultural virtue, oscillating convulsively among a variety of intertwined counter-narratives: the originary myth of purity and virtuous struggle is invoked therefore to consecrate his own personal history and to defend the integrity of colonial Jamaica against metropolitan political and rhetorical assaults. For this he finds a congruent and confirmatory image in the durable significations of the sugar cane: 'through all its different stages, [it is] the most uncertain production upon the face of the earth' (II: 11). Here it is not sugar's value as an economic commodity that is being advertised. Rather, it is its ability to deliver from the complex semiosis of its 'sweete negotiation' an outward visible sign of Creole virtue, a sign that grounds that virtue in the founding myth of unremitting toil coupled with uncertain rewards.[19]

This mythic value of incertitude is likewise extended to colonial climate. From that source he raises a set of correlated images that are as intrinsic to the Creoles' identity and this moment of crisis in their cultural consciousness as sugar itself. Encodings of 'sweete negotiation's defining oscillation and flux are recognized too in the very temporalities of diurnal nature, as the mists at dawn are dissipated by warming sunbeams, and 'the eye is presented with an enchanting variety of new and brilliant images' (I: 176). While the cooling mists and showers of November bring welcome relief from blazing heat, they also occasion perplexity that a season so agreeable to the feelings should be so 'prejudicial to the health of the white people, and inimical to the constitutions of the negroes' (I: 179). At the level of poetics, the *negotium* extends its capacity to contain a similar variety of culturally significant narrative modes that become implicated in the author's desire and design to use them as counter-agents or stays against the unravelling of civilization: these modes conveniently accommodate the myth of incessant labour to produce cultural value (georgic), while masking the darker inflections of social decadence and disease (picturesque).

And in this connection may be observed the equally resilient necessitarian myth by which African enslavement was traditionally rationalized. Where Beckford makes any noticeable concession to African displacement he does so not to critique slavery or the slave trade but to rationalize both as part of a larger civilizing activity. His argument taps into a familiar pro-slavery narrative: Africans enjoyed demonstrably higher social and moral benefits from transplantation to the West Indies than they would have if abandoned to the presumably less desirable fate of greater oppression, misery and ignorance in Africa. This argument constructs displacement as historical necessity, citing in its corroboration certain climatic infelicities like tropical heat and the constant threat of 'languor', to which Europeans were especially vulnerable and Africans more adaptable by virtue of their superior physical constitutions. African displacement, then, is historicized as a natural precondition to the greater good of white-dominated civilization in Jamaica. Slavery and its consequences are naturalized to the supreme purposes of the Creole *negotium*.

With the axiomatic foundation established for Beckford's slavocracy of virtue, he proceeds to support the edifice of his discourse with sturdy pillars of rhetoric, oblique counterpoints to the dire predictions of corrosion and moral decay emanating from the enemies of the West Indians. While the abolitionists were loudly proclaiming their vision that a slavish tyranny at the margins of empire would inevitably seek to absorb the freeborn at the centre,[20] Beckford was rhetorically designing an architecture of Creole slave-based civilization that drew its virtue from local and translated sources, and defined itself against the creeping exhaustion and internal contradictions of Europe. He reiterated his defence that a civilization built on the ethics of slavery/negation would mean social displacement of house slaves and collapse of the economy.

The oppressiveness of existing debt laws offered him a repeated arena in which to contest England's much-vaunted liberties. His counter-narrative is tendentious in its defensive representation of Creole society while systematically constructing a polemical critique of European orthodoxy. His analysis subjects the essentialisms of freedom and social equality to searching inquiry, exposing an oft-cited pro-slavery boast the originary source of which can be traced in this study to Ligon's paeans to the egalitarianism of early Barbadian settlers. Jamaica progressively gains the cultural advantage over eighteenth-century Europe because, by Beckford's lights, it is not quite as complexly stratified as Europe:

In European communities there is a chain of subordination that descends from link to link, which, while it preserves the strength of the whole, gives ease and motion to some particular parts; and which, without constraint, ensures obedience: whereas, the levelling principle that obtains among the white people in Jamaica, entrenches upon the duties of society, and annihilates the bonds of power, and the good effects of subordination. (II: 348)

This comparative sociological analysis is not in the least a disinterested one: it brooks no divergence from the existent model of bi-racial stratification. In fact, it consciously elides the existence of the lower orders of all those white people below the occupations of mechanics and field attendants, identifying them with 'vagrants', 'shadows' and 'dregs' of a community which might 'overcharge' his ideal picture with gloom. The reductive vision proceeds:

It was my first intention to draw a line of separation between the white people and the negroes in Jamaica; but as they are so intimately connected and blended together, I find it almost impossible: as far therefore as there seems to be a natural dependence of one upon the other, I shall consider them as one mass; nor let the pride of colour be offended, when I observe that the planter is infinitely more indebted to his slave, than this latter is under obligations to him.

Both sides are ennobled by this idealization of their mutual bondedness:

and if the first be humane from interest, and the last be industrious from principle, I will only ask on which side does the merit lie? (II: 281)

In his determined attempt to paint the situation of the African slave as an 'enviable' one, he formulates a fictive equality and assimilation of the races one to another. Narratively, this places the slaves safely beyond the reach of the abolitionist. More broadly, it thoroughly defamiliarizes the presumption of privilege instituted in the European social paradigm. In the same voice, it elevates the culture-ratifying values of Jamaican farming above British, painstakingly documenting the rigours of the former in extended (digressive) sections of volume II (pp. 227–355), contrasting the life of an English farmer ('an occupation of pleasure and content, and independency, at least, if not abundance') to that of a Jamaican farmer (beset by risks of mismanagement and loss, a prey to 'misconduct' and 'villainy').[21]

If the old myth of tireless, risk-laden labour is constantly invoked to ratify the legitimate social reality of Creole Jamaica, so too is that legitimacy sought in the aesthetic processes of that labour which is the enterprise of narrative creation. Beckford's poetics become implicated in the polemics of cultural controversy by the sheer reach and heterogeneity of the aesthetic formations embodied in the text. The four passages to follow are drawn from a section of Volume I (22–31) whose ostensible object is to describe the views of a part of the island named Sixteen-mile Walk. They invoke so many of the key structuring categories of late eighteenth-century representational practice, in them the aesthetic cannot without great difficulty be detached from the political. I have arranged them in pairs 1A, 1B: 2A, 2B to illustrate a pattern of shared conceptual values and similar conflictive resolutions. In 1A, 1B, the descriptive impulse seeks its desire in the implied topos of a picturesque tourist whose painterly imagination surveys primarily to comprehend and recontextualize the displayed scene:

1A The banks of the river are ornamented with a variety of beautiful productions, which exhibit an infinite diversity of breaks and foregrounds; and that part of it over which a bridge is thrown, is, in my opinion, the most striking: it is flat and simple, and seems peculiarly adapted to the features of the scene: it communicates, as it were, disjointed beauties, and hardly appears to interrupt the progress of the stream, although the current is always seen to ripple, sometimes to break in foam, and in the rainy seasons to rush with such a violence, as oftentimes to carry it away, or to deposit its ruins among the docks and sedges. Indeed the whole stream runs through, and enriches, as many delightful scenes as a lover of Nature can anywhere meet with, or the most enthusiastic artist could possibly desire. (23–4)

(*A description of the view from the village of Bath to the Fountain of the Medicinal Spring*):

1B . . . in [the] journey is most pleasingly united every object that can call forth the charms of retirement, in the murmurs of the stream which invite to meditation; in the cooings of the dove that awakens sensibility; in the trillings of the nightingale that soothe despair; or in the clamour of the crows, the shrieking of the parrots and the perroquets, and the dismal croaking of the toads that overcome, with the sounds of tumult and discordance, the assuasive melody of softer tones. (28)

The landscape tantalizes with the promise of accessibility, while certain integral features remain elusive, fraught with menace or outright peril. The activity of the perceiving subject is almost instantly identified as an attempt to colonise natural space and objects with covert emotional needs and political motives.

In the second pair (2A, 2B), the ideal of variety is intensified by darker colours and profounder reflections, staging the widest ambitions of the negotium in its blending of pleasure with terror, desire with content, and activity with retirement:

2A On the left-hand of this romantic valley there runs a narrow road, the sides of which are covered with hills of an almost perpendicular height, and from whence there trickles, at every turn, a slender rill, which winds its prattling course among the trees and shrubs that over-hang the almost invisible and tremendous chasm below.(27)

(*A description of a shady glen near the Bath House*)

2B How sweetly adapted is this charming retreat to midnight contemplation, silence, and the muse! The Penseroso *here* had found *his* paradise – the afflicted, consolation – the patient, hope – and the philosopher an oblivion of all the world and all its cares. (31)

Beckford insists on calling forth the full panoply of topoi found in contemporary practices of natural description. He translates to Jamaica some of the major structuring categories of pre-romantic sensibility – melancholy, the sublime, gothic, solitude, and retirement – thus revaluing the pre-existing view of colonial nature, colonial history and the *translatio* itself. And elsewhere in the book, as his narrative designs progress from mapping the timeless on to the temporal, synchrony on to diachrony (I: 338), his pace and rhythm are varied according to mode and activity: the delightful pleasures of fishing and hunting are counterpointed to the meditative. They are all resolved in Beckford's attempt to produce a single seamless narrative fabric. But the ostensibly disinterested proposition that Jamaica engenders all of the major structuring categories of eighteenth-century representational practice must be revalued beyond mere aesthetic reference. The ideological desire thereby accomplishes the most fearful myth of anti-slavery and anti-imperialist ideologues – that the economic interests and cultural integrity of England would become conflated with the upstart pretensions of colonial margins like Jamaica. Empire could be subversively (aesthetically) assimilated into one of its dissonant parts.

Thus, the natural economy of Creole Jamaica is advanced to stand its own competitive ground in the arena of aesthetic values. In the same way, the social and political economy of slavery is affirmatively opposed to the normative ideals of liberty, equality and social justice. The challenge Jamaica poses to the Old World is the inconvenient spectacle of the colonial cultural parvenu presuming to interrogate the privileged aesthetic principles and practices of its imperial hierarch. The peculiarities of light and shade on the island, its dews and heats, its sea breezes and sunsets, all argue new ways of looking, new ways of seeing and representing, stretching the possibilities of conventional perspective and practice. In framing this as a problem with the potential to reshape conventional representational practice, Beckford apprehends a defining concept that might be called a 'fidelity gap', the difference, as he puts it, between 'running a line over the extremities of Nature and filling up those lines with truth and judgment; and it even requires some art to express Nature in such a manner, that she may not be deemed unnatural' (I: 17).

This radical use of the *negotium* to assimilate to itself not only the political and economic prerogatives of the empire but also to contest and supplant its aesthetic criteria brings the poetics of reaction to participate in the narrative of exhaustion. One of the key rationales for the reactionary practices of this poetics is to be found in the high incidence of *aporia* (the trope of inexpressibility) invoked typically to cope with mystification and novelty engendered by Jamaican nature. The landscape and the revisionist practices uniquely required to depict it propose themselves as the indefeasible grounds on which the Creole ethos stakes its claim to supplant the traditional imperium. In effect, it is by these inscriptions in the narrative of the *Descriptive Account* that the text aesthetically usurps the metropole's imperium over that sphere of colonial life. It persistently reaches beyond the restricted confines of Jamaica's quarrel with her particular mother country England, extending this contest for the imperium to other European countries. Beckford pours civilized scorn on Spain, characterizing it as a nation only just emerging from cultural darkness. He attributes the revolutionary turmoil of France to a lag in civilization and liberty. His argument turns on the theory that with the aging of cultural institutions in Europe, novelty would become harder and harder to find; copying, imitation and aesthetic monotony would result: 'the views of Tivoli and Frascati, and Albano, have furnished for years the same ideas and imitations. Their beauties and varieties have been too frequently copied, and are hence too generally known to promise to the artist any further charms or novelty . . .' (I: 270); 'the views of the islands of the West Indies may give scope to a new expansion of picturesque ideas' (I: 271). As he imagines the empire of pictorial representation shifting, his conception shapes a metaphor for displacing European artists from their long-standing hegemony in the representational domain. One of the text's distinctive structuring leitmotifs, a picturesque painter–tourist documenting the 'sweete negotiation' of land and landed, sugar and slaves, furnishes his image of the kind of aesthetic sensibility best suited to publicize the politico-cultural values of the Creole imperium. The artist named here functions at least partly in a generic role: 'the colours of Loutherbourg are better calculated for the expression of such varieties than those I should imagine of any modern artist; and he might there meet with several falls, the surrounding scenery of which might eclipse the boasted waters of Schaffhausen, the brilliance of Pisvacha and the gloom of Terni (I: 12). Beckford may be assumed to have associated this scenery with Philippe Jacques de Loutherbourg (1740–1812) as much for the landscape's affinities with the artist's picturesque practice as for Loutherbourg's relation to period landowners.

What these structural and descriptive features demonstrate therefore is the extent and the efficiency with which the aesthetic practices of this text realize its desire to assimilate the two controlling tropes of colonial power (the *translatio* and the imperium) at a moment when local Creole interests were under determined assault from metropolitan sources. Beckford's topos of the migrated painter–tourist is his analogue to Grainger's perplexed desires for muse and poets: they are the later-eighteenth-century Creole expressions of the *translatio*, all the more urgently appropriated here, though for purposes somewhat transformed from its original usage. Beckford's need is occasioned not by a cultural state of pre-literate barbarism, but by the inadequacy of existing aesthetic language and representational forms to image a totally novel reality. By virtue of his knowledge and experience, he therefore assumes the role of learned orator, the primary historian–narrator–painter, giving legitimacy to a new imperium, and at the same time infusing its revitalizing spirit into an old imperium under threat of exhaustion. Such ironic inversions of the *translatio* are especially revealing of how this text's aesthetic practices disrupt the traditional discourse of empire and then use that discourse to construct its own: in effect, to make the empire 'talk back'. It produces a kind of ambiguity which Cheyfitz points out is inherent to imperialism's conflictual economy: the conflict is 'between what this ideology represses (that imperialism is always acting in the interests of its own power) and what it admits (that imperialism is acting in the interest of enlightening the other)'.[22] In this case, the deceit runs both ways. The first, the older, is familiar enough. The second, the latter-day Creole power, represented in the *Descriptive Account*, illustrates the ideology-repression nexus in the assimilated narratives of the text's aesthetics, and illustrates its enlightening interest precisely by establishing Jamaica as a new order of knowledge. Both defining activities of the *translatio* (the *translatio imperii* and the *translatio studii*) are reproduced in the Creole appropriation. The text demonstrates that the transfer or alienation of the old imperium's power could at least be imagined. For the latter the text demonstrates that the imperium's prerogatives over learning and culture could also be interrogated, and persuasively so, on the grounds of a discourse of sound epistemological and aesthetic principles.

With respect to the imperium, in so far as it can be treated as a quasi-autonomous factor (because never entirely divorceable from the *translatio*), what the foregoing analysis illustrates is the ideological potency of the argument commonly formulated in that extended talk-back that ensued as the Creoles responded to the metropole's discourse on control and reform. As Beckford framed it in the *Descriptive Account*, the economic ramifications of abolition would impact just as heavily on England as they would on Jamaica and the colonies. The colonies were one of the major tributaries flowing into the mainstream of the mother country; abrupt changes in their historical arrangements would bring severe social and economic dislocation, reducing slaves to penury and psychological insecurity;

working ruin on bankers, creditors, merchants and other commercial interests, along with thousands of others employed in or dependent upon the trade:

It seems to be forgotten that the colonies were planted, were peopled, and encouraged, by provisional laws enacted in their favour by the legislature of England, under the faith and guarantee of which many thousands of people have emigrated from their native countries, taken up and purchased lands in those regions, cleared, built, settled and planted at their own expense, depending upon the shipping of Great Britain and of Ireland for supplies and freighting those vessels home with a barter that has opened a new channel of wealth, which for a century at least has flowed with one rich and augmenting stream to fertilize the mother country. (II: 317)

Viewed through these aesthetic lenses, the Creole imperium (or perhaps, more properly, neo-imperium), emerges as a construct of Beckford's privileged thematics constituted from and affirmatively foregrounded in his text as land, labour, sugar and slaves. The combined power of these factors needs no further recitation, except to point out a relevant structural relationship to the inversion dynamic associated with the *translatio*. In subsuming the imperium with the *translatio*, the imperium displays another crucial factor of the counter-narrative. Because it is itself appropriated and translated, the imperium is a very steadfast inversion, a very obdurate institution of translation as a political practice. As such it demonstrates how, by a series of logical inferences, this primarily linguistic (here aesthetic and cultural) practice can be refigured into the political sphere. The exegetical text is Walter Benjamin's theory of translation which suggests some potential ways of reconceiving land, labour, slaves and sugar to constitute themselves as a single language of neo-imperium. Benjamin's discussion refers properly to language, its aims and intentions, and the ultimate impossibility of true translation: 'It is the task of the translator to *release* in his own language that pure language which is under the spell of another, to *liberate* the language *imprisoned* in a work in his recreation of that work' (italics mine).[23] Beckford's reconstitution of himself in the *Descriptive Account* as the eloquent and sufficient translator has already been shown. Benjamin's definition of the translator's role is so couched in a figurative language of bondage and work it is hard to resist its creative elucidation of the present text. Certainly if Beckford is a translator his work has already been shown to be searching to display and validate the originary myths on which the Creole imperium could be founded (Benjamin's *release* and *liberate*). The language imprisoned is the narrative of colonial aspiration struggling to make its voice heard above the din of determined adversaries and political hierarchs ('under the spell of another'). The language imprisoned in the *Descriptive Account* is the ideological–cultural potential of the text's aesthetic dimensions, its desire to legitimate Creole culture and autonomy.

Having laid out the dynamic of structural processes that defines the operation of the *negotium* as it adjusts to evolving cultural and political challenges, we can now turn to define the major aesthetic formations of the text in an attempt to understand their role in supporting the *negotium*'s objectives and their complicated relationship to Creole interests and desires at this critical moment.

Previously defined as a poetics of reaction, the picturesque emerges in Beckford's design as the language best suited to produce the effects implied above. By that design Beckford performs his own version of migration and translation for aesthetic purposes. Expressed as both immanent aesthetic form and thematic preoccupation, the picturesque fulfils the functions outlined above by (1) demonstrating its character as ideological and political praxis; (2) aestheticising into an image of Creole cultural idealism the true nature and relationships existing among land and landowners, labour, sugar and slaves, and (3) revalorising itself to ratify the specific conditions of colonial culture and civilization. This critique of aesthetic practice and function will illuminate the kinds of strategies and structures in which cultural ideology is embedded in the text. It will also reveal how the picturesque mainly (but significantly in aggregation with georgic and the sublime) succeeds in producing the powerful aesthetic and economic values of sugar, transforming it from material object to mythic talisman. The text thereby will be shown to transcend the disinterested pursuit of abstract purity, its aesthetic mixtures producing the *Descriptive Account* as a discourse on culture and civilization.

The narrative manifestations of the picturesque in the *Descriptive Account* are overt and abundant enough to be self-evident, but the picturesque's value as ideology and as a vehicle of cultural politics bears placing in some relevant theoretical and historical contexts. Together with the *translatio* and the *imperium*, the picturesque creates and occupies a discursive space of meaning that meets the definition of ideology James Donald and Stuart Hall offer: that which allows us to 'make sense or give meaning to the social and political world . . . defining a definite discursive space of meaning which provides us with a perspective on the world'.[24] As it inserted itself into the representational vocabulary of the late eighteenth century, the picturesque disclosed its historical tendency to align with ideologies of containment, producing culture in conditions of contestation, revisionism and reaction. Ann Wallace offers a pertinent historicist reading of its rise and appropriation under analogous conditions in England. She points to its function as a collusive agent in the social and economic changes surrounding land use, its tendency to subsume and assimilate, to inhibit progressive or revolutionary action and the ideological formations through which the landed classes asserted their right to property control and cultural representation. Wallace's definition of the picturesque as 'subsuming the literal activities of ploughing, seeding etc into a mindless naturalized labor, assimilated into an aestheticized landscape'[25] concurs with a similar subsuming tendency in Beckford's assimilation of the *translatio* and imperium to the *negotium*.

More pertinent still to its identity as ideological and political praxis is the picturesque's politico-historical alignment with landowners who were 'intent on asserting their rights to enclose, pale in, extend, and appropriate public land for private purpose'.[26] What Worral here documents for the nineteenth century is prefigured and historically reproduced in Beckford's persistent recourse to the aesthetic; it coexists in his ideology in collusion with a determined anti-abolitionist posture, laying the aesthetic site for political contestation of those issues central to that struggle recently joined between the metropole and colonial Creoles. If in its central metropolitan production 'Land [was] the material which provided the basis for the symbolic practice of the picturesque aesthetic',[27] so in the marginal colonial places of plantation societies, as aesthetically reproduced in the *Descriptive Account*, land also becomes a critical site for political contestation. A further parallel may be drawn between the picturesque's association with a metropolitan moment of crisis, and a corresponding shift in dependent relationships in the colonies. In the picturesque's contemporaneity with what Ann Bermingham describes as a shift from a social system of 'paternalistic, quasi-feudal rights and duties to an industrial employer'[28] may be discerned an analogue with the slave plantation economy's impending transformation by abolition and emancipation.[29]

The centrality of land and landowners to Beckford's picturesque poetics emerges in his representation of these narrative elements within an aesthetically determined setting which occludes the true historical relationship of the one element to the other within the West Indian context. In this way the picturesque is brought into the complicitous ethic of the work's reactionary objectives as it furnishes a form in which to represent the Creole slavocracy of virtue. On the one hand, Beckford's persistent recourse to the picturesque can be shown to aestheticize a determined anti-abolitionist posture. On the other, it is related to an ideological motivation whose end is to add value to both land and landowners. As a reaction to abolitionist contestation, the *Descriptive Account* inserts the Creole slavocracy into an ongoing agrarian discourse in which some early nineteenth-century practitioners of the picturesque aligned themselves politically with the landowners and improvers referred to in the previous paragraph, and formulated an ideology of land use that stood in radical dissent to traditional notions of social responsibility.[30] The slavocrats formulated a similar argument about their right to use their human property to work the sugar lands in furtherance of their private economic interests.

In contributing to this discourse, Beckford explicitly reveals his desire to migrate the picturesque, its practices and practitioners, to support Creole cultural objectives. He repeatedly voices his burning desire to transport major picturesque painters like Claude Lorraine (1660–82), Salvator Rosa (1615–73) and Nicolas Poussin (1594–1655) to the Jamaican landscape, a migration he envisaged would yield both painters and colonized a place of reciprocal value.[31] In an ironic inversion of the degeneration charges heaped on the colonies, Beckford proposed this migration as an anodyne for a decadent European pictorial tradition. By his lights, it would broaden the range of images and ideas available to artists, thus adding value to their works and enhancing the aesthetic experiences of all intelligent audiences. Most of all, though, the ideological motivation of the picturesque in this work is to add value to all the structures of work in the text (sugar production, literary, cultural production): a kind of negotiated arrangement that would settle all that value on the land and landowners as cultural and political entities.

Throughout the text, the conventional picturesque topos of an aesthetically educated traveller exploring the Jamaican landscape is repeatedly imagined. From the title-page advertisement, Beckford announces that his description of place and his didactic account of sugar-cane cultivation will be 'chiefly considered in a picturesque point of view'. This prefigures the definitive ordering principles of the work, while preparing readers for his compulsive habit of imposing a painterly perspective even on factual and functional activities. One plot of the touring topos figures a planter taking a business-like survey of his property at year's end. Even on this very secular figure performing a set of very mundane duties Beckford insistently imposes a painterly perspective: 'I suppose the planter to be setting out to take a view of his estate in the month of November; and shall accompany him through the various occupations of the negroes from that time until the commencement of the crop; and shall suppose that he looks with a painter's eye at the sky above, the plains below and upon the various scenes that shall at different times, and in different situations surround him' (1:175).[32] This conceit alternates with another of similar persistence, in which he invents a painter in search of the picturesque or expresses a desire for a painter's presence to experience and record Jamaica's picturesque scenes: 'I cannot help thinking that a young artist, particularly if he be of an inquisitive and an enthusiastic turn of mind, may devote a few years of his life with as much pleasure and profit to the imitation of the beautiful and romantic scenery of that island' (1:268-9).

The function of the creolizing text as prospecting propaganda or promotional advertising has been discussed in chapter 1. Its efficacy in attracting new settlers and solidifying white political control had been proven for wellnigh four hundred years. Now, overlaid with picturesque filiations, that narrative is invoked, as it were, to gentrify slave-owning and plantation economy, and thereby posit the existence of a high state of cultural progress in Jamaica. How Beckford deploys the aesthetic for narrowly subjective purposes and how he positions marginal entities (slaves and lower orders) within his pictorial-narrative frames bear more than passing continuity with intersections of landowning, empire and morality in Pope's aesthetics. Pope, too, distinctly contrives to efface the labouring poor or to aestheticize the conditions of their relationship to his landscapes. This connection places Beckford's aesthetics of reaction in an old conservative tradition, although now, because of his relationship to the colonies, it is a markedly ironic relationship.[33] In the meantime, what the place lacked in authentic painters he would compensate for with his considerable aptitude for narrative painting in prose and his flair for art criticism of the picturesque genre. Beckford held out the thematic, structural and stylistic features of his narrative as tangible proofs that the material and aesthetic constituents for producing a picturesque civilization were already in place and that he, as a Creole author, personified those proofs. The picturesque transforms with great detail, colour and imagination the narrative realism of land and landowners, portraying each of these elements in its didactic relation to life and action. Both the picturesque's desire and its capacity for fullness and presence, depth and variety are notably exemplified in this word picture of the legendary Port Royal:

Every situation that commands the harbor of Kingston, takes in a prospect that can hardly be surpassed in any quarter of the world, as in that prospect are strongly varied and magnificently brought together, the pleasing and romantic, the extensive and sublime.

The majestic sweep and beautiful curve of the Bay of Port Royal, the numerous sails that catch the wind in every direction, the romantic projection of the town that gives it name, the dotted houses that mark in the situation of Kingston, and the numerous masts of vessels that rise above their summits, present a scene of business and variety. . . (I:20–21)

Here the narrative painting is richly allusive: it constructs a pointed metonymy of Beckford's larger ideology of place, and manifests the creolizing text's role as a producer of knowledge and a source for extending sensibility. Evoked as a site of commerce and urban prosperity hedged around by beautiful vistas, Port Royal comprehends a complex formation of cultural desire. That 'majestic sweep and beautiful curve' recuperates its historic associations with opulence and power. Those 'tall masted vessels, with numerous sails that catch the wind in every direction' recall Port Royal's storied past of buccaneer exploits, affirming its present identity as a place of progress, even while its link with that past endures in its use as a colonial stronghold and naval station. The union of past and present, business and pleasure recuperates that earlier criterion of civilized value from the Augustan age, the union of common urban and rural ease. More importantly for the present discussion, it reproduces the *negotium*'s function as a mediating instrumentality, one that eminently serves the creolizing narrative's economy of progress.

The second series of elements – labour, sugar and slaves –

constitute a powerful aggregation of aesthetic and economic values whose combined power sustains Creole cultural myth, and reveals the constructed nature of the picturesque in its tendency to mask social reality. What follows will explore the specific role these mixtures play in producing the *Descriptive Account* as a discourse on culture and civilization, with necessary references to ideological connections with the politics of land and labour.

At the level of pure description, Beckford offers the reader ample instruction in the nature of colonizing agricultural activity in Jamaica: cycles of planting and growing, harvesting and grinding, the rhythms of active and restful life inscribe Jamaica into the paradigm of Western cultural history that owe some of its primordial literary foundations to georgic. These pursuits are by definition predicated on the performance of labour. And labour in georgic representations symbolizes the imperative of wringing not only material sustenance but essential cultural–historical meaning from the land. Subsumed here within picturesque structures, georgic produces sugar's value as both material artefact and transcendent idea, yoking the necessity to work (the struggle with tangible, material form) with an equally compelling necessity to extract some transcendent meaning from that work: what Heinzelman says of the georgic writer may here by an easy metaphor be applied to the Creole author on sugar: 'the poet of the Georgics writes rather than sings, suffers the exigencies of making not just a living but a whole field of meaning in a cultural context that includes the sociopolitical justification of his own compositional project'.[34] In thus appropriating georgic values to itself, the picturesque constructs sugar in a narrative myth of struggle, survival and cultural progress.

The desire to verify Jamaica as a locus of authentic culture and civilization finds recurrent expression in the picturesque modes of narrative. And, typically, that desire manifests itself in collateral proximity with the structures of desire that sugar has been shown to engender in the eighteenth-century imagination. In Beckford the idealizing rhetoric participates in a familiar bourgeois enthusiasm usually reserved for the growth of European cities and the expansion of commerce and consumerism within them: 'A sugar plantation is like a little town: and I have often been surprised, in revolving in my mind the necessary articles that the cane requires and consumes, how intimately connected is everything that grows, and everything that labors, with this very singular and at one time luxurious, but very necessary, as it is deemed to be a highly useful and wholesome, plant' (I: 141).

The passage resonates with Defoe's faith in the capacity of free trade to accomplish a harmonious global culture, while its verbal glow recalls Addison's rhapsodizing over the Royal Exchange in the *Spectator* (69), and his warm effusions over the thriving economic metropolis of London (*Spectator* 454). Sugar-plantation culture could argue its legitimacy and its indispensability with any other: in fact, the material goods it produced penetrated the consuming habits and transformed the life-styles of all Atlantic and some Mediterranean cultures: those it consumed expanded the economies of producing countries. The Creole culture's participation in this exchange facilitated livelihoods, earned its elites new status and mapped identities for a whole new class of persons whose civilization found apologists like Beckford to argue its legitimacy.

Nor is this rhetoric of cultural mythmaking, this hypotyposis in the language of the passage quoted above, to be found only in reference to the commodity market value of sugar. It crops up in contexts so unexpected as to appear to subvert the text's very formative negotiation between sugar and civilization. Like Ligon and Grainger, Beckford comments at length on the hazards and frustrations that attend sugar-cane breeding and cultivation. In terms that come close to humanizing the plant, he describes it as 'treacherous' and 'perverse', a plant 'so liable to accidents, and attended with injury, that very little dependence can be placed upon its returns' (I: 142). For the next ten pages, his exposition on the extreme care and attentions required in the months of the plant's growth is replete with references to incertitude and ambivalence, deceit and flattery, perverseness and false promise. In the georgic narrative of work and struggle, this language is unmistakably calculated to establish an inverse relationship between the difficult conditions of cane culture and the supreme value of the social and economic polity it sustained. And to reinforce the integrity of that civilization, Beckford reasserts sugar's singularity by appropriating further the resources of that idealizing rhetoric that sugar engendered from Jimenez through Ortiz.

Differentiating it from 'almost every production of the earth', he adverts to its inherent capacity to regenerate itself from a state of extreme physical debilitation. For example, even if allowed to remain unreaped past normal ripeness, when the rind dries and the juice evaporates ('in short, [taking on the] appearance of stubble, [which] would burn like tinder'), there still inheres in it a capacity to 'reinvigorate and revivify itself from such an appearance of vegetative decay'. And to drive home his affirmation of its singularity, he caps the passage with that persistent trope whose effect, if not conscious intent, is always to raise the cultural value and capital of the colonizing economy, even as, inevitably, it interrogates the continuing hegemony of an imperial government whose councils were being increasingly influenced by forces inimical to the slaveholders: 'I hardly know a plant in Europe that would recover, and yield perhaps as much or more produce after its resuscitation than it would if taken in its prime' (1:152). The anthropomorphic resonances in parts of the cited passages invest the cane with volitional agency and with a philosophical attribute of mind; they thereby imbue it with the capacity to participate in that mythic struggle that is the mark of all great civilizations: to confront adversary forces, to encounter fate and to prevail.

Slaves and their labour bear a natural and indivisible relationship to the Creole economy, and that relationship is commensurately aestheticized to achieve Beckford's cultural and political objectives.[35] As a reactionary structure deployed to blunt political pressure, the representation of Africans as picturesque objects in a consciously sanitized landscape mitigates the physical hardships and social issues of slavery. Naturalizing them to coerced labour and to a permanently alienated autonomy, implicates the picturesque in a complexly constructed legitimation of Creole culture.

The slaves' robust physicality and their children's irrepressible spirits offer ready-made opportunities for enlarging picturesque ideas. Under the imperium of the Creole picturesque, the effect of these features is to naturalize their presence in the rural landscape of labor, to make them an integral part of colonized nature, as natural as trees, shrubs, dales and hills:

A negro village is full of those picturesque beauties in which the Dutch painters have so much excelled; and is very particularly adapted to the expression of those situations, upon which the scenes of rural dance and merriment may be supposed with the greatest conveniency to have happened. The forms and appearances of the houses admit of every variety which this particular species of rural imagery requires; and the surrounding objects of confined landscape, with the vulgar adjuncts of hogs, poultry, cats baskets, chairs, and stools, are always at hand to fill up the canvas, and to give sense to nature, and truth and novelty to the representation of the scene. (I:228)[36]

Scenes like this unfold the complex layered design of ideology wrapped into picturesque practice. The referential force of the 'scenes of rural dance and merriment' in Dutch paintings equates the black slaves with the type of rustic labour familiar to European experience. In abstracting the slave quarters from any physical reference to other human habitations that would contextualize their status, Beckford naturalizes them to the coercive economy of slavery.[37] In commingling them with the 'vulgar adjuncts' of hogs and poultry, he extends the system of affinity to lower nature. This reduction at once neutralizes and displaces the durable narrative of primitivism which served both sides in the slavery debate. From that ground the abolitionists made persuasive appeals on the basis of sensibility and natural virtue on behalf of the suffering slave. Conversely, primitivism embodied the source of an equally resilient and widely disseminated pro-slavery libel. Thus the aestheticized images of the slaves seen in the picturesque landscape mask political values. They allow Beckford to reinterpret that scene for a wholly anti-abolitionist project coded as 'truth and novelty'. By assimilating the slave village to the canvas of Dutch painters, he domesticates and normalizes slavery, while arguing the landscape's congeniality to the type of those same painters whom he invites to Jamaica. ('There are many parts of the country that are not much unlike to, nor less romantic than, the most wild and beautiful situations of Frescati, Tivoli and Albano' (I: 9); Nature here achieves what Lorrain, Poussin and Salvator Rosa achieves 'with pleasure and pains' in Europe (I: 11). Beckford's translation of the picturesque to this arena of contested culture and politics is neither incidental to his text nor to the ideological history of the aesthetic. His conception of the Jamaican landscape as a theatre for reactionary politics stages a resistive response not only to the antagonisms of anti-slavery but also to the omens of revolutionary France.[38]

In the interests of balance it ought to be recorded that Beckford expresses feelings of compassion and concern for the slaves. From motives of sensibility he appeals for more food and better, sturdy clothing to protect the watchmen at the cattle pens from the chill of the night air (I: 198–200) ('That they think, that they feel, that they act – who can be so foolish or so impious as to deny?' I: 200). He levelled condign moral strictures against specific incidents of mutilation and excessive 'corporal infliction' on slaves, recommending mandatory imprisonment or fines for white people guilty of such treatment. By the same token, in his definitive pro-slavery stance, he attributed the bulk of such allegations to the personnel engaged directly in the procurement and transportation of slaves: he exonerated the planters themselves on the rationalization that they would not mistreat their economic investment (II: 323–33).

With the allusion to the 'scenes of rural dance and merriment' from the Dutch painters, the text implicates the picturesque in a very complexly constructed legitimation of Creole culture. Beckford repeatedly calls attention to the plight of the European peasantry: low-paid, ill-fed, ill-clothed and poorly housed, their liberties continually eroded by greedy landowners and their futures rendered bleak by industrializing trends in agriculture. Against such dire disabilities, he typically depicts the living conditions of the West Indian slaves in a favourable light, vigorously contending that the slavery system's provision of free clothes, housing and food somehow privileged the slaves in the comparison. Yet, on the crucial distinction that the peasants were free and the slaves were not, he maintained a disingenuous silence.

All this discourse on comparative ethnography encode in the *Descriptive Account* a complementary nexus of private and public purposes as it seeks to construct a model of Creole culture. The narrative content itself and the manner of its presentation signal the author as a figure of enlightenment, knowledge and cultural sophistication. The text deploys the picturesque as a mythos of individual desire: the desire of the individual to claim a place and define a relationship to that place.[39] Furthermore, the text signs ethnographic alterity and variety as highly commodifiable values. The picturesque construction of the slaves is laid in evidence here for its probative value in establishing the exceptional cultural sophistication of the author, figuring at once his knowledge of place, his sensibility to its aesthetic contents and his benevolence to a despised race. The public purposes commodify all these cultural values and qualifications for the consumption of his objective audience, those who might be well placed to redeem his personal plight, and those whose money, power and influence could be enlisted to prop up the Jamaican slavocracy, and thus affirm his vision of viable civilization there.

The grand, lively scenes of picturesque invention might well have served to defer the social and political exigencies that circumscribed

Beckford's consciousness and the cultural ideal his book desired. Mills, works, houses peeping among the branches of tree-covered hills or buried amidst their shades (I: 7) compose a physical scene, an ideal space designed to reproduce a particular kind of aesthetic and (by extension) social order. The literary skill and extensive knowledge exhibited in this considerable work establish the publicist's authority at least as a countervailing voice in an arena of contested discourse. But the apparent solidity of Creole affirmations is ultimately fractured by the internal contradictions of the very aesthetic which seeks its legitimacy. Prone by its very nature to hypotyposis in language and emotion, the picturesque is equally liable to mute and efface its objects, and is therefore unreliable as a final instrument with which to stabilize social truth. It must proceed by selecting and suppressing – colluding in loss, occluding displacement. Homi Bhabha calls this fracturing of univocity the 'ambivalence of colonial authority [which] repeatedly turns from mimicry to menace'.[40] Muting pain and suffering, burying history in nature, the picturesque places itself under threat from those very fearful subterranean energies it seeks to subdue. In Beckford's case, these energies materialize as those dimly remembered Indian remains imaginatively located in caves, as memorials to Spanish atrocity, and as a weeping slave woman whose cries are deliberately aestheticized by the superimposition of a waterwheel's sound.[41]

The picturesque has already been demonstrated in its capacity to assimilate an enabling modality like georgic (with constructive effects). Now, likewise, it attempts to assimilate these phenomena whose defining qualities mark them as belonging to the sublime. Masked and conflated into a single metaphoric identity, the picturesque veils its potential terror beneath 'the humble pleasures of quiescent scenery' seducing the unsuspecting observer into a pleasurable melancholy along a river's course, until that course emanates into the disruptive transformations of the sublime.[42] For the 'quiescent appearances' of the waters lull that fictive observer into the treacherous security of melancholy and contemplation. As s/he follows the river's course, it becomes 'a deep and capacious bason' which turns into a waterfall which cascades into a whirlpool which retreats into a cavern:

down falls at once the accumulated, heavy and resounding stream; the waters below seem to dread the impending fall, and shrink, as it were, from the weight of the inundation: the cataract descends with noise and fury: it forms a tremendous whirlpool underneath, in which uprooted trees of the most early growth and ponderous size, are instantly ingulphed, are buried for a time in the watery grave, and emerge at last at a considerable distance from their place of descent, and load with their contents the adjoining banks: it works its way under the rocks, and forms deep caverns at the bottom of the stream. (II: 57–8)

Experienced on the physical and refigured on the metaphysical, this trope preserves a durable continuity in Jamaican history, as attested by a modern Jamaican scholar, Jean D'Costa, who offers the witness of her childhood memories of 'secret maroon caves through which rivers sank into the unknown to rise again beyond the mountains'[43] to historicize this dialectic of descent, disappearance and reappearance, which stands as an emblem of these larger cultural meanings. This repeated pattern accomplishes an ironic unity with the earliest references to caves in the text. Now in Beckford's eighteenth-century production of this moment in Creolized history, these caves rematerialize on this scene, only now represented as fearful subterranean energies with a capacity to disrupt the totalizing voice of imperial authority. Edward Said's formulation in *Culture and Imperialism* provides a theoretical construction of narrative power that admits such interventions into the cultural discourse of colonial sites. It is as relevant to Beckford's Indian 'narrative' here as it is to his narrative of Creole resistance to slavery and metropolitan imperialism.[44] The interplay of pleasure and treachery, silence and noise, peace and trouble occasions an affective confusion, creates a cognitive gap at the place 'where consciousness encounters the world'. At this exotic scene of difference, the colonial sublime is strikingly produced in defiance of the colonizing authority. It defamiliarizes and overpowers the sensations, as the trees are uprooted and 'ingulphed'; the colonial sublime stages one of the most acute scenes of difference-in-defiance.[45] It leaves the narrating voice of the text in a state of quasi-aporia, managing only this platitudinous utterance to mask its deflated desire: 'Nature there partakes more of the terrors of the sublime, than of the humble pleasures of quiescent scenery.'[46]

One further, still more dramatic, production of the sublime will suffice to complete this illustration of how Beckford's desire for an ideal of creolized culture is effectively compromised by the powerful energies of natural phenomena that defy human intelligence and exceed human scale. The tropical play of sun and rain theatricalize the performative in nature as a 'great variety of beautiful and aerial forms' (II: 295). But they also hold the power to affect his imagination as tropes for those forces that could endanger his ideal of cultural construction. That profound impact is reflected in the extensive space (well over fifty pages, with small digressions) occupied by his account of the hurricane of 3 October 1780. The following excerpt depicts the sheer, all-pervasive might of the hurricane as a natural phenomenon: 'From the morning until four o'clock in the afternoon, the wind continued to blow with increasing violence from the north and east: but from that time, having collected all its powers of devastation, it rushed with irresistible violence from the south; and in about an hour and a half after that period, so general and persevering were its accumulated effects, that it scarcely left a plantain-tree, a cane, or a building, uninjured in the parish' (I: 94–5). The terror and foreboding – the high winds and torrential rains, the widespread destruction of human lives and material property – all these, by themselves, would furnish sufficient motive for sublime pity and fear. However, Beckford's compulsive subjectivity internalizes these events, refiguring them as eschatological signs. This section of the narrative is one of the most multi-voiced in the whole text: concrete representation alternates with sombre reflections; the grim toll of general human mortality alternates with and gives rise to intimations on his own personal mortality. These intimations are transvalued as potential disruptions of colonial order, or worse, as the demise of Creole social and political formations. 'In the space of a few days, the independent were reduced to penury, and the needy became affluent. He who the day before had not a house to put his head in, laid the foundation in that scene of indiscriminate calamity, of a dwelling without expence, and of goods without the necessity of credit. It seemed as if the fortune of individuals was jumbled together, and that *he* had the best right of possession who could boast the most successful arm in the day of plunder' (I: 134).

The language of the passage invests that 'scene of indiscriminate calamity' with certain markers for social disorder, signifiers of political revolution. Though thinly disguised under dark allusions to reversals of fortune (the rich made poor and the high brought low), the passage's deft understatements are redolent with an unmistakable apocalyptic biblicism. A social order rearranged by violent cataclysmic events, of slaves seizing the initiative to right long-suffered wrongs, of mulattos and free coloureds taking the opportunity to vent class tensions, of civil peace dissolved in an orgy of looting and plunder – all these are images that had wide currency in slavery propaganda. Their lurid forms haunted the imaginations of slavocratic interests and general conservative publicists in the late eighteenth century. With the ominous unfolding developments in nearby Saint Domingue and those already realized in France, it is not impertinent to trace the imprint of those fears in Beckford's anarchic picture of the post-hurricane lawless 'dwelling without expence, and [enjoying] goods without the necessity of credit'.

These images invite further connections with the French Revolution. The specific image suggested by the above quotation is an ironic inversion of Edmund Burke's 'uncertain anarchy of the moral world'.[47] Burke's subject would by definition cower in the presence of traditional power. Beckford's revolutionary subject, empowered by the sublime of natural disaster, assumes at least aesthetic equivalency with that power. The roles are reversed; the slaves realize what Beckford most wistfully demurred.

In the *Descriptive Account,* Beckford advances the *negotium* to imagine, at least aesthetically, the cultural consequences of subsuming within it an imperium translated from the metropole to the colony. Framed admittedly in highly idealized structures of desire, the text seeks at least a dividend of the imperium potent enough to secure the status quo of Jamaica's slavocratic economy and institute a Creole ideal of picturesque culture. The sublime notwithstanding, the irresistible pull of reactionism draws Beckford repeatedly over ploughed ground, even when, by his own admission, his narrative is running well past the limits of his original intention. He neither resolves his anxiety for lost history nor does he transcend his terror of the potential in radical abolitionist thought to incite race war and install a revolutionary culture that would invert the relative status of slaves and masters. The outward signs of the text's formal closure suffer hopeless protraction by Beckford's personal unwillingness to countenance any form of Creole economy that was not based on slave labour. The *negotium* would have to await the arrival of 'Monk' Lewis before any author-publicist would exploit its potential to imagine and embrace a truly revolutionary image of Creole history.

CHAPTER 6

Lewis: personalizing the 'negotium'

Though with markedly divergent intensities and though qualified by a sensibility more inclined to romantic revolution than to reactionary politics, the picturesque and the sublime which so centrally informed Beckford's vision of Creole culture persist in the next and final text, imaginatively shaping Matthew 'Monk' Lewis' desire to appropriate 'sweete negotiation' for both private and public purposes. Situated at the end of the line of literary and cultural history traced in this book's design, Lewis' *Journal of a West Indian Proprietor, Kept During a Residence in the Island of Jamaica* (1834) fittingly incorporates certain key desire formations of the *negotium*, some identical with Ligon's originary source, others accreted in the process of creolization. Imprinted now in Lewis' *Journal* with the consciousness of a reformist slave-master and the revolutionary potential of freedom-expectant slaves, the *negotium* diffracts and redefines these formations into modes and constructions of cultural desire consonant with the existing shape of creolization and major historical transformations taking place in early nineteenth-century Jamaica. Lewis reinvents and redefines 'sweete negotiation' to meet the objectives of a very private kind of romantic idealism. At the same time, he appropriates it to serve the wider social purposes of reforming slavery and accommodating certain desires and belief systems of the slaves. The *Journal* ultimately transforms the *negotium* to such an extent that it envisions an image of Creole culture liberal enough to countenance the inevitability of slavocratic decline, a personal myth so far divorced from the origins of the *negotium* as to intuit a reformed colonial public sphere.

When Matthew Lewis the elder, former Deputy-Secretary at War, died in 1812, he willed to his youngest son Matthew Gregory ('Monk') Lewis two slave estates in Jamaica: Cornwall in the western and Hordley in the eastern part of the island. In the *Journal* (1834),

'Monk' Lewis left behind a narrative history of his two visits to those holdings.[1] So little, if anything, in Lewis' objective experience prepared him for the workaday reality of life on a slave plantation, it is not surprising that in the journal he filters the discrete images and events of his colonial sojourn through the prism of a romantic imagination, refiguring them as allegories for a displaced subject's desire to formulate new terms of order for an illiberal social polity defined by the ethics of tyranny, exploitation and social death.[2] Composed during the two visits he paid (four months during 1815–16, and six months during 1817–18) to familiarize himself with conditions on his estates, the *Journal* records mainly the objective particulars of daily life and experiences on his properties, together with Lewis' subjective critiques of slavocratic order and African manners and beliefs, critiques that assume increasing complexity as Lewis struggles to mediate the disparate roles of slave-master, liberal aesthete and romantic idealist.

In Lewis, some of the earliest characteristic functionalities of the *negotium* are seen to converge and transform themselves. Without attributing them to direct influence or conscious emulation, the following continuities between Lewis' *Journal* and the other four main texts can be remarked. From Ligon, the *Journal* continues the founding narrative of profit and purity, the one (*the neg*) implicating Lewis the liberal subject in the conflicted business of owning slaves, the other (the *otium*) struggling to impose on this scene of cultural conflict and political contestation an ideal of romantic revolutionary ethics forged from the confident integrity of his own egotistical sublime. As a culutral text, then, the *Journal* reflects an unbroken continuity with Ligon by exploiting the definitive dualism of the *negotium*. But to the extent that it objectifies an exceptionally literate slaveowner's sensibility, it adapts the *negotium* to serve both the demands of a highly subjective idealism while attempting to mediate a public historical moment of far-reaching cultural and political change. From Rochefort, the *Journal* recuperates the trope of *premiers temps*, in a fashion that is distinctive to the very process of creolization, at once shaping its author's idealism and being redefined by it. With the indigenous now all but a faded memory, Lewis is free to focus all the energy of his cultural and ethnographic interest on the African slaves, often perversely reimagining them, their true meaning and identities after incongruous classical paradigms, but ultimately domesticating the notion of *premiers temps* to his own solipsistic cultural experimentation. In this respect, he echoes and responds to the paradigm of the benevolent, paternalistic Creole slaveholder prefigured in Grainger's Montano. The resonance of Montano's self-reproduction in Lewis' valorization of ambient nature affords a point of structural and thematic contrast to Beckford. Unlike Beckford, Lewis does not privilege the luxuriance of Jamaican nature to bury the natural plenitude of the slaves' humanity. Indeed, he implies that slaves and nature constitute a moral economy that has the potential to redeem the Creole slavocracy from total degeneracy. Thus his relation to the picturesque is a divergent one in that he does not use it to mute and obscure the authentic voice and face of slavery. Similarly, where in Beckford the sublime's intimations of revolutionary order are strenuously demurred, in Lewis it enables the romantic subject fairly to court a radical image of reformed Creole culture. That image is entirely consonant with those idiosyncratic features of Lewis' personality which prompted Byron to describe him as 'paradoxical', and with those effects of creolization which Brathwaite defined as identification with and commitment to a specific West Indian cultural locus, and from which Glissant derived his critique of dissensus and diffraction.

Paradox, dissensus and diffraction are by these lights the distinctive marks of his creolizing sensibility, and their functions in imprinting his self-consciousness on the process of reshaping culture will be developed in due course. But here it is instructive to examine how Lewis attempts to alter the fundamental terms of cultural reference in creoledom by altering the narrative value of sugar itself. We have seen how in the foregoing chapters sugar functioned as the core signifying system of these texts, and as the narrative object that consistently claims the single highest descriptive and figurative value. In his turn, Lewis exhibits no compelling narrative interest in sugar either as an object of natural history or for its long tradition of engendering metaphysical and aesthetic ideas. His references to sugar are by no means continuous or extensive; in fact they are really quite disparate and, by comparison with the other authors, surprisingly few in number. As though to assert his dissensus or to exhibit a perverse desire to differentiate himself from the legacy of Creole publicists, Lewis downplays the referential proportion and consequence of sugar. In the *Journal* sugar diminishes in inverse proportion to the author's growing fascination for the singularities of the slaves, his appreciation for their human value, and his personal interest in securing their comfort and welfare.

Only two or three references may be characterized as mediated by normal proprietary (economic) interest, or plain secular information-gathering. One such didactic entry describes the division of labour between slaves carrying canes on their heads to the mill and others removing the trash after the juice has been extracted. A second entry describes the process of grinding the canes and of making the byproduct, rum.

The other entries all evidence a persistent imagery of conflictual values. Even in the case of the didactic entry what seemed to transfix his attention was how thoroughly the productive economies that sustained Creole culture depended on a deliberately gendered selection and exploitation of labour, and how thoroughly Creole pretensions to purity were disrupted by ever-present sources of contamination. Only the 'cleanest' slave women were chosen to feed canes into the mill to separate the pure from the impure, but, to produce a marketable body of finished secondary products, the impurities of scum, trash and other 'feculent' parts were necessarily and inextricably commingled.[3]

In another series of references gathered from separate occasions and incidents the recurrent themes are reducible to carnivalesque misrule, fire, and aggravated disputes degenerating into rebellion. Marked by typical abandon and revelry, improvisation and role-playing ('puttin' on ole massa'), the John-Canoe festivities charm and stir Lewis' predisposition for indulging the slaves' recreative merrymaking, but they also engender anxiety about an orderly start to a profitable sugar crop.[4] The slaves are granted a holiday with 'as much rum, sugar, noise and dancing as they chose' (73). But the preparations for reaping and grinding are interrupted by a fire. And to add to Lewis' anxiety, Charles, an old coachman, missed his step and fell into a boiling-house siphon, horribly scalding himself.

Significantly, the most violent disruptions occur at the boiling house or around the mill, those very highly contested sites which Ligon so rhapsodized and Tryon pronounced his dire warnings about. A dispute in the boiling house between a bookkeeper and a slave resulted in an exchange of blows, at the end of which the bookkeeper was knocked down (196). Tempers flared among the onlooking slaves; they stopped servicing the mill, and the whole situation escalated into what Lewis himself whimsically described as a 'petticoat rebellion' (139–41).

These examples unerringly illustrate that by the first two decades of the nineteenth century the *negotium* had become imbricated in the wider climate of cultural change and political instability occasioned by the politics of abolition and anti-slavery. Lewis' language is laced with heavy cultural and political ironies, his tone varying little beyond flat detachment and dispassion. As further analysis will demonstrate, those effects function as oblique criticisms of the ethics of a culture produced from that conflicted negotiation of slaves and sugar. The recurring linkages of riotous play, verbal altercations and full-blown 'industrial unrest' disrupt the vaunts of purity and social harmony which the pro-slavery apologists and their political leaders in Parliament commonly employed as counterpoises to anti-slavery attacks. Lewis' documenting of the common incidence of rat-gnawed canes exposed the vulnerability of the manufactured product to disease and contagion, and added fuel to the anti-saccharite narrrative of taint, infection and social threat. This image of a rodent plague recuperates the vehemence with which Johnson rebuked Grainger's poetic allusion, but in the altered aesthetic context of the Creole narrative and the altered political climate of the Creole slave plantation the spectre of silent plague produced a sense of terror that prefigures the political function of the sublime (to be discussed later), and figuratively intimated the collapse of Creole power.

Lewis' distinctly solipsistic attitude to the traditional narrative value of sugar embodies a metaphor for the broader project of re-engineering Creole structures.[5] In his *Journal*, the social parameters of the *negotium* are expanded to make the term 'creole' a more inclusive social marker. The (social and political) reforms Lewis implements at Cornwall and the aesthetic revisions encoded in the *Journal* all work together to renegotiate that term to signify a cultural ideal comprehensive enough to include the reformist impulses of a 'Monk' Lewis and to image a romantic imagination transformed by practice and aesthetic.

In approaching the dynamic ideal of cultural transformation as represented in the *Journal*, it should be remembered that Lewis inherited a legacy in which the *negotium* has already demonstrated its capacity to subsume pre-existing cultural and political practices and to make itself hospitable to emergent (creolizing) ones. It has not only subsumed but also subverted practices meant to further the hegemonic aims of the metropole. Now appropriated by a consciousness given to paradox and dissensus, irony and ambivalence, the *negotium* stands susceptible of further transformations to serve the ends of a very particular kind of cultural idealism.

Besides the testimony of Byron cited earlier, a further buttress for Lewis' particular kind of emotional and mental constitution can be found in the critique of another intimate of Lewis, Lord Holland, a fellow slaveholder who echoes an identical note in his use of the words 'paradox' and 'perverseness' to characterize Lewis' thought and conversation. Holland also reports certain 'peculiarities of egotism' that appeared in his behaviour and affected his friendships around the time of his father's death.[6] Lewis had identified himself with social activism for the humane treatment of animals and for environmental preservation against the onslaughts of industrialization. The voyage and the journal that documents it, then, gave him a chance to explore further his personal myth of freedom, to displace the vision of class conflict and Satanic rebellion from the European ethos of *The Monk* to the site of the creolized Other in the *Journal*: his two sugar estates seemed to offer Lewis a site on which to perform his peculiar domestication of the *translatio*: a radical practice for liberalizing colonial culture. Jamaican Cornwall and Hordley proved to be fertile ground on which to plot the demise of repressive structures, and to subvert rationalist, conservative modes of thought.

These motives are clearly signified in the Latin epigraph affixed to the opening page of the *Journal*: 'Nunc alio patriam quaero sub sole jacentem' [Now I seek a new fatherland lying under another sun]. The words are an almost exact borrowing from Virgil (*Georgics* II, 512), announcing the intentional moment of another seeker, another founder and mythmaker, with whom Lewis signals shared purposes by appropriating and adapting the references (he changes Virgil's third person '*quaerunt*' [they seek] to a first person '*quaero*' [I seek]). In this dialogized 'translation' of Virgil, both *translatio* and *imperium* are signified. The classical authority is invoked to legitimize Lewis' own objectives of constructing place; the liberties he takes with the original text images the free play of the *negotium* as it assumes control over its own constituted order. In staging its reinterpretation of the *imperium* for highly subjective ends, the *Journal* hereby asserts its function as a critique of Creole forms. Lewis situates himself not as the type of the proto-imperialist civilizer but as a benevolent lawgiver. The journal of another creolized author provokes an illuminating contrast. John Gabriel Stedman's relation to the imperium, as its workings can be reconstituted from his *Narrative of a Five Year's Expedition against the Revolted Negroes of Surinam* (1796), hovers always at the *neg* pole of the *negotium*, staging violence, sexual licence, perfidy and death. It offers an oblique point of reference from which to refine Lewis' complex critique of European culture from the Creole margins.[7]

Inscribed in the allusions to classical sources is Lewis' determined desire to reinvent the *negotium* for a very private kind of romantic idealism. It is hard to establish with final certainty whether Lewis meant that Virgilian epigraph to stand as a literal statement of conscious intent to actually implement some kind of concrete social structure, some sort of community or polity. Mrs Baron-Wilson, one of Lewis' earliest biographers, asserts that his unequivocal motive for travelling to Jamaica sprang from the 'very practical conclusion' of desiring to witness with his own eyes the actual condition of the five hundred slaves on his estates. She is emphatic that this decision arose neither from 'transient impulse' nor 'visionary illusions'.[8] His actions and achievements too disclose a very clear model of conscious cultural engineering.

Cornwall, his principal slaveholding, embodied in its social and economic constitution some very determined elements of what Lewis must have imagined could be an early-nineteenth-century version of a neo-classical polis. In Cornwall three principal tropes of the Creole cultural narrative converge, the *negotium*, the *translatio* and *premiers temps*, together producing subjective and concrete social effects (formations).

Picturesque and fruitful, relatively stable and prosperous (*neg*), Cornwall immediately recommended itself to Lewis not only as the first choice for his principal residence in the Tropics, but also as a seigneurial seat with infinite potential to fulfil his fanciful desire for a *locus amoenus* (*otium*).

While Lewis steadfastly repudiates the crasser forms of bourgeois emulation, he does not escape the powerful inducements 'sweete negotiation' offers to sustain the Creole consumption ethic. This unabashed production of the gastronomic ethos of colonial Jamaica dramatically affirms his growing creolization. The abundant fresh air, dappled waters and fertile soil of that island afforded sources that could be appropriated for aesthetic enjoyment and economic profit, but also exercised an even more essential power on his imagination. On the physical level of appetitive gratifications, Lewis revels in the sumptuous fare served daily at his dinner table: Nature yields him her bounty in the produce of the earth, the birds of the air, the fish of the sea and the plenteous fruit of various trees – all which he finds so 'excellent', and available in such profusion, that he confesses 'I never sit down to table without wishing for the company of Queen Atygatis of Scythia, who was so particularly fond of fish, that she prohibited all her subjects from eating it on pain of death, through fear that there might not be enough left for her majesty' (104–5).

If that narrative instance identifies him unambiguously with the self-indulgent *neg* of Creole culture, the one to follow poignantly recuperates the *otium*, even as it asserts the romantic subject's perverse resolve to domesticate the imperium. Ironically, and as though to render impertinent those neo-classical rules of decorum so much revered by his eighteenth-century literary predecessors, Lewis inserts an entry recording his visit to the family mausoleum, on a page adjacent to this rhetorical indulgence on food. What the entry lacks in prescriptive decorum, it supplies by harmonizing fully with the moralized reflections on the theme of mortality and dissolution intrinsic in the entry celebrating food. Built of pure white marble and surmounted by a statue of Time, the family mausoleum suggested to Lewis 'a theatrical representation of the tomb of all the Capulets . . . so perfectly divested of all the vestiges of dissolution, that the sight of it quite gave me an appetite for being buried . . . I never yet saw a place where one could lie down more comfortably to listen for the last trumpet' (102). Written during the very first days of his first visit, it is clear that Lewis early discovered in Cornwall the idea for an enduring myth of family and personal place. His quest for authentic cultural origins would find its fulfilment at the paradoxical intersection of food and death. The rediscovery of his ancestral roots at that aesthetic meeting-place seals his acculturation as surely as the tomb seals the mortal remains of his predeceased Creole kin. The common signs of each fuse together to remake Cornwall into a place where vision is given and insight achieved into the moral unity of seemingly disparate and disagreeable ideas.

The mausoleum signs its cultural value in its strange silent power. Lewis would receive overt and living testimonies of his creolized identity from the irrepressible discursivity of his slaves. In his first consciously ironic act of seigneurial beneficence, he declared a holiday to accommodate the festive high spirits of his slave family. The events that followed the ceremonies of arrival and welcome are recollected in the terms of a messianic advent. As might be expected, the slaves could hardly contain their emotional excitement: gripped in the transports of this historic spectacle, an old retired slave woman appropriated the biblical voice of Simeon and sang her own *nunc dimittis*, declaring that she could now expire in bliss, for her eyes had seen her salvation. Some allowance must be made for at least some hyperbolic content in Lewis' record of this event: his predisposition to self-parody and exaggerated sensibility are widespread throughout the *Journal*. But the evidence of slave writers and transhistorical scholarship on slavery powerfully corroborates this representation of the profound impact the master's presence exercised on the self-image and identity definition of the slave. The author of the *Journal* represents seigneurial presence as a powerful sublimity destabilizing normal plantation order. The related consequences of this will be conclusively produced in further substantive discussion of the sublime. Further analyses of slave behaviour uncover the extent to which the theme of creolization as a process of cultural immersion constructs Lewis' subject position in his text.

Entries in the *Journal* for the first visit portray the slaves as seeking every excuse and opportunity to be in Lewis' presence, to touch and to talk to him, eager to affirm their identity as his property and to be reassured that he was their patriarch. Orlando Patterson identifies this behaviour as an expression of a kind of 'fictive kinship', in which the language of kinship is used to acknowledge authority, to express loyalty and, ironically, to express duplicity and psychological manipulation.[9] In entries for the second visit Lewis records similar behaviours, but his search for meaning now leads him to interpret the whole phenomenon of the slaves' invention of excuses and complaints as a desire to talk to him for the sheer pleasure of it: 'They plump invent them only to have an excuse to "talk to massa," and when I have given them a plump refusal, they go away perfectly satisfied, and tank massa for dis here great indulgence of talk.'[10]

The mixed tones of bemusement and perplexity in Lewis' words evidence a less than total understanding of the psychological and political dimensions of the slaves' behaviour. But he gradually came to understand how his indulgence and participation in these forms were transforming his consciousness and identity. The next passage

documents his full-throated identification with the place and therefore an explicit expression of consciousness concerning his own
creolization:

> If I were now standing at the banks of Virgil's Lethe, with a goblet of the
> waters of oblivion in my hand, and asked whether I chose to enter life anew
> as an English labourer or a Jamaican negro, I should have no hesitation in
> preferring the latter. For myself, it appears to me almost worth surrendering
> the luxuries and pleasures of Great Britain, for the single pleasure of being
> surrounded with beings who are always laughing and singing, and who
> seem to perform their work with so much nonchalance, taking up their
> baskets as if it were perfectly optional whether they took them up or left
> them there. (101)

As an arena of symbolic action, Cornwall advances the trope of
premiers temps beyond mere allusive aesthetics or self-validating antiquity. Lewis' very firm commitment to translate liberal ideals into
practical public good prompted him to experiment with an ideal of
order constituted by mapping certain reimagined contrivances and
lost originals of classical antiquity (with certain intimations of the
Golden Age and the Greek *polis*) on to the peculiar human and
material economies of this Jamaican property. These disparate
elements converge in the author's consciousness as an image of
transculturation, a uniquely realized expression of his migrated self's
attempts to mediate the competing claims of public good and private
interest.[11] In this gesture of reprodcing himself on the stage of public
action, he consistently enacts the practices of the *translatio*, though
his relation to that tradition is necessarily ironic, and often perverse.
In the Ciceronian myth, the *translatio* is conceived as a civilizing
practice that leads savage human nature into cultural enlightenment.
In Lewis, the practice is creolized to mediate the tensions between
the slaves' desire for freedom and social justice and the slavocrats'
resistance to that desire. Lewis situates himself between these two
politically conflicted constituencies. He negotiates between the
ideologies and institutions of enlightened polity allied with subversive contestation on one side (the anti-slavery ideologues), and
exploitative economic interests allied with oppressive politics on the
other (the pro-slavery interests). The *Journal* accommodates these
conflicted impulses by its formal capacity, as narrative, to sublimate
Lewis' revolutionary impulses, and to redeem them from the category of mere atomistic collisions with the status quo by transforming

them into aestheticized constructions beyond the disquisition of material history.

The *Journal* furnishes abundant evidence for the claims of cultural construction in the politics and aesthetics Lewis practised to bring about his objectives. We shall return to extended discusion of these presently. But here some rationalization for identifying Lewis' project with the Greek *polis* is in order.

In the ensuing discussion, the *polis* must be understood to function as an intrinsic structure which complements an extrinsic domain of political actions through which Lewis reproduced himself in a highly individualistic myth of the public sphere. An imagination already habituated to a highly valorized classical ethos had little trouble reinventing its own idiosyncratic idea of a Greek *polis* on the New World stage of a West Indian slave plantation. Of course, the *polis* (a term approximately signifying 'city state') was a very specific form of community organization peculiar to seventh- and eighth-century Greek antiquity. And while there is no attempt here to posit a literal-minded equation between that political system and Lewis' slave community at Cornwall, certain structural and operational affinities between the two invite the analogy. The identification of the *polis* with the invention of Greek civilization through the establishment of rights under the law (Starr calls it the 'hothouse for Greek civilization' [vii]) resonates clearly in Lewis' legal reforms.[12] The *polis*' distinctively small size, its definition as a 'one-celled' community structure, 'both more and less than a state',[13] and its ideal of autonomy are all replicated in Cornwall's narrow confines. Lewis' arrogation of the romantic gesture to define himself radically against other slaveowners and to interrogate the broader political culture that prevailed in colonial Jamaica is equally harmonious with the spirit of the *polis*.

The classical political concept of the *polis* is undeniably valuable as an interpretive tool.[14] It offers a conceptual framework for understanding one facet of the *Journal*'s critique of culture as self-reproduction. It also re-emphasises the continuing philosophical and pragmatic range of the *negotium*. If the *polis* facilitates our search for a conceptual model by which to define Lewis' ideology, it inevitably leads us back to the larger containment structure of the *negotium* in which it is comprehended and from which it draws its conceptual power.

We can now return to those political and aesthetic manifestations that inform the construction of the *negotium* as cultural praxis. This analysis clearly discloses how the *negotium* adapts itself to accommodate the author–romantic aesthete–slaveowner's reformist impulses.

For his part, Lewis set about a busy programme of reform and amelioration: reprimanding or dismissing autocratic or abusive overseers, baptising and catechizing slaves, adjudicating grievances and complaints, visiting the sick, improving the plantations' facilities and enhancing the slaves' general living and working conditions.

Foremost among his reforms were the new regulations to abolish whipping and replace it by confinement. That this measure originated from a judicious observation of methods and effects rather than from romantic whim is evidenced in Lewis' explicit rationalization that confinement seemed to make a more 'lasting impression upon the slaves' minds; while the lash makes none but upon their skins; and lasts no longer than the mark' (383). In addition, he owned such a strong a revulsion to the use of the cart-whip that he wrote, 'I have positively forbidden the use of it on Cornwall and if the estate must go to rack and ruin without its use to rack and ruin the estate must go' (119). Other reforms stipulated that penalties meted out to slaves should be recorded in a register of punishments; that no slave was to be struck or punished without the trustee's express orders; and that slave women should be protected against exploitation by white employers and their entitlements to food and clothes codified. The case of a bookkeeper whom he dismissed for striking a slave argues forcefully his determination to treat these rules not merely as private-sphere political dilettantism, but to translate them into the tangible, socially transforming terms of public-sphere interest. In his desire not merely to do justice but also to be seen to dispense it forthrightly, Lewis diligently gathered the evidence by securing eyewitnesses and as much corroboration as he could muster. In his reprimand, he warned the bookkeeper that 'if he grounded his claim to being believed merely upon his having a white skin, he would find that on Cornwall estate at least, that claim would not be admitted' (197).

By this unequivocal declaration, Lewis anticipated the eventual transformation of a legal ethos traditionally dominated by a narrow sphere of plantocrats into a public sphere enlarged to enfranchise blacks and coloureds: a reformed sphere in which the sign for membership or participation would be not colour or race but an identity of interests in pursuing the ends of cultural redefinition.

Cornwall thus comes to be defined not so much in the literal terms of an autonomous state but of an invented ideal, a New World paradigm of the Habermasian public sphere, in Nathans' words, 'a defensive zone set off from the state, a demarcation rather than a positive definition'.[15] Predictably, these reformist tendencies drew censure from the slavocracy and their partisans: at the opening of the Cornwall Assizes on 4 March 1816, the Presiding Judge of Trelawny delivered a thinly veiled but deliberately aimed admonition in which he alluded to persons 'promoting disorder and confusion', 'infringing the established laws', propagating 'insidious practices' and 'dangerous doctrines.' His allusions seemed to point unerringly at Lewis. Though a subsequently issued disclaimer seemed to exempt Lewis as an exclusive target, the disclaimer did not entirely mask its disingenuous intent to preserve at least his apparent association with that whole class of persons.

Lewis' commitment to building a liberalized social order and to extending the principles of law and justice to black slaves did not preclude a due vigilance for hard economic self-interest. The *Journal* documents his enthusiasm for implementing more efficient labour-saving devices, and reveals a similar progressive vision about how such mechanization might improve management and productivity. The 30 January 1818 entry records a plan to introduce the plough and oxen to supplant slave labour; the same entry speculates about improving the estate's breeding stock with an initial shipment of four English bulls. Such innovation was not without its vicissitudes: Lewis concedes his failure to forecast problems and formulate solutions; to anticipate the need for an English ploughman to superintend the slaves' work with the cast-iron ploughs, and for other skilled mechanics to repair them.

Private wealth and its attendant power enabled Lewis to translate the inherent opportunities of 'sweete negotiation' into an ameliorated image of slave culture on his own estates. Both in itself and in the value of its translated social power the *negotium* posed a stout critique of slavocratic ethics. In the *Journal*, it positions itself to contest the legitimacy of a longstanding practice of Creole culture – absentee proprietorship. Lewis constructs the space of absence in two ways, both of which further weaken the aspirations of Creole elites to cultural integrity in the eyes of anti-slavery advocates.[16] On the one hand Lewis appropriates the *negotium*'s capacity for moral and ironic ambivalence by dissociating himself from the absentee legacy, a gesture most dramatically staged in his symbolic home-coming ceremonies, and then in radicalizing his Creole marginality by the highly subversive reforms he implemented. On the other hand, he figures absence in its most detestable (and contestable) expression, the signs of negation and dereliction of responsible behaviour which to him were epitomized in mulatto ownership and abuse of slaves. Lewis' critique infers a clear connection between absence and social disorder, between social disorder and economic ruin, between economic ruin and moral anarchy (117; 366–7). A number of very striking examples established this chain of causation in his mind. Especially probative of this thesis was the case of an absentee owner who delegated the affairs of his estate to an overseer-attorney who in turn delegated his responsibilities to an otherwise very intelligent subaltern who in turn mistreated the slaves, causing many of them to run away. The moral and economic consequences are pronounced with the dogmatic finality of an immutable law: 'The property was nearly ruined and absolutely in a state of rebellion' (117). Here the conjunction of negligence, cruelty and disorder verify for Lewis an inexorable descent into cultural anarchy.

Prefiguring the major treatment of the sublime to follow, it may be observed here that contemporary theoreticians emphasize the sublime's function as a mediator between the subjective consciousness and the world of mundane reality,[17] and define its role in unmasking the self to the self.[18] These dynamics of the sublime may help to explain how Lewis finds the aesthetic distance and candour not to exempt even himself or his own private history from the ultimate confronation with slavery's collapse. Thus, he does not shrink from holding up Hordley (his trouble-prone estate) as a symbol of the real threat of social anarchy and economic disaster that could result from seigneurial detachment and subaltern neglect.

On his second visit, in March 1818, he found Hordley 'in perfect uproar', with widespread discontent among the slaves and heedless indifference among the overseers: 'All the blacks accused all the whites, and all the whites accused all the blacks.' Into this scene of human history-turned-chaos, Lewis inserted his own efficient reason and decisive good judgement to reform specific managerial practices and improve the general social order of the plantation (he removed the trustee, the physician, the four white bookkeepers and four black governors 'within five days and a morning' (365)). Complementing the exercise of these higher faculties with a robust vein of irony, he parodies his disbelief at the image of himself caught in the moral dilemma of a slaveholder: 'I felt strongly tempted to set off as fast as I could, and leave all these black devils and white ones to tear one another to pieces, an amusement in which they appeared to be perfectly ready to indulge themselves' (366).

Lewis pursues his deconstruction of slavocratic order beyond the culpability of white masters and overseers into the peculiar race–sex–class ethos that produced mulatto slaveowners, in his eyes another category of devilish tyranny. One mulatto mistress, by his report, gave a little girl thirty lashes with a horsewhip for exposing the mistress' theft. In the relation of this incident Lewis reserves for this mulatto and her entire class a degree of rhetorical vehemence and moral revulsion nowhere heaped on any individual white owner in the *Journal*: 'Nothing would contribute more to the relief of the black population, than the prohibiting by law any mulatto to become the owner of a slave for the future' (401). Closely read and interpreted, Lewis' narrative commentary on this and other manifestations of the mulatto identity complex gives us an insight into the causes and presuppositions that shaped and informed his revisionist ethics for the culture of slavery. Striking as it is in its own right, the critique of mulatto excess intuits greater organic signification; it stands as a critical metonymy to the development of Lewis' larger reformist ideology. The brutality and inhumanity of the mulatto mistress is deconstructed as a powerful sign of moral, political, and cultural degeneration, and an equally powerful argument for reform.

The condition of one other group of freed persons represented to Lewis a degraded image of freedom in an unreformed plantocracy. As reports of his liberality and the reformed order at Cornwall spread, Cornwall became a focal point for all manner of complaints and grievances against the system. Travelling across Jamaica and into a few of the larger towns, Lewis was able to see at first hand that while some free people of colour had become property-owners and some free blacks had acquired skills in crafts and trades, both classes were afflicted by carelessness and improvidence; they lacked the incentives for creative self-improvement that Lewis thought a reformed ethic of freedom would afford them.

Though Lewis neither advocated general immediate emancipation for all Jamaican slaves nor granted it to his own, and though his reasons are no doubt as involved and complex as the conundrum of slavery itself, some credibility may be attached to his persuasion that any sudden emancipation would place whites under the dire threat of large-scale massacre from the overwhelming disproportion of blacks. Thus, contemplating the equally undesirable alternatives of tyranny and repression on one side and race war on the other, he invents a paradigm that allows him to imagine and assay the ideal of a reformed community, albeit one narrowly restricted to the confines of Cornwall.

Even in the absence of absolute legal freedom, the desire to imbue Cornwall with the symbolic marks of enlightened culture imprints itself on the *Journal* by means of persistent paradox and enigma. On one hand the ethos of reformed methods and incentives engenders and promotes *civitas*, an impulse to order community on civilizing, enlightened principles. The best illustration of this enlightening paradigm is to be found in Lewis' institution of the Order of the Golden Girdle to reward mothers with a medal for every child they successfully carried to term and christened properly. He assessed the social and economic value of this institution in only thinly veiled self-congratulatory terms: 'I expected that this notion of an order of honour would have been treated as completely fanciful and romantic; but to my great surprise my manager told me, that he "never knew a dollar better bestowed" than the one which formed the medal of the girdle' (125–6).

If the demonized backdrop of Hordley stood as an allegory for moral evil and social anarchy, if thirty lashes inflicted with a horse-whip on a little girl so graphically imprinted on Lewis' mind a vision of moral authority devolved to brutish tyrants and oppressors, then the ideal of Cornwall could shine forth as an image of order, a carefully controlled experiment in social engineering. If Hordley was 'an absolute Hell', Cornwall could be made Paradise.

In a characteristic defiance of the stubborn polarities separating these two moral orders, Lewis flirts with an accommodation (a negotiation) between the two that at once subverts and enriches the texture of his own social idealism, redefining the *negotium* to accommodate the cult of obeah, a much maligned and equally feared African heterodoxy.

Despite the devoted and earnest work of Christian missionaries, the innate moral universe of the New World African slave continued to be informed by traditional African belief systems. In the case of Lewis' Jamaican slaves, the persistence of obeah practices and beliefs among them posed a challenge of resilient contestation to Cornwall's accommodationist ethics.[19] Widespread among West Indian slaves, obeah (a term of Ashanti and Fante origin) was a system of beliefs about the indwelling supernatural powers of the universe; its practitioners (African priests who became obeahmen) and their adherents attempted to harness those powers to confront and combat the presumptive sorcery or powerful magic of the white man which had inflicted on them the trauma of forced migration and enslavement.[20] More typically, though, its rites were invoked to resolve interpersonal disputes, to repay private grudges and injuries, to visit sickness and even death on private enemies, and to cast and remove spells.

Lewis exhibited a characteristic laissez-faire response to the categorically incompatible economy of these two belief systems. That the *Journal* is largely free of the typical rhetorical strictures against obeah's primitiveness or of legal regulation against its subversive practice among the plantation slaves may be attributable to Lewis' fanciful attempt to install at Cornwall an experiment in religious heterodoxy that would reflect his philosophical indifference to a privileged, conformist denominationalism. Clearly obeah, with its use of poison, spells and other weapons of spite, revenge and paranoia was antithetical to the Christian precepts of charity and forgiveness. But the author of the *Journal* was also the author of *The Monk*, the creator of Ambrosio, an apostate protagonist of illicit lust and nefarious stratagems, who wields his hypnotic power within religious cloisters, consecrated spaces which mask a fearful topography of subterranean vaults and a spiritually decadent climate of superstition and moral aberration. Given that capacity for conceiving paradox and conflict, Lewis appears to have had little compunction in contemplating (even puckishly orchestrating) the moral anarchy of a nonconformist slave plantation. To the awesome power of obeah's mortal and spiritual threats, Lewis brought a gothic and romantic fascination strikingly expressed in his representation of Adam, an incorrigible obeahman and troublemaker. Just before Lewis' second visit, Adam had spread terror over the whole estate, hiding slaves, scheming, conspiring and poisoning 'left and right'. All these seditions earned him veritable rebel-hero status. Lewis' tone betrays less righteous indignation or moral reproach than bemused indulgence and wonder: 'I found the whole estate in an uproar about Adam' (350 ff.). Lewis marvels at Adam's extraordinary physical strength and reports with an almost flat affect the bare facts of his arrest for unlawful possession of a weapon, his trial, sentence and transportation (possibly to Cuba) (354).

Lewis' attitude to the phenomenon of obeah was compounded of several distinctive strains in his emotional and intellectual makeup. The idealist master and architect of Cornwall positioned himself astutely to mediate feuds, disputes and allegations involving obeah. From that position of political vantage he could play the cultural anthropologist, study obeah's nature, probe its mysteries and anatomize its workings. He could discover the identity of its chief professors and cultists, and by such intelligence acquire foreknowledge of conspiracies and threats to communal well-being. The ironic interpreter of signs, rituals and ceremonies perceived immediately obeah's utility as an expedient form of resistance and counterpoint. He saw intuitively that the slaves needed a meaningful source of empowerment in their struggle for justice, freedom and survival. Tolerating obeah would put elements of the African slave's native myth and cosmology into the play of diverse cultural elements that shaped creolization. Conversely, the ironist who permitted the coexistence at Cornwall of both obeah and Christianity collusively (if tacitly) provided the African slaves with the opportunity to evolve an adaptive strategy which could manipulate and negotiate between the two belief systems, appropriating Christianity as an alternative efficacious magic to protect them against obeah, to allow them to take oaths on the Bible to enhance their credibility, and to give them the power 'of humbugging the white people with perfect ease and convenience' (375).

Finally, these complex synergies of belief, ideology and desire dramatize two metaphysics in tension, a tension which the aesthetic imagination resolves through its intimations of 'romantic revolution'. And this prompts us to ask two questions which are necessary to fix the sources and origins of Lewis' revolutionary consciousness. Did Lewis think of himself as a revolutionary? Did he seriously perceive the reformist ideas he implemented at Cornwall as a model for revolutionary action?

Well connected with royalty, nobility and an ample circle of titled and wealthy personages, Lewis served briefly (May–December 1794) in his country's diplomatic mission to The Hague, and as a Member of Parliament for Hindon. That background would seem to render him an unlikely figure to contest the institutions of propertied wealth and power. True, in *The Monk* he seemed to relish the fictionalized images of apostasy and gothic rebellion personified in Ambrosio and the seductive magnetism of Satan. There the very marks of artistic genius that won him the plaudits of esoteric and discerning readers also worked powerfully to identify him in the minds of certain critics (Thomas James Mathias and Coleridge among them) with the forces of licence, irreligion, and nonconformity which some feared could plunge England into political upheavals similar to those which shook France in 1789.[21] Questions on the slave trade were tabled in Parliament during Lewis' tenure, and he is reported to have had extended conversations and some correspondence with William Wilberforce on questions of abolition and emancipation.[22] Likewise, there was mutual admiration between himself and Charles James Fox, that sworn adversary of the slaving interests, and an even closer friendship with Fox's nephew, Lord Holland, who embraced the abolitionist cause while himself owning slaves.[23] Holland House, where Lewis was a frequent guest, numbered within its circle other prominent opponents of the slave trade.[24]

Taken singly, none of these affiliations provides a sufficient rationale for Lewis' foray into reformist politics. My sense of Lewis' relation to this idea of romantic revolution is necessarily qualified by the peculiar distinctions of his temperament, motives, self-interest, and sensibility, and all these singularities are inextricably intertwined with his historical situation at a cultural watershed between the late Enlightenment and the Romantic Age. The identity that emerges from that relationship is at once transitional and transgressive: it renders the quest for clear-cut answers at best elusive.

This returns us to the theme of the sublime, foregrounded earlier in this chapter. Lewis' sublime appears to emanate from the nodal point formed by the post-Enlightenment/Romantic nexus. The themes of ambivalence and liminality implied in this attempt to fix Lewis in a defining cultural moment have been intuited in earlier references to the signs of paradox and instability in his disposition. Now these themes can be further defined in relation to cultural and aesthetic shifts associated with the displacement of the eighteenth-century sublime by nineteenth-century romanticism. Some bearings of post-Burkean criticism may instruct our attempts to understand the persistence of the sublime in the cultural and aesthetic formulations of Lewis' *Journal*. The signs of personal flux and ambivalence are figured in the *Journal* as a persistent pattern of destabilization in images and meanings. Lewis' atypical relationship with his slaves, his indulgence of obeah and the concomitant tensions generated by his disassociation from the Jamaican slavocrats are tangible illustrations of this problem of destabilized meanings. David B. Morris has identified this kind of destabilization precisely with the cultural and historical frames of reference delineated above, making the distinction that the eighteenth-century sublime 'occurs in a world of received relatively stable meanings, where interpretation is not openly at issue' while the romantic sublime 'involves an experience in which words and images grow radically unstable, where meaning is continually in question . . . promising new dimensions of insight.'[25] As an aesthetic construction, the sublime permits Lewis to address an otherwise threatening encounter with otherness, to discover self in other and thereby to transcend otherness. Lewis' reproduction of the sublime enacts a phase of that modality defined in Martin Price's conception as an 'heroic ascent into transcendence' and an 'act of self-discovery'.[26] The sublime is produced in the *Journal* as a destabilized and destabilizing modality, powerful enough to subvert an existing sociopolitical order but too deliberately aestheticized in its various constructions to disrupt history with revolutionary action.

As a countercultural discourse, the sublime in Lewis' constructions undermines the 'metaphysical certitudes' of Ligon's rigid socio-cultural hierarchies, supersedes Rochefort's search to legitimize and stabilize an emerging Creole ethos by locating Carib ethnography in *premiers temps*, and contests the similar recourses to georgic and picturesque modes in Grainger and Beckford respectively. In effect, the sublime dramatizes most sharply in the *Journal* those functions of the *negotium* which have been displayed in the gradual transformations illustrated in the authors above.[27]

Most distinctively in the description of his symbolic 'homecoming', but also in other common interactions with the slaves, the author of the *Journal* represents seigneurial presence as a powerful sublimity destabilizing normal plantation order. And yet the combined effects of historical forces, private interests and subjective temperament so operated on his consciousness that the *Journal*'s manipulations of the *negotium* stop just short of revolutionizing slavocratic order. The *negotium*'s potential revolutionary energies are instead displaced on to the compelling romantic image of a rebel slave.

That slave, classically named Plato, though dead for some three decades by the time of Lewis' visit, arrested his imagination by those heroic attributes that defined him as a sublime figure. Embodying the power of occult knowledge, the will to defiance and autonomy inhering in marronage, and a counter-cultural political relationship to Creole authority that defines dissensus, Plato clearly instances the sublime's tendency to inform phenomena that exceed normative scale and defy human comprehension.

A runaway who had escaped to the Moreland Mountains in the 1780s, Plato wreaked terror and material depredations on the surrounding properties and persons. His gallantry and daring magnetized other male slaves to his banditti and women to his retreat, a place reputed to have been, as Lewis writes, 'as well furnished as the haram [*sic*] of Constantinople' (95). Both the manner of his life and the circumstances of his death suggest the most dramatic realizations of the revolutionary sublime in Lewis' *Journal*. He supported the women's resistance politics by offering them refuge and status: 'Every handsome negress who had the slightest cause of complaint against her master, took the first opportunity of eloping to join Plato where she found freedom, protection, and unbounded generosity; for he spared no pains to secure their affections by gratifying their vanity' (91). Fearsome highwayman, desperado, and 'professor' of the African occult science of obeah, Plato personified to the surrounding slavocrats the sublime's threat of personal and systemic extinction. Lewis' narration records his deeds and profiles his forceful personal essence in a language that suggests the awe and admiration Plato commanded: 'He died most heroically; kept up the terrors of his imposture to the last moment; told the magistrates, who condemned him that his death should be revenged by a storm, which would lay waste the whole island that year. Before the year was over the most violent storm took place ever known in Jamaica.' Lewis reports that his gaoler's imagination was so affected by the realization of the threat that he 'gradually pined and withered away, and finally expired before the completion of the twelvemonth' (94). The association of this extraordinary figure with mountains, mystery and superhuman scale invokes, contests and displaces Burke's formulations about the sublime and about the nature of revolution. Where, in the Burkean aesthetic, mountains engender moral terror, and the French Revolution stages a 'monstrous tragi-comic scene', filling its observers with 'scorn and horror',[28] Lewis' journal aestheticizes the tragi-comic sense into a parodic romance wherein Plato personifies the sublime of righteous political terror. Plato embodies that irrational will to power of the lower masses which Burke's conservative instincts so categorically abhorred.

With Plato and the revolutionary convulsions of the sublime, Lewis' *Journal* manifests the most volatile oscillations of the *negotium*. The romance of Plato the revolutionary hero and folk legend provides a model for the romantic subject to contemplate the excess of desire embodied in the *negotium*, to appropriate it for subjective aestheticism, for purposes private and social. Impelled by the vision of threat Plato posed to Creole culture, Lewis aestheticizes a model of culture dissolving into terror and anarchy. Cornwall and the enlightened social order instituted there stand as the solid indefeasible reproduction of Lewis' self into a highly particularized definition of public-sphere politics and cultural practice. Yet at the other end of the island there stood Hordley, volatile and tense, continually threatening to collapse, defying the most earnest attempts at pacification and social order. The sublime therefore served to aestheticize the image of Hordley and Lewis' total politico-cultural programme into a microcosm of the larger convulsions that were threatening to shake the island and the regional slavocracy: major uprisings closely predating emancipation were to occur in Barbados (Bussa's Rebellion, 1816), in Demerara (1823) and in Jamaica (the Baptist War 1831–2).

Still one more critical construction of the socio-political nature of the romantic temperament serves pointedly to rationalize Lewis' embrace of anarchy and social dissolution. Carl Woodring writes:

The Romantics did not recoil from a world without order. They recoiled from philosophies that attributed superficial, geometric order to a living universe that is profoundly if impalpably ordered. They hesitated when confronted with visions of volcanic revolution as the natural center of organic growth, but they were unanimous in accepting volcanoes as more natural in the life of man than Malthusian segregation into male and female workhouses. Their spiritual condition did not require that the universe continue under mathematical laws of order. . .The aesthetic changes occurring in the romantic era made the asymmetries of earth acceptable to seekers of the sublime and the sacred.[29]

In their fortuitous contingency with Lewis' sublime, the formations, functions and consequences of 'sweete negotiation' are decisively altered. The *Journal's* emphatic preoccupation with social duties and Lewis' frequent musings about the distribution of affective and sentient capacities among the African slaves all invest the original and evolving definitions of the *negotium* with a crucial moral dimension. This moral reference is both politically and culturally constituted. These extended parameters broaden the social references of the *negotium* to a value not hitherto observed in the foregoing texts' construction of Creole culture.[30] In their broadest cultural construction, these shifts in the *negotium* are not restricted to the moral and social realm; they have equally significant economic implications, for as the *negotium* takes its primary point of departure from the 'desire for the sweete things' newly aroused in the incipient bourgeois-capitalist culture of Ligon's Barbados so, in Lewis, it revisits those bourgeois roots, only now to disrupt the originary consensus (that the *negotium* should be the preserve of planters and an aspiring middle class), mediating it with the sublime which destabilizes those rigid exclusivities. Where in Ligon, Rochefort, Grainger and Beckford 'sweete negotiation' remained the epitome of mimetic desire for the planter class and allied interests directly concerned with the sugar trade, Lewis expands and transcends the bourgeois construction of 'sweete negotiation' to attain the ultimate representation of the Creole dissensus through his sublime. Terry Eagleton defines this quality of the sublime as 'the anti-social condition of all sociality'.

This anti-social/sociality paradox reproduces the defining tensions of the *negotium* in terms that reveal how the *negotium* is radicalized by Lewis' politics and social ideology. The anti-social (the *neg*) may be construed from Lewis' categorical dissociation of himself from the reactionary politics of the slavocrats and their apologists in the emancipation era. Lewis' reformist postures antagonized fellow-slaveholders, imprinted as those postures were with that dynamic of the sublime Eagleton calls 'something of the challenge of mercantile enterprise to a too clubbable aristocratic indolence'.[31] But out of the same conjunction of sublime aesthetics and the cultural adaptability of the *negotium*, Lewis also imagined sociality (the *otium*), founded from the earliest moments of his first visit on the slaves' idea of fictive kinship and solidified progressively by his own expressions of paternalistic liberality.

The *negotium*'s engagement with the sublime concentrates the intrinsic ironic capacities of both ideas to mediate and humanize the machines of Ligon and Beckford. Where in those two authors the slaves' role in 'sweete negotiation' is cheerfully naturalized to the imperatives of production (and even self-sacrifice) to serve the superordinate interests of the master and mercantile class, now in Lewis it is mediated by a special kind of moral imagination in which the rigours of slave labour have become aestheticized in a private myth of sociality. In Lewis' conception of an ideal social order, meaning has become so destabilized that his pleasure at being surrounded by happy, amiable slaves privileges an illusion of ease and nonchalance over the arduousness of labour. All parties are depicted as a harmonic body 'so that I can hardly persuade myself that it is really work that they are about. The negro might well say, on his arrival in England – Massa, in England everything work! For here nobody appears to work at all' (I: 101). This use of the illusionary power of language and the romantic imagination affirms the durability of those values characterized by Glissant as Creole 'dissensus.' Historicized to the changing colonial context of early-nineteenth-century Jamaica, that dissensus acts in congenial collusion with the shifts and oscillations of the *negotium* to produce a myth of revolutionary order.

Lewis' relationship to revolution remains a mythic one. However compelling the heroic sublimity of Plato, Lewis never pursues that slave-rebel's paradigm of revolution to any substantive empirical replication. Cornwall aside, the final exegesis of the *negotium* is only fully tested on a scene of romantic consciousness. Lewis' choices remain firmly rooted in the aesthetics of social relations and of revolution.

From the first, his appetite for the inducements of the sublime permit him to derive from the *negotium* a reformed image of Creole cultural forms grounded in the total aestheticization of all social relations. This subjective relationship is a metaphor for action that offers a way to constitute cultural desire from the social and moral dimensions of the aesthetic. Again Eagleton elaborates a social theory of the aesthetic that is illuminating here. He associates such total aestheticization of social life with an emerging public sphere, locating therein a social order 'so spontaneously cohesive that its members no longer need to think about it'.[32]

From the second category, we have already adverted to those images and resonances that bear the imprint of the most dramatic political upheaval to affect Lewis' generation in Europe, the French Revolution. Yielding to the constraints of objective historical action, Lewis opts to ground his idea of revolutionary action in the eminently more controllable domain of symbolic language. Out of the resources of his own proven discursivity and the pleasure his slaves demonstrated in talk for its own sake, he fashions Eagleton's public sphere of a 'community of sensibility', a desire to root social power 'in the sensuous immediacies of empirical life, beginning with the affective, appetitive individual of civil society, and tracing from there the affiliations which might bind him to a greater whole'.[33]

In this sense the *Journal* becomes the site on which Lewis' revolutionary energies are displaced; those energies that could not be expressed in palpable historical action are thereby sublimated in a distinctive tendency of the romantic consciousness to privatize and aestheticize experience.[34] With reference to post-French revolutionary European culture, Nathans historicizes this tendency by formulating a relationship between language and politics deployed to achieve legitimacy where revolutionary power 'unable to find an institutional or even visible locus, came to be invested in language and signs'. 'Politics' ceased to reflect the competition of interests and became a contest of 'discourses for the appropriation of legitimacy'.[35]

'Monk' Lewis died on his return voyage to England at the end of his second visit to Jamaica. It had been his resolute intention to return to Jamaica to advance his reforms. The literal liminality of his death and burial at sea between Jamaica and England stands as a striking metonym for the chronic ambivalences which qualified the *negotium* of his thought and action. The scene of his demise enacts a kind of tragic parody on the possibilities and limitations of creolizing the *negotium*. Transformed to its highest romantic epitome in Lewis, 'sweete negotiation' transcends the original and successive emanations of the exclusive bourgeois myth of planters and traditional Creole elites, but untimely death leaves it hovering in the ineluctable formative element of West Indian culture ('the sea that diffracts'), at one with the nascent, fluid state of creolizing change at the dawn of emancipation.

Postscript and prospect

The West Indian colonies furnished an efficient proving-ground for the satisfaction of European cultural and historical impulses. Texts documenting this convergence mirror not only the potential of the colonies to expand political and economic aspirations, but also to cause a whole range of intellectual consequences to flow from the experience of colonial novelty. Sugar figured this novelty in complex ways. The foregoing chapters have explored the subtle signs, the desires and desire formations that would percolate from the sites of its production and generate other forms of production in the near two-century continuum defined by the chronological parameters of this book. The six major authors figured here collectively embody, reflect and diffract the actualities, contradictions, and idealisms of an inherently conflicted social reality. Their work illustrates an unfolding and changing pattern of literary representation distinctively identified with colonialist discourse. 'Sweete negotiation' subsumes within itself the essence of these complexities in its obvious allusion to sugar as natural object, prized commodity and metaphysical idea.

As if mesmerized by the precision and imaginative reach of his own verbal invention, Ligon repeats the phrase in this expansion of its possibilities on page 96 of the *History*, where he cites its involvement in the great fortunes of two of Barbados' early, most prominent, planters, Colonel James Drax and Colonel Thomas Modiford: 'Now if such estates as these, may be raised by the well ordering this plant, by industrious and painful men, why may not, such estates, by careful keeping, and orderly and moderate expending, be preserv'd, in their posterities, to the tenth generation, and by all the sweet negotiation of sugar?' Ligon's ambitious dream of a colonial plantation legacy durable enough to extend for ten generations seems both prescient and pointed when tracked along the trajectory described by this study.

Sound management, prudent or shrewd methods and highly productive slave labour did in fact ensure that slavocratic heirs in the Beckford and Lewis families (among others) could continue to benefit from that 'sweete negotiation' of owning sugar estates well into the nineteenth century. The tangible evidences of architectural history are persuasive enough of sugar's capacity to reproduce itself. In every island its physical 'estate' survives, if only often as relics, in a private sphere of elegant plantation houses (Drax Hall and Nicholas Abbey, Barbados; Worthy Park, Jamaica), ruined homesteads and slave huts, and in the public sphere of capital resources (canefields, sugar mills, boiling houses and refineries).

No less persuasive, though far more subtle, because interior and permeating, are the constructions of cultural identity and ideology contained in the persistence of the *negotium*, the theoretical instrumentality which helps us to chart the evolution of Creole cultural consciousness in the six principal texts of this study. Deep seated in the allusive structures of 'sweete negotiation', the *negotium* subsumes and diffuses the properties of a complex signifying system, figuring at once the material values that propelled individuals to risk and enterprise, and the mythic virtues that eluded demystification so persistently as to generate its own highly durable mythology and its own cultural pretensions.

Though the analyzed contents of all the major texts reveal their capacity to figure relationships and unmask meanings, one final perception of Rochefort might be singled out which matches Ligon's for its appreciation of the power of that mythology and the comparative value of those pretensions. In a voice of confident self-consciousness which we have come to identify with early Creole publicists, Rochefort proclaims his estimate of sugar's importance in terms that only Ortiz and Mintz so far have sought to test and validate: anticipating their insightful appreciation of its place in Western discursive and cultural history, Rochefort adjudges the invention of sugar to be equal in importance to if not greater than 'the invention of clocks, the sea compass, the art of navigation, prospective glasses, printing and artillery'.[1]

The point and purpose of this present study has been to place a previously unnoticed or under-noticed selection of texts into a discourse of colonialist cultural ideas, recuperating that discourse from diverse spheres of human activity – political, economic, ethnographic and aesthetic, to name the main ones – represented in the

principal authors examined. The critical interpretations and theoretical supports advanced illuminate the nature, meaning and
consequences of sugar's relation to the textual construction of
cultural desire. Out of that dense organicism, the *negotium* emerges, a
theoretical tool at once dynamic and functional, plastic and adaptable to the interest-inflected consciousness of each successive author,
oscillating sharply between modes of reaction and revolution.

Those two political postures may seem incompatible as markers
for the Creole slavocracy's search to establish uncontested authority
and cultural authenticity. And yet, reaction and revolution are
grounded in the very dissensus and diffraction that define the
concept 'creole'. In this book's theory of the *negotium* those political
postures are crucial markers for the concept of hybridity so central
to current colonialist theory. In addition, the polarities of reaction
and revolution strategically reemphasize what this study has manifested: that creolization produces special kinds of perception, errant
sensibilities, as Glissant concludes, never really producing 'direct
synthesis', but typically suggesting 'another way', 'something else'.[2]

Thus, the descriptions of those constituent activities of culture
listed above as 'spheres of human activity' comprehend, like the
negotium which gives them significant form and coherent function,
the inherent diversity and instability of Creole process and the
dynamic forces of history that link them to the formation of ideas in
any given cultural context. Diversity and instability emphasize the
predominating dynamic energies of these texts, illustrating the
supreme values of creolization as its tendencies privilege the
protean, and define itself through process rather than fixity or stasis.
Each major author's work covered evinces a pattern of struggle
against and varying degrees of adaptation to this process, but the last
chapter shows that the consummate subject of this identity is 'Monk'
Lewis, who personified the exceptional combination of paradoxical
disposition and ideological commitment which problematize his
relation to thought and action.

The last of the indices crystallized in the reference to the
formation of ideas underlines again the extent to which the dialogic
power of Ligon's originary idea persists across a landscape of cultural
and political change, displaying the capacity of the *negotium* to absorb
those vagaries, to transform them into the higher inventive possibilities of creolization. Ultimately, 'sweete negotiation' alludes to and
prefigures those possibilities in some of the implied propositions of

this book's thesis. Those implications lie in the potential of the *negotium*, as it manifests itself in the structural functions of these texts, to suggest a working paradigm for an early-stage history of Caribbean cultural ideas. Gordon K. Lewis reminds us that such an intellectual history is born out of two processes, both pointedly reproducing the poles of thought and feeling between which our *negotium* has been shown to oscillate. On the one hand such a systematization of cultural ideas would draw from that overarching reference point, the metropole, to which every one of these Creole publicists recurred both as a source of legitimation and contestation for their ideas. On the other hand, the subtle, transforming process, referred to consistently as 'creolizing', would furnish the second major tributary of modes, thoughts and ideas to be 'absorbed and assimilated . . . [and then] reshaped to fit the special and unique requirements of Caribbean society as they developed from one period to the next'.[3]

What specific contribution each of these authors might make to such a project for systematizing the history of cultural ideas around the discourse on sugar has already been prefigured in the foregoing chapters. But here some singularities might be identified. The power of Ligon's inventive imagination has already been demonstrated in his ownership of the idea that set this book in motion. 'Sweete negotiation' would remain definitive and essential. Rochefort's collusion, however complicit in the ideological purposes of colonization is amenable to enlightened reconstruction: its own definition marks it as always already imprinted with the hybridity of creolization. From Grainger the conflations of myth surrounding the idealized figures of Montano, Junio and Theana would add the philosophical values of broad social good and the paradigm of a Creole aesthetic of tragedy. The persistence of a pretension to undiluted British essence as the hallmark of cultural value in Schaw would reinforce the much-debated dialectical tension that surrounds the definition of West Indian social evolution after emancipation. Beckford's prospectus for importing European picturesque painters to formally locate Jamaica in that tradition would conceivably not escape the *negotium*'s creolizing power. Lewis' untimely end leaves his articulation and implementation of a reformed ideology of Creole culture equivocal and truncated. Still, the energy of his intellect and the agility of his imagination would dominate the aesthetic, social and political contexts. The Cornwall experiment, his interest in discursive possibilities between master and slave, his fascination with the sublime of romantic revolution in Plato all bespeak the capacity of his superior talents to animate and inform the outline of that history of ideas.

The reference to Cornwall and discursive possibilities prompts one final speculative turn to consider how such a history could draw on Lewis' relation to public sphere theory. Studies over the last two decades have documented that coffee houses, salons and the digestibles consumed within them have played a critical role in defining and expanding the public sphere. Sugar penetrated this informal but highly accessible public sphere from the outset of its wide availability as a popular consumer good. In a 'sweete negotiation' with tea, coffee, chocolate and other digestibles, it made itself indispensable in spaces of discourse and sociability, thus participating in the dissolution of social barriers and the promotion of new ideas.[4]

All together, Lewis' historical activities and the aestheticized forms they take in the *Journal* reproduce two principal expressions of public sphere myth. The first is to be seen in the representational character of his ceremonial appearances in January 1816, as well as in his subsequent public appearances at visitations and court hearings. Lewis' calculated use of these occasions to alter (even subvert) traditional formal relationships radically revise Jurgen Habermas' first typology of the public sphere, in which absolute monarchs and nobility create arenas for spectacle and display of authority. The other expression of public sphere representation intimated in the *Journal* also modifies Habermas' second typology.[5] This connection is figured in Lewis' succession to ownership of productive property in sugar and slaves and his identity as a published author. To the extent that Ligon, Rochefort, Grainger and Beckford similarly personified various permutations of such property holding, authorship and publicity, they may be associated theoretically, like Lewis, with Habermas' economic classes 'producing commercial capital' and modifying the structure of the public sphere by creating their own identity. 'Sweete negotiation' invents the theme on which the identities of their publics and their own are created. The oscillations of the *negotium* mimic the transformative processes of creolizing history.

The Creole *negotium* as evolved in these texts, and distinctively mediated by Lewis, invents a public sphere in which participants reproduced the activities Habermas formulated as 'pursuing their interests through written forms of communication that represented the views of private individuals'.[6] Forged from the inherent cultural values of flux and dissensus, the creolized form of 'sweete negotiation' argues its own legitimacy as a source of cultural theory and practice in colonial West Indian studies.

Notes

INTRODUCTION

1 The fundamental definitions of dialectical structure in Caribbean social formation which have influenced social and historical thinking about the problem foregrounded here have been set out in the work of two scholars: Peter J. Wilson has formulated the idea as a struggle between value systems in his *Crab Antics: The Social Anthropology of English Speaking Negro Societies of the Caribbean* (New Haven: Yale University Press, 1973); and in 'Afro-American Slave Culture' *Roots and Branches: Current Directions in Slave Studies*, ed., Michael Craton, *Historical Reflections*, VI (1979) 131–34, Monica Schuler has derived a dialectical analysis from a perceived structural conflict between ruling class and subordinates (slave-owners, blacks and coloureds during this period). The concept has been usefully summarized (and problematized as to its limitations) in William A. Green, 'The Creolization of Caribbean History: The Emancipation Era and a Critique of Dialectical Analysis', in Hilary Beckles and Verene Shepherd, *Caribbean Freedom: Economy and Society From Emancipation to the Present* (Kingston, Jamaica: Ian Randle Publishers, and London: James Currey Publishers, 1993).

2 Edward Brathwaite, *The Development of Creole Society in Jamaica 1770–1820* (Oxford: Clarendon Press, 1971), p. xv. In a subsequent collection of essays, Brathwaite supplies a succinct formulation of the term 'Creole' as applied to the West Indies as those who had 'intimate knowledge of and were in some way committed by experience and attachment to the West Indies'. See his *Roots* (Havana: Casa de las Americas, 1986), p. 129.

3 Gordon K. Lewis, *Main Currents In Caribbean Thought: The Historical Evolution of Caribbean Society in Its Ideological Aspects, 1492–1900* (Baltimore: The Johns Hopkins University Press, 1983), p. 24.

4 Geoffrey Scammell, *The First Imperial Age* (London and Boston: Unwin Hyman, 1989), p. 174.

5 Philip Boucher, *Les Nouvelles Frances: France in America, 1500–1815, An Imperial Perspective* (Providence, RI: John Carter Brown Library, 1989), p. 53.

6 Lewis, *Main Currents*, p. 25.

7 Whistler, 1655, quoted in Handler and Lange, *Plantation Slavery in Barbados, An Archaeological and Historical Investigation* (Cambridge, MA: Harvard University Press), p. 17. See also Edward Littleton, *The Groans of the Plantations* (London, 1689), and Dalby Thomas, *An Historical Account of the Rise and Growth of the West India Colonies* (New York: Arno Press, 1972).

8 The distinguished Caribbean cultural theorist and scholar Rex Nettleford attributes this persistence to 'the tenacious hold of a superordinate metropolitan power over the cultural apparatus of the Caribbean'. Nettleford further identifies it with an 'agonising process of renewal and growth that marks the new order of men and women who came originally from the Old World cultures (European, African Levantine, Oriental) and met in conflict on foreign soil'; see his *Caribbean Cultural Integration: The Case of Jamaica: An Essay in Cultural Dynamics* (Los Angeles: Center for Afro-American Studies and UCLA Latin American Center Publications, University of California, 1979), p. 2.

9 Lewis, *Main Currents*, p. 70. Robert Markley makes a related point about the conflict between desire and ownership of property and about exchange as a necessary condition of the individual's existence in these early *negotium* economies in his paper 'Desire, Technology and Alienation' delivered at the South Central Society for Eighteenth Century Studies Annual Meeting, Lubbock, Texas, 1992.

10 Lewis, *Main Currents*, p. 70.

11 J. R. Ward, *British West Indian Slavery: The Process of Amelioration 1750–1834* (Oxford: Clarendon Press; New York: Oxford University Press, 1988), p. 1.

12 Ibid., p. 13.

13 Lewis, *Main Currents*, p. 89.

14 Ibid., p. 89.

15 For a valuable gathering of pictorial images figuring such liveried slaves in their relation to this desire for high social recognition, see David Dabydeen, *Hogarth's Blacks: Images of Blacks in Eighteenth Century English Art* (Surrey: Dangaroo Press, 1985). Pictures aside, Dabydeen's study provides a clear cultural and historical context in which these images were constructed. Peter Fryer summarizes the practices and purposes surrounding these retinues in *Staying Power: Black People in Britain since 1504* (Atlantic Highlands, NJ: Humanities Press, 1984), pp. 18–21. The meaning of these images within the dynamic of consumption and fashion is discussed in the more recent work of John Brewer, *The Consumption of Culture, 1600–1800: Image, Object, Text* (London; New York: Routledge, 1995).

16 Walter Adolphe Roberts, *The French in the West Indies* (New York: Bobbs Merrill, 1942), p. 66–67.

17 Scammell, *First Imperial Age*, concedes that this idealism was only 'imperfectly achieved'.

18 Historians have commented widely on the climate of political activism and revolt that created these premature hopes of freedom among the

slaves. Michael Craton provides a good case study for Barbados in his chapter titled 'Bussa's Rebellion: Barbados, 1816' in *Testing the Chains: Resistance to Slavery in the British West Indies* (Ithaca and London: Cornell University Press, 1982), 254–66.

19 Jerome S. Handler and Frederick W. Lange, *Plantation Slavery in Barbados*, p. 15.

20 Ibid., pp. 22–3; Philip Curtin, *The Atlantic Slave Trade: A Census* (Madison: University of Wisconsin Press, 1969), pp. 53–6.

21 Eric Eustace Williams, *Capitalism & Slavery* (New York: Russell & Russell, 1961), p. 25.

22 J. R. Ward, *British West Indian Slavery*, p. 12.

23 Rochefort's work covers affairs principally in Martinique and Guadeloupe (colonized with other islands of the Lesser Antilles between 1625 and 1635), but the subject-matter and references also include St. Christopher (settled by the French in 1625 and partitioned between the French and the English in 1627: see Herbert Ingram Priestley, *France Overseas through the Old Regime* (New York and London: D. Apple-Century Company Inc., 1939), p. 79.

24 The French completed the expulsion of Caribs from Guadeloupe by about 1641, but in 1653 the Caribs ravaged plantations on the smaller island and almost drove the French out of Martinique (Eccles, *France in America* (New York: Harper and Row, 1972), p. 31.

25 Philip Boucher, *Les Nouvelles Frances*, p. 32.

26 The Carib natives of that island divided their allegiance so that the leeward side of the island supported the English, while the windward side supported the French.

27 Boucher, *Imperial Perspective*, p. 27.

28 Though considerably smaller in numbers when compared with the English in Barbados, French populations grew notably, and by 1683 stood as follows: Martinique 16,254; Guadeloupe 8,698; Saint Christopher 7,793. Figures for all the Fench Antilles at about the same time stood at 18,888 for whites; for blacks and mulattos the figure was 28,534, of which 27,000 were slaves); Priestley, *France Overseas*, p. 91.

29 Stewart Lea Mims, *Colbert's West Indian Policy* (New Haven: Yale University Press, 1912), p. 280.

30 Williams, *Capitalism & Slavery*, pp. 113–14.

31 F. R. Augier, *et al. The Making of the West Indies* (London: Longmans, 1961), p. 92.

32 Williams, *Capitalism & Slavery*, p. 40 and *From Columbus to Castro: The History of the Caribbean, 1492–1969* (London: Deutsch, 1971), p. 88.

33 Williams, *Columbus to Castro*, p. 88.

34 Burns, *History of the British West Indies* (London: Allen & Unwin, 1965), pp. 499; 510.

35 C. Duncan Rice, *The Rise and Fall of Black Slavery* (Baton Rouge: Louisiana State University Press, 1976), p. 155.

36 Lowell J. Ragatz, *The Fall of the Planter Class in the British Caribbean, 1763–1833: A Study in Social and Economic History* (New York and London: The Century Co., 1928), p. 251. For a discussion of the use and frequency of petitions as a tool to affect public opinion during this period, see Seymour Drescher, 'Paradigms Tossed: Capitalism and the Political Sources of Abolition' in Barbara L. Solow and Stanley L. Engerman, eds., *British Capitalism and Slavery: The Legacy of Eric Williams* (Cambridge University Press, 1988), pp. 204–7.
37 Anthony Pagden, *Lords of All the World: Ideologies of Empire in Spain, Britain and France c. 1500–c. 1800* (New Haven, CT: Yale University Press, 1995), p. 112. Pagden cites sources in Adam Smith, Botero, Campomanes, Lycurgus and Arthur Young.
38 Annette Kolodny, *The Lay of the Land: Metaphor as Experience and History in American Life and Letters* (Chapel Hill: University of North Carolina Press, 1975); Mary Louise Pratt, *Imperial Eyes: Travel Writing and Transculturation* (London: Routledge, 1992).
39 Edouard Glissant, 'Creolization in the Making of the Americas,' in Vera Lawrence Hyatt and Rex Nettleford, eds., *Race, Discourse, and the Origins of the Americas: A New World View* (Washington: Smithsonian Institution Press, 1995), pp. 273–5.
40 Homi Bhabha, 'Representation and the Colonial Text', in Frank Gloversmith, ed., *The Theory of Reading* (Sussex: Harvester Press; Totowa, NJ: Barnes & Noble, 1984), p. 202.
41 Barbara Bono, *Literary Transvaluation From Vergilian Epic to Shakespearean Tragicomedy* (Berkeley: University of California Press, 1984).
42 Thomas Kent, 'The Classification of Genres', *Genre* 16 (1983), 11.
43 Terry Eagleton, *The Ideology of the Aesthetic* (Cambridge, MA: Basil Blackwell, 1990).
44 Kurt Heinzelman, 'Roman Georgic in the Georgian Age: A Theory of Romantic Genre', *Texas-Studies-in-Literature-and-Language* 33 (1991), 183.
45 Alastair Fowler, 'The Beginnings of English Georgic', in Barbara Kiefer Lewalski, ed.,*Renaissance Genres: Essays on Theory, History and Interpretation* (Cambridge, MA: Harvard University Press, 1986) and Annabel M. Patterson, *Pastoral and Ideology: Virgil to Valery* (Berkeley: University of California Press, 1988).
46 Ann Bermingham, *Landscape and Ideology: The English Rustic Tradition* (Berkeley: University of California Press, 1986).
47 Gordon K. Lewis, *Main Currents*, p. 25.
48 Herder, cited in Clifford Siskin, 'Gender, Sublimity, Culture: Retheorizing Disciplinary Desire', *Eighteenth Century Studies* 28 (1994), 37–50.

1 LIGON: 'SWEETE NEGOTIATION'

1 R. B. Le Page and Andrée Tabouret-Keller, *Acts of Identity: Creole-Based Approaches to Language and Ethnicity* (Cambridge University Press, 1985), p. 38.

2 These formative scenes of both text and colony bear a formal structural resemblance to the concept Bakhtin theorizes as a body in the act of becoming. Bakhtin seems especially apposite to theorize this relationship between textual production and its objective cultural production, because his analysis turns so decidedly on history's potential for producing cultural crisis. Standing as it does at a crucial moment in the early development of capitalism and mercantilism, Ligon's *History* exhibits similar relations to those crises in the social and economic sphere, with repercussions for history, speech and language. That this founding text of Barbadian Creole culture should appear so inextricably mired in the negations of its defining structure and those of the very object it pursues is specific but not unique to colonizing.

3 Raymond Williams, *Keywords: A Vocabulary of Culture and Society* (Oxford University Press, 1985), p. 77.

4 Michael McKeon, 'Andrew Marvell and the Problem of Mediation', in Harold Bloom (ed.), *Andrew Marvell*, Modern Critical Views Series (New York and Philadelphia: Chelsea House Publishers, 1989), pp. 205–27.

5 Michael Shinagel, *Daniel Defoe and Middle-Class Gentility* (Cambridge, MA: Harvard University Press, 1968), p. 130.

6 Anon. *The Present State of the British Sugar Colonies Considered* (1731).

7 *Description Géographique des isles possedees les Anglois*, p. 79.

8 David Richards, *Masks of Difference: Cultural Representations in Literature, Anthropology, and Art* (Cambridge University Press, 1994).

9 Thomas, *An Historical Account*, p. 9.

10 Thomas Tyron, *Tyron's Letters upon Several Occasions for the Merchant, Citizen, and Countryman's Instructor* (London: Printed for Geo. Conyers and Eliz. Harris, 1700), p. 215.

11 For further discussion of information-gathering practices and motives see Geoffrey Scammell, *The First Imperial Age*, p. 175.

12 Fernando Ortiz, *Cuban Counterpoint; Tobacco and Sugar*, trans. Harriet de Onis (New York: A.A. Knopf, 1947).

13 Mary Douglas, *Purity and Danger: An Analysis of Concepts of Pollution and Taboo* (London: Routledge, 1966), p. 2.

14 Richards, *Masks of Difference*, p. 80.

15 Ortiz, *Cuban Counterpoint*, p. 6; 16. Annette Kolodny, *Lay of the Land*, associates this metaphoric deployment of the land with the female principle of gratification. She designates this gendering as 'America's oldest fantasy'. A similar gendering is evidenced in Ligon's designation of the place where his gaze was transfixed by those black females in the Cape Verde Islands as a 'valley of pleasure' (15). Kolodny describes the female principle as enclosing the individual in 'an environment of total receptivity, repose, painless, integral satisfaction' (4).

16 Anthony Pagden, *Lords of All the World*, p. 69.

17 David Richards' discussion of the erotic male gaze as an instrument of

colonial hegemony with reference to *Oroonoko* illuminates my point here: see *Masks*, p. 78.

18 Francis Barker, *The Tremulous Private Body: Essays on Subjection* (London and New York: Methuen, 1984), p. 62.

19 In another critique of the paradox of cultural inventions, David Richards identifies that paradox with a deep-seated sense of loss of self and displacement, calling this an attempt to fashion a 'consequential political identity, a social value in an appropriated [contested] space' (*Masks*, p. 47). For a further connection of this anxiety-ridden identity with colonial capitalism, see Eric Cheyfitz, *The Poetics of Imperialism: Translation and Colonisation from The Tempest to Tarzan* (Oxford University Press, 1991), p. 85.

20 Rex M. Nettleford, *Caribbean Cultural Identity*, p. 4.

21 Tryon, *Letters*, p. 201.

22 Keith Ellis, 'Images of Sugar in English and Spanish Caribbean Poetry', *Ariel* 24 (1993), 149–59.

23 Rene Girard, *Violence and the Sacred*, trans. Patrick Gregory (Baltimore: John Hopkins University Press, 1977), p. 7.

24 Michel Foucault, *Discipline and Punish: The Birth of the Prison* (New York: Pantheon Books, 1977), p. 136.

25 Orlando Patterson, *The Sociology of Slavery; An Analysis of the Origins, Development, and Structure of Negro Slave Society in Jamaica* (Rutherford, NJ: Fairleigh Dickinson University Press, 1969).

26 Gilles Deleuze and Felix Guattari, *Anti-Oedipus: Capitalism and Schizophrenia* (New York: Viking Press, 1977), p. 37. R. Young glosses this idea of a machine of fantasy in the context of colonial desire constituted socially and collectively. His conclusion is that colonialism, in short, was not only a machine of war and administration, but also a desiring machine (*Colonial Desire: Hybridity in Theory, Culture, and Race* (London: Routledge, 1995), p. 98).

27 Cheyfitz, *The Poetics of Imperialism*, p. 85.

28 Tryon, *Letters*, p. 187.

29 McKeon situates the various kinds of mediation entailed in the larger imperialist enterprise in a 'terrain of crisis.' What he calls a 'crisis of secularization' is especially pertinent to my argument for the roots of Creole cultural foundation, particularly as that concept helps us to theorize the relationship of Ligon (and other authors) to their colonial experiences and to develop a critique of their identification with Creole aspirations. The present selection of texts is equally intimated in McKeon's formulation of the desire of colonizing politics and epistemology as reducible to a 'process of mistranslation, in which reformation amounts to deformation, purification to corruption – in which to know and experience now amounts to a crudely 'imperialistic' act of comprehension . . .' ('Andrew Marvell and the Problem of Meditation' 206).

2 ROCHEFORT: FRENCH COLLUSIONS TO NEGOTIATE

1 The full English title of the work *is The History of Barbados, St Christophers, Mevis, St Vincents, Antego, Martinico, Montserrat and the rest of the Caribby Islands in all XXVII in Two Books.* It was translated by J. Davies of Kidwelly(1666). Subsequent references to this work will be abbreviated as the *Histoire.*

2 In the principal editions available, Poincy is mentioned only as the dedicatee of the work and commended for his distinguished service to and efficient administration of early French Antillean colonial settlements. Davies speaks in his preface of the 'authors' of the work, but gives no further specification of their identity beyond an acknowledgement that unnamed eyewitnesses and collaborators contributed 'testimony' from their travels and experiences. Among such persons, described as 'disinterested' and of 'known integrity,' Davies names Father Raymond Breton, the first French missionary to Dominica who lived there for many years and thus supplied first-hand knowledge of the Caribs. His work, edited by Joseph Rennard, is entitled *Les Caraibes* (1929). Breton is credited as the compiler of the Carib vocabulary appended to the conclusion of the work. Davies also acknowledges that the *Histoire*'s two-part structure is in imitation of Jose de Costa's *Historia natural y moral de las Indias* (1616). The 1665 French edition of Rochefort's *Histoire,* published in Rotterdam, is dedicated to Monsieur de Beveren, a governor of Tobago, and signed by Rochefort. The 1666 edition, translated by Davies, is dedicated by him to Sir Edward Bysche.

3 My use of 'heterological' as an analytical term to examine cultural and linguistic interactions is drawn from Michel De Certeau's *Heterologies: Discourses on the Other,* tr. Brian Massumi (Minneapolis: University of Minnesota Press, 1986); see p. xiii.

4 One of the finest recent studies on European–Carib relations with very well-researched historical sources and critical insights on the French political and cultural contacts is Philip P. Boucher's *Cannibal Encounters: Europeans and Island Caribs, 1492–1763* (Baltimore and London: Johns Hopkins University Press, 1992); see p. 24.

5 See Peter Hulme and Neil L. Whitehead (eds.), *Wild Majesty: Encounters with Caribs from Columbus to the Present Day* (Oxford: Clarendon Press, 1992), 117–18.

6 Elsa Goveia, *A Study on the Historiography of the British West Indies to the End of the Nineteenth Century* (Washington, DC: Howard University Press, 1980), 24–5.

7 Lévi-Strauss' view is that narrative historiography is itself the myth of Western modern intellectual thought, and that it is especially allied to bourgeois, industrial and imperialistic processes. See Hayden V. White, *The Content of the Form, Narrative Discourse and Historical Representation* (Baltimore: Johns Hopkins University Press, 1987), p. 34.

8 For the most part I have used the common standard ethnographic name 'Carib' to describe these indigenous Antillean people. In a few places, however, I have preferred Rochefort's usage 'Caribbian', especially where his voice and sense add dimension to the particular context.

9 Hayden V. White, *The Content of the Form*, p. 45.

10 Vlad Godzich, quoted in Michel de Certeau, *Heterologies*, p. iii, and Raymond Williams, *Keywords*.

11 These phrases are attributed to Raymond Williams, *Keywords*.

12 de Certeau, *Heterologies*, p. xiii.

13 Philippe Jacquin's essay 'The Colonial Policy of the Sun King' offers a very succinct rendering of these economic and cultural developments. See Robert R. McDonald, ed., *The Sun King: Louis XIV and the New World*, Studies in Louisiana Culture, vol. III, (New Orleans: Louisiana State Museum, 1984), 73–6.

14 Jacquin, 'Colonial Policy', 75–6.

15 This practice is well documented in traditional histories of Spain and the New World, but two contemporary discussions are illuminating: Valentin Y. Mudimbe, 'Romanus Pontifex (1454) and the Expansion of Europe' in Vera Lawrence Hyatt and Rex Nettleford, eds., *Race, Discourse and the Origins of the Americas: A New World View*, p. 63 (Washington: Smithsonian Institution Press, 1995), and Mary B. Campbell, *The Witness and the Other World: Exotic European Travel Writing, 400–1600* (Ithaca: Cornell University Press, 1988), 200–1.

16 This reference corresponds closely with the species Rochefort identifies in his catalogue as an 'Indian Fig Tree': a tree of thick bushy leaves, estimated to shelter two hundred men, bearing a small fruit similar in taste to the French fig.

17 Judith P. Butler, *Subjects of Desire: Hegelian Reflections in Twentieth-Century France* (New York: Columbia University Press, 1987), p. 9.

18 Ibid., p. 123.

19 James Clifford and George E. Marcus (eds.), *Writing Culture: The Poetics and Politics of Ethnography* (Berkeley: University of California Press, 1986), p. 114.

20 The main list, entitled a Caribbian Vocabulary, is included as an appendix to the text, and is divided into ten sections covering, among other things, words and usages for the parts of the body, kinship terms, actions and passions, animals and plants. The second is a shorter list inserted in Book 2, chapters ten and eleven, whose items are constituted more as a descriptive grammar, covering lexicon and phonology.

21 de Certeau, *Heterologies*, p. 78.

22 For further discussion of the heterological tradition in its relation to knowledge, language and epistemology, see de Certeau, *Heterologies*, p. xx. In *The Writing of History* (New York: Columbia University Press, 1988), de Certeau analyzes the way that primitive voice/language

'relativizes' prior convictions and affirmations into a radically transformed scientific or philosophical system (225).
23 Clifford and Marcus, *Writing Culture*, p. 00.
24 Edward Said, 'Representing the Colonized: Anthroplogy's Interlocutors,' *Critical Inquiry* 15:2 (Winter, 1989), 212.
25. Ryan, 'Assimilating New Worlds', traces these comparative practices to
travel writing of the early sixteenth century: 'ancient paganism served
as a template of error which provided missionaries with a mode for
comprehending the Indian' (527).
26 Homi Bhabha, 'Representation and the Colonial Text: A Critical
Exploration of some Forms of Mimeticism', in *The Theory of Reading*, ed.
Frank Gloversmith (Sussex: Harvester Press, 1984), p. 203, relates this
assimilation of difference to a cultural crisis evidenced by repression
and substitution; he lists this transfiguration as one of two attitudes
colonial discourse assumes in the presence of external reality, dis-
avowing reality and replacing it with 'a product of desire that repeats,
rearticulates "reality" as mimicry.'
27 Two valuable articles that help to clarify issues of Carib origin and
cultural anthropology are Neil L. Whitehead, 'Carib Cannibalism. The
Historical Evidence,' *Journal de la Société des Americanistes* 20 (1984),
69–70, and Arie Boomert, 'The Arawak Indians of Trinidad and
Coastal Guiana, 1500–1650,' *Journal of Caribbean History* 19:2 (1984), 128.
28 Cheyfitz, *Poetics of Imperialism*, p. 144.
29 This 'playing back' of customs, beliefs, and mores of ancient peoples is
a commonplace of West Indian colonial cultural narratives. It appears
as well in Renaissance and later historical and travel accounts describing the indigenous peoples of the non-European world. It became
conventional to compare and assimilate the manners and habits of the
Native American to those of the ancient Hebrews, Greeks, Romans,
Egyptians, and others. For further discussion of this mapping of *premiers
temps*, see James Clifford, 'On Ethnographic Allegory', in Clifford and
George E. Marcus, eds., *Writing Culture: The Poetics and Politics of
Ethnography* (Berkeley: University of California Press, 1986), p. 101.
30 Reversing the order would have been faithful to the order of physiological
digestion; for the present purposes, however, the term assimilation–
consumption is meant to suggest another related sense: first, a careful
visual examination and scrutiny followed by cognitive comparison, then
a sniffing – suggesting a desire for almost total sensory knowledge –
before final ingestion, the ultimate act of cultural assimilation.
31 Michael T. Ryan, 'Assimilating New Worlds,' 529.
32 Butler, *Subjects of Desire*, preface, ix.
33 Young, in *Colonial Desire*, discusses this persistent tendency in culture to
oscillate between 'poles of sameness and difference, comparison and
differentiation' as produced by a characteristic internal 'dissension' of
capitalist economies, p. 53.

34 See my essay '"Our Caribs are not Barbarians": The Use of Colloquy in Rochefort's *Natural and Moral History of the Caribby-Islands, Providence*': *Studies in Western Civilization* 2:1 (Fall 1993), 69–85.

35 There are close to ten pages of illustrations, each page containing several different species: the artist is not identified except to say that the illustrations were a deliberate decision of 'the authors and publishers' to represent 'the things themselves to help the readers imagination.' Preface, np).

36 De Certeau lays out a searching interpretation of these structures and displays, drawing certain philosophical relationships to visualization and edibility, and making certain allusions to translation. I am particularly indebted to his discussion of Jean de Lery's narrative objectives in the *Histoire d'un Voyage faict en la terre du Bresil* (1573), particularly as he shows how that narrative serves the ends of analysis and consumption 'back home'; see *Writing of History*, 224.

37 Robert J. C. Young, *Colonial Desire*, p. 53.

38 Described as a red or yellow-red dye widely used among Antillean Indians for body-painting and ornamentation, roucou is derived from the pulp surrounding the seeds of the annato tree.

39 Cheyfitz, *Poetics of Imperialism*, p. 105.

40 McKeon identifies and locates this challenge as posed in the question of 'how to transform use-value into exchange-value', 'Andrew Marvell and the Problem of Mediation', 215.

41 De Certeau, *Heterologies*, p. ix.

3 GRAINGER: CREOLIZING THE MUSE

1 An informed sketch of Grainger's life can be found in the *Dictionary of National Biography*, vol. III, 368–70; a memoir containing recollections by Percy, with selections from his poetry and letters, appears in John Bowyer Nichols, *Illustrations of the Literary History of the Eighteenth Century*, vol. VII (London 1848), pp. 225–99. These two volumes are the primary sources for my account of Grainger's life and his medical and literary career. A valuable source for anecdotes of Grainger's relations with Johnson's coterie and their reception of his *Sugar Cane* is Boswell's *Life* of Johnson, ed. G. B. Hill and L. F. Powell, vol. II, pp. 453–5; 532–5; a review of *The Sugar Cane* attributed to the joint collaboration of Johnson and Percy appeared in the *London Chronicle* 5 July 1764, p. 12 [continued pp. 20, 28] and another, attributed to Johnson, in the *Critical Review*, October 1764. Percy, Shenstone, Lord Kames, and Johnson were the first to read the poem in manuscript.

2 Johnson held Grainger in high personal esteem and greatly admired his Latin verse translations. He had strong reservations, however, about *The Sugar Cane*. As a subject for serious discourse he thought the plant 'unpoetical', and reportedly derided Grainger's introduction of rats into

the poem. Still, in an apparent attempt to win favourable reception for the work and to forestall hostile attacks from critics like Smollett(who had splenetically censured Grainger's translations of Tibullus and Sulpicia in the *Critical Review* of December 1758), Johnson co-authored with Thomas Percy a largely affirmative review of *The Sugar Cane* in *The London Chronicle* (July 1764). Motives of sympathy and personal affection aside, Johnson could not excuse Grainger for failing to repudiate the West Indian slavocracy in his poem. And so, consonant with Johnson's principled stand against slavery, he denounced that part of *The Sugar Cane* which revealed Grainger's complicity in a system that made a commerce of 'fellow-creatures'. For Grainger's relations with Johnson and Percy, see respectively James Boswell, *Life of Johnson*, ed. George Birkbeck Hill, rev. L. F. Powell, 6 vols. (Oxford University Press, 1934), and John Bowyer Nichols, *Illustrations of the Literary History of the Eighteenth Century*, 8 vols. (London: J. B. Nichols and Son, 1848), VII: 225–99.

3 Boswell's reference is indefinite as to the date of the Oxford speech, but see *Life*, II: 312.

4 Smollett's personal attacks notwithstanding, the work received very high commendation from Johnson: *Life*, vol. II, p. 454.

5 According to Boswell, *Life*, Grainger lost this annuity as a result of some falling out with Borryau.

6 Some further works of Grainger's may be mentioned: 'Bryan and Pareene' (1764), a ballad about West Indian life; between May 1756 and May 1758, he made regular contributions to the *Monthly Review* on drama, poetry and medicine. Some further poems appeared in the *Gentleman's Magazine* (1758).

7 Quoted in Boswell, *Life*, II: 312.

8 Despite the expedient of aesthetic effacement in this work, the Caribs persistently made their desire for history felt. The colony changed hands in persistent Anglo-French struggles seven times between 1666 and 1713; Richard Dunn gives a succinct historical account of these vagaries in Sugar and Slaves, pp. 117–120, 135–136, 146–148. See also *History of the Leeward Islands*.

9 All textual references to *The Sugar Cane* are to the first edition [1764]. References to Grainger's notes accompanying the poem will bear the label *ver*, followed by a line number, in keeping with his practice.

10 Grainger's note is both instructive on the subject and illustrative of his negotiating intentions: 'Sugar is twice mentioned by Chaucer, who flourished in the fourteenth century; and succeeding poets, down to the middle of the last, use the epithet sugared, whenever they would express anything uncommonly pleasing: since that time, the more elegant writers seldom admit of that adjective in a metaphorical sense; but therein perhaps they are affectedly squeamish' (Bk. I, *ver* 22).

11 Butler, *Subjects of Desire*, p. 155. Though this study has not positioned its subject with the same philosophical (abstract, self-reflexive, Hegelian)

focus Butler pursues in hers, my interest in the role of narratives in material and cultural production has benefited from the light Butler throws on that role.

12 Jennifer Morgan places the development of these attitudes within the framework of that crisis in European identity I have identified in my previous chapters. See her essay '"Some Could Suckle Over Their shoulder": Male Travellers, Female Bodies and the Gendering of Racial Ideology, 1500–1770', *William and Mary Quarterly*, 54: 1 (January 1997), 167–192.

13 In figuring these delicate negotiations among intersecting cultures, the poem mirrors what Scammell describes as cultural 'parodies', pressures produced by the effects of colonization and empire, and experienced as the colonists' need to acculturate and the metropolitan authorities' need to regulate: see *First Imperial Age*, pp. 165–6.

14 My initial insights for the concept of the *translatio* are indebted to Cheyfitz, *The Poetics of Imperialism*, and McKeon, 'Marvell'.

15 James Kinsley, trans., Introduction, *The Works of Virgil*, ed. John Dryden (Oxford University Press, 1961), p. viii.

16 Based on secondhand authority, Boswell's account of this supposed gathering at Sir Joshua Reynolds' rooms has been disputed; see *Dictionary of National Biography*, 369.

17 Besides its standard classical meanings applied generally to economic and social contexts, Cheyfitz's interpretation of the term *oikoumene* as a concept of the ideal civilized community governed by reason and distinguished from barbarous hordes on the outskirts is pertinent to my reading of Grainger's social and cultural idealism.

18 Cheyfitz, *The Poetics of Imperialism*; McKeon, 'Andrew Marvell' pp. 113–114.

19 Grainger's call for the return of absentee Creoles is an oblique admission that sources of enervation had already set in upon Creole society. Indeed a vexed polemic identifying those sources with the adverse effects of empire on the nation was already raging at the metropole. See Kathleen Wilson, 'The Good, the Bad and the Impotent. Imperialism and the Politics of Identity in Georgian England', *The Consumption of Culture 1600–1800: Image Object, Text*. Eds. Ann Bermingham and John Brewer (London and New York: Routledge, 1995), 237–262. Mckeon holds that the *translatio* suffers a 'degeneration' as each 'new vessel of empire' is forced to 'accommodate' to the imperium, p. 213.

20 Identifying this diffractive effect with transience, Glissant dissociates it from exclusion, in that it 'does not imply the intense entrenchment of a self-sufficient thinking of identity, often sectarian, but of relativity, the fabric of a great expanse, the relational complicity with the new earth and sea', p. 269.

21 Mintz, *Sweetness and Power*, p. 158.

22 James Donald and Stuart Hall (eds.), *Politics and Ideology: A Reader* (Milton Keynes and Philadelphia: Open University Press, 1986).

23 Heinzelman, *Roman Georgic*, p. 202.

24 Ibid., p. 203.

25 Orlando Patterson discusses this identification as one of the marks to which timocratic societies aspire in their desire for honour and social distinction, *Slavery and Social Death*, pp. 58–60, 94–7.

26 Erasure of the indigenous has usurped their identity not only with the land but also with its lore: at the level of discourse this control manifests itself as an imperium over signs which directly contests the presumptive imperium of the centre. This redefined relationship revises the references of an earlier historian of colonization in a way that is strikingly ironic and prescient: 'In general one may observe that ignorant country people and barbarous nations are better observers of times and seasons, and draw better rules from them, than more civilized and reasoning people, for they rely more upon experience than theories, they are more careful of traditionary observations, and living more in the open air at all times, and not so occupied but they have leisure to observe every change, though minute, in that element, they come to have great treasures of useful matter, though as it might be expected, mixed with many superstitious and idle notions of the causes', Charlevoix, p. 292.

27 For a further pertinent elaboration of how such symbolic ideas function, with special references to the meaning of work in slavocratic systems, see Orlando Patterson, *Slavery and Social Death*, pp. 11, 98–9.

28 Sylvia Wynter's analysis of Columbus' 'discover and gain' deeds offers a penetrating insight into the history of the colonization ethics that lay behind Grainger's slavocracy of virtue. Her reading (with necessary qualifications parenthesized) is illuminative of a slow evolution (devolution) to meritocratic-noble (timocratic) status; see Wynter's essay '1492: A New World View' in Hyatt and Nettleford, *Race, Discourse*, pp. 23–4.

29 This utilitarian construction of the utopian ideal evinces a remarkable durability. Its coincidence here with a discourse on revisionist notions of empire and the advancement of learning bears more than a superficial allusion to Baconian colonization themes. For a further discussion of this link, see Francis C. Haber, 'New Jerusalem and Technological Progress', in Sessions, *Francis Bacon's Legacy of Texts: The Art of Discovery Grows with Discovery* (New York: AMS Press, 1990), 85–8.

4 SCHAW: A 'SACCHAROCRACY' OF VIRTUE

1 The *Journal*, eds. Evangeline Walker Andrews and Charles McLean Andrews (New Haven: Yale University Press, 1934) records Schaw's travels to Antigua, St Kitts, North Carolina and Portugal during the instanced years. As the continental material falls outside the scope of this study, it is noticed only in passing. Up until its first publication in

1921, the journal was circulated privately. Both editions are identical as to substance, but the second differs in the addition of two appendices, one containing two Rutherfurd letters and the other some supplementary editorial notes. All textual references will be to the second edition and will appear in parentheses within the text of this chapter. References to the 'Journal' are to the day-to-day entry-writing process. References to editorial material will be labelled 'Andrews' followed by a page number. Since the surnames of the editors are identical, in the interest of brevity I shall refer to them jointly as 'the editors'.

2 Constitutionally, Scotland became one with England in the Act of Union of 1707. Schaw recognizes and embraces the consequences of that relationship by commonly conflating her Scottish with her English identity, particularly in matters of large imperial scale. Undifferentiated uses of the two nationality descriptives in this chapter will reflect that attitude. Typically, though, she particularizes the Scottish element in her pursuit of the ethnic essentialism and cultural exclusivism she seeks to establish for her fellow Scots in the colonies discussed here.

3 Simon Gikandi's work on the broader reaches of this subject is incisive. His specific comment on Scots mediation of British colonial objectives in East Africa makes good comparative reading alongside my study of the West Indies. See Gikandi, *Maps of Englishness: Writing Identity in the Culture of Colonialism* (New York: Columbia University Press, 1996), pp. 33–5.

4 Here a necessary distinction must be made between Schaw's apparent disengagement from local politics in the West Indian portion of her journal and her clear expressions of loyalist partisanhip in the American part, a distinction directly attributable to the imminent revolutionary eruptions on the Continent.

5 For the substantive biographical information included here I am indebted to the sterling research on Schaw by the editors of the *Journal*. The calibre of their scholarship is as distinguished as its value to later generations is esteemed. They are meticulous and informed on matters of accuracy and authenticity. Thorough and persistent in their methods, they pursue sources and leads in Great Britain, North Carolina, and the West Indies, interviewing descendants of some of the eighteenth-century figures, or visiting the modern owners and trustees of properties and materials in the Carolinas and the West Indies related to Schaw and her journal. The finished product is an example of the finest traditions of literary and historical research.

6 Andrews and Andrews, eds., *The Journal*, pp. 1 and 10.

7 Ibid., p. 10.

8 Ibid., pp. 336–7.

9 Ibid., p. 306.

10 Ibid., pp. 319–20.

11 Lord Mansfield is best known for his far-reaching legal opinion on

slavery in the Somerset case (1772) (the landmark case protecting the liberties of slaves in England).

12 For a good source on the social history of Scotland with some discussion on the education of young women, see Marjorie Plant, *The Domestic Life of Scotland in the Eighteenth Century* (Edinburgh University Press, 1952); a more recent work with special references to the role of family in and the particularistic content of Scottish education during the period, see Charles Camic, *Experience and Enlightenment: Socialization for Cultural Change in Eighteenth Century Scotland* (University of Chicago Press, 1983), pp. 126–198.

13 Colin Kidd's discussion of the 'shared contours' of Britishness between the English and the Scots is relevant to the present discussion. See his *British Identities before Nationalism, Ethnicity and Nationhood in the Atlantic World, 1600–1800* (Cambridge University Press, 1999), p. 281. Kames' relevant ideas on Scottish history and constitution can be found in *Essays upon Several Subjects Concerning British Antiquities* (Edinburgh, 1747), and his ideas on property in *Sketches of the History of Man* (Edinburgh 1778).

14 It must be emphasized that in Adam Smith's analysis the slave economy is characterized as inefficient and slavery as a moral and legal aberration. See *An Inquiry into the Nature and Causes of the Wealth of Nations*, 1772 (New York: Modern Library, 1937), Book I, Chapter 8, pp. 80–82. But Smith historicized the natural emergence of slavery systems in close association with the growth of leisure, wealth and display (Book III, chapter 2, pp. 364–6).

15 Hume's opinions on Africans were added in a 1753 footnote to his essay 'Of National Characters.' See *Essays, Moral, Political and Literary*, eds. T. H. Green and T. H. Grose, 2 vols (London: Longman, Green, and Company, 1907), vol I, part I, no. xxi, p. 252.

16 Adam Ferguson treats the subject of subordination in his *Essay on the History of Civil Society* (Edinburgh, 1767; Boston: Hastings, Etheridge and Bliss, 1809), pp. 303–309.

17 Bruce Lenman, *Integration, Enlightenment and Industrialization: Scotland 1746–1832* (University of Toronto Press, 1981), p. 11.

18 The passage reads, 'I hear a boat alongside. I hope it is my brother and that he has brought us something for Supper . . . This is a delightful evening, I hope to have a sound sleep, wishing you good night, I will go to my state room once more' (p. 76). The qualities of presence and immediacy are clearly reminiscent of Richardson's epistolary experiment, but the style of *Pamela* is not replicated in Schaw with any significant consistency.

19 Most of these evicted tenants on Schaw's ship were bound for North Carolina, but a small number settled in the West Indies. David Dobson gives 150,000 as a 'conservative estimate' of total Scots emigrants settling in North America before 1785, with a figure of 10,000 emigrating annually by the 1700s. Precise numbers for Scots emigrating to

the West Indies during the period are hard to come by, but Dobson's research indicates that they were highly desirable workers eagerly requested by local officials (notably the government of St Kitts) from the earliest years of settlement. *Scottish Emigration to Colonial America, 1707–1785* (Athens and London: University of Georgia Press 1994), pp. 125–8.

20 See also Gordon Donaldson, *The Scots Overseas* (Westport, Connecticut: Greenwood Press, 1976), pp. 40 and 57. Between 1707 and 1763 more than 600 Scots, mainly prisoners from the two intervening Jacobite uprisings, were transported and sold as indentured servants in Barbados, Jamaica and Antigua The finest tuning we are able to obtain for the Leeward Islands signals a 'steady influx' there through the early years of the eighteenth century, with Antigua the prime beneficiary (Dobson, *Scottish Emigration*, p. 128). That colony received a significant infusion of Scots from the 425 prisoners transported to the West Indies after the 1745 uprising. In the context of very small population numbers for whites (fewer than two thousand when Schaw visited), the predominance of Scots in Antigua was highly probable. See also Bruce Lenman, *Integration*, p. 26 and Duane Meyer, *The Highland Scots of North Carolina, 1732–1776* (Chapel Hill, NC: University of North Carolina Press), p. 25.

21 Compare Olaudah Equiano's growing awareness of the compassionless ethics of the slave trade in his account of a sale-and-separation scene: 'O ye nominal Christians . . . Are the dearest friends and relations now rendered more dear by their separation from the rest of their kindred, still to be parted from each other and thus prevented from cheering the gloom of slavery, with the small comfort of being together, and mingling their sufferings and sorrows? Why are parents to lose their children, brothers their sisters, or husbands their wives?' *The Interesting Narrative of the Life of Olaudah Equiano* (1789) in *The Classic Slave Narratives*, ed. Henry Louis Gates, Jr. (New York: Penguin Books, 1987), chap 2, p. 38.

22 As the editors remind us, the captain would then have the right to sell that indenture to a master in the colonies with whom the emigrant would spend a set number of years of service. For a further discussion of Scottish emigration and indentures, see Bernard Bailyn, *Voyagers to the West: A Passage in the Peopling of America on the Eve of Revolution* (New York: Knopf, 1986), pp. 166–89.

23 Colin Kidd offers further insight into this complicated aspect of Scottish identity and its relations to empire. *Subverting Scotland's Past*, p. 213.

24 The following table supplies some statistics on the two colonies' geographical size, and on sugar production for the years 1770–1779.

Colony	Area	Tons of sugar
Antigua	108 sq miles	7,398
St Christopher	63 sq miles	9,165

25 While the political and ideological reasons are evident enough, it must

be said that this attitude was at odds with a prolific body of sentimental, primitivistic and humanitarian literature.

26 Patterson, *Slavery and Social Death*, pp. 30, 44.

27 Schaw is strikingly at variance with contemporary leading Scottish thinkers. Adam Smith speaks admiringly of the 'virtues in distress' of savage peoples; their capacity to endure pain, torture and hardship without flinching or lament is assigned to wholly different causes, and markedly redound to their moral credit. Smith wrote: 'a contempt for death and pain prevails among all savage nations . . . There is not a negro from the coast of Africa who does not, in this respect, possess a degree of magnanimity which the soul of his sordid master is too often scarce capable of conceiving' (*Theory of Moral Sentiments*, 1759; introd E. G. West, Indianapolis: Liberty Classics 1976; part V, chap. 2, p. 337).

28 Charles H. Hinnant, *Purity and Defilement in Gulliver's Travels* (London: Macmillan, 1987), pp. 16–17.

29 Schaw's cooption of Scots may be narrowed to Lowland Scots. She is particularly associated with an elite group of educated, fashionable Edinburgh women, some of whom were then living in the colonies. The larger implications of such Scottish identification with British imperial intentions is discussed at greater length in Eric Richards, 'Scotland and the Uses of the Atlantic Empire' in *Strangers within the Realm: Cultural Margins of the First British Empire*, Bernard Bailyn and Philip D. Morgan, eds. (Institute of Early American History and Culture, Williamsburg, Virginia, Chapel Hill and London: University of North Carolina Press, 1991), pp. 91–8.

30 Compare Ligon, *A True and Exact History*: 'They are a happy people, whom so little contents', p. 45.

31 Elizabeth Bohls explores the role of the picturesque in her chapter on Schaw in *Women Travel Writers and the Language of Aesthetics, 1716–1818* (Cambridge University Press, 1995).

32 Gikandi, *Maps of Englishness*, pp. 34–5.

33 *Ibid.*, p.35; Gikandi also illuminates at some length and with fine insight the other side of the picture – those who explicitly identified themselves as Creoles – using the case of Mary Seacole, a Jamaican Creole, as a critical point of contrast, pp. 125–43.

34 Burns, Alan Cuthbert, *History of the British West Indies* (London: Allen & Unwin, 1965), p. 510.

35 A good study for general purposes that is applicable to the present discussion is Gordon Donaldson, *The Scots Overseas*. For a substantial work of scholarship concentrating on the Scots' emigration to America in the years around Schaw's travels, immediately preceding the American Revolution, see Bernard Bailyn, *Voyagers to the West: A Passage in the Peopling of America on the Eve of the Revolution* (New York: Alfred Knopf, 1986).

36 E. V. Goveia, *Slave Society*, pp. 203–14.

37 Goveia, *ibid.*, quotes a persuasive selection of historical sources whose very reliable accounts corroborate Schaw's faith in the ability of these classes to reproduce a culture of quality through their economic achievement.

38 George Pinckard, quoted in E. V. Goveia, *Slave Society.*

39 Luffman, *Brief Account of Antigua*, quoted in Goveia, *Slave Society*, p. 208. James Ramsay, *An Essay on the Treatment and Conversion of African Slaves in the British Sugar Colonies* (Dublin, 1784) who served as a naval chaplain in the West Indies, gives a similar profile of this lower rank of white colonists.

40 Bohls, *Women Travel Writers*, pp. 63–4.

41 Anthony Pagden's lucid historical study, *Lords of all the World*, sets out the philosophical foundations for these attitudes; see especially pp. 103–9.

42 Ferguson, *Essay on Human Characters*, pp. 306–307; Hume, *Treatise of Human Nature* (Oxford: Clarendon Press, 1975), pp. xiv–xviii, pp. 272–73.

43 See David Barry Gaspar, *Bondmen and Rebels: A Study of Master–Slave Relations in Antigua* (Baltimore and London: Johns Hopkins University Press, 1985), p. 205.

44 Andrews and Andrews, eds., *The Journal*, p. 81 note.

45 Martin is the author of *The Essay on Plantership*, father of Josiah Martin, a Carolina governor. The editors add another son, notorious for having fought a duel with Wilkes; see Andrews and Andrews, eds., *The Journal*, pp. 259–73.

46 See Gaspar, *Bondmen and Rebels*, p. 130–1, and Gordon Lewis, *Main Currents*, pp. 168–9.

47 I discuss this notion at greater length in the Lewis chapter.

48 In similar sketches Bryan Edwards provides a useful comparative reading, though he insistently dignifies the term 'Creole' whereas Schaw's objectives have the effect of downgrading it. See *The History Civil and Commercial of the British West Indies*, vol. II (London 1819), pp. 11–18.

5 BECKFORD: THE AESTHETICS OF NEGOTIATION

1 Again, Ortiz's comprehensive vision prefigures my analysis here. He characterized tobacco as a 'liberal reformer' and sugar as a 'reactionary conservative': *Cuban Counterpoint*, 12.

2 Kurt Heinzelman, 'Roman Georgic in the Georgian Age', 182–214.

3 That these highly constructed aesthetic 'packages' are unconscious vehicles for ideology is hardly in dispute both from the totality of their functions in this text, and from the attention given them in theoretical writing. See Louis Althusser, *For Marx* (London: Allen Lane, 1969) and *Lenin and Philosophy and Other Essays* (London: New Left Books, 1971), and

a useful overview of Althusser's formulations in James Donald and Stuart Hall, *Politics and Ideology* (Philadelphia and Milton Keynes: The Open University Press, 1986), p. xvii.

4 Annabel Patterson offers a lively illustration by using a Burns poem to show how pastoral aesthetics like those Beckford cultivated may be implicated in 'cultural conspiracy' and support 'conservative ideology': see *Pastoral and Ideology*, 193–4.

5 Selwyn H. H. Carrington, 'The American Revolution and the British West Indies Economy' in Barbara L. Solow and Stanley L. Engerman (eds.), *British Capitalism and Caribbean Slavery: the Legacy of Eric Williams* (Cambridge University Press, 1988), p. 145.

6 Eric Williams, *From Columbus to Castro*, p. 226.

7 Carrington, 'The American Revolution', p. 139.

8 Ibid., p. 152.

9 Chief among the causes for concern was a black–white population ratio of 25:1 in Hanover. The plot failed, the ringleaders were captured: some were executed, some were flogged, and others were transported. Craton, *Testing the Chains*, pp. 174–5.

10 Ibid., p. 175.

11 Ibid., p. 165.

12 Ibid., pp. 180–2.

13 Seymour Drescher, 'Paradigms Tossed', in Solow and Engerman (eds.), *British Capitalism*, p. 203.

14 In addition to Eric Williams' magisterial work *From Columbus to Castro* already cited, the following titles are most useful: Thomas Clarkson, *The History of the Rise, Progress, & Accomplishment of the Abolition of the African Slave Trade, by the British Parliament*, 2 vols. (1808; rept. London: Frank Cass, 1968); Roger Anstey, *The Atlantic Slave Trade and British Abolition 1760–1810* (Atlantic Highlands, New Jersey: Humanities Press, 1975). A good essay collection covering the subject in its international, racial, class and cultural aspects is Christine Bolt and Seymour Drescher, *Anti-Slavery, Religion and Reform: Essays in Memory of Roger Anstey* (Folkstone: William Dawson, 1980). Drawing on the important critiques of feminine sensibility and the category of the 'domestic', Charlotte Sussman offers an effective postmodern reading of anti-saccharite discourse in her essay 'Women and the Politics of Sugar, 1792', *Representations* (Fall 1994), 48–69.

15 Pagden, *Lords of All the World*, p. 103.

16 Ibid., p. 6.

17 Herder is an important contributor to this narrative. His dogmatic view that unchecked imperial expansion ('indiscriminate, unrestricted migrations') inevitably resulted in 'dangerous commingling and social degeneration', was to become normative for this chapter in the philosophy of the cultural history of empire: 'We shudder with abhorrence when we read the accounts of many European nations, who, sunk in the most

dissolute voluptuousness and insensible pride, have degenerated both in body and mind and no longer possess any capacity for enjoyment and compassion.' (Johann Gottfried Herder, *Outlines of a Philosophy of the History of Man* (1784), trans. T. Churchill (New York: Bergman Publishers, 1966)).

18 The reference here is to propaganda spread by Protestant sources about Spanish atrocities against New World indigenous peoples, propaganda commonly driven by motives of political and economic rivalry: for a recent re-reading of *la leyenda negra*, see Sylvia Wynter, '1492: A New World View', p. 6.

19 This unequal relation between labour and return is one of the primordial references of georgic; see Heinzelman 'Roman Georgic'; Anne D. Wallace 'Farming on Foot: Tracking Georgic in Clare and Wordsworth', *Texas-Studies-in-Literature-and-Language* 34:4 (1992), 509–40.

20 This vision was emboldened by power the Creole interests had accumulated through outright purchase of seats or strategic influence secured with allies in Parliament. Both Houses of Parliament counted among their number owners of slaves and members with direct commercial interest in the trade. Beckford's affluent and powerful extended family numbered among its political luminaries William Beckford, twice Lord Mayor of London and MP for Shrewsbury. By Eric Williams' account some fifty-six MPs had a personal interest in slavery by the year 1823: *Capitalism & Slavery*, 92–5. Peter Fryer sketches the names and connections of the West India lobby in Parliament in *Staying Power: The History of Black People in Britain* (London: Pluto Press, 1984), pp. 44–50.

21 These two instances of assimilation (Creole planter to British farmer and colonial slave to European peasant) were set pieces in pro-slavery writing. The incongruities and exaggerations of the argument are clear enough and need not detain us here, but they were widely rebutted in anti-slavery texts. The eminent abolitionist, Wilberforce's associate, James Stephen, maintained that the European peasant undertook his exertions from necessity of a moral kind, retaining freedom over his family, time, and will, while the slave 'cast his hoe from no impulse but that of fear', *The Crisis of the Sugar Colonies* (1802: rept. New York: Negro Universities Press, 1969), pp. 48–54. Sidney Mintz also debunks these claims, allowing for some linkages but denying exact comparisons: *Sweetness and Power: The Place of Sugar in Modern History* (New York: Viking, 1985), pp. 57–8.

22 The *locus classicus* for this civilizing, instructive function of the *translatio* is, of course, Cicero's *De Inventione*. Cheyfitz's highly illuminating discussion (*Poetics*, pp. 113–14) of *De Inventione* and its relation to imperialist discourse has been an invaluable help in my reading of this text. See also Cheyfitz, *Poetics*, pp. 160–1.

23 Walter Benjamin, *Illuminations: Essays and Reflections*, ed. with intro-

duction by Hannah Arendt, trans. Harry Zohn (New York: Schocken Books, 1969), p. 80.

24 James Donald and Stuart Hall (eds.), *Politics and Ideology: A Reader* (Milton Keynes and Philadelphia: Open University Press, 1986), p. ix.

25 Anne D. Wallace, 'Farming on Foot', 509–40.

26 David Worral, 'Agrarians against the Picturesque', in Stephen Copley and Peter Garside (eds.), *The Politics of the Picturesque: Literature, Landscape, and Aesthetics since 1770*, (Cambridge University Press, 1994), p. 257.

27 Ibid.

28 Ann Bermingham, *Landscape and Ideology: The English Rustic Tradition 1740–1860* (Berkeley: University of California Press, 1986), p. 74.

29 Bermingham, ibid., takes as her primary context the agrarian revolution of late eighteenth- and early nineteenth-century England, but she lists other conditions which parallel those reproduced in slavery: tension between old country families and new industrialists, the existence of absentee gentry situated remote from the site of labour, the change in agriculture from a labour-intensive to a capital-intensive pursuit. Eric Williams (*Capitalism and Slavery*, p. 76) attributes the collapse of the slave sugar-economy system to industrializing forces. His thesis is re-evaluated in essays in Christine Bolt and Seymour Drescher (eds.), *Antislavery, Religion, and Reform*.

30 For further discussion illustrating how this new economic position was inscribed ideologically, see Bermingham, *Landscape and Ideology*, pp. 74–76.

31 For a discussion relating such practices to eighteenth-century English descriptive practice, see John Barrell, *The Idea of Landscape*, pp. 35–46.

32 Beckford's deliberate descriptive choices here are identifiable with the conservative impulses and certain class exclusive implications found in Dryden and Pope. In the context of her discussion on the eighteenth-century history of literary forms related to work, Annabel Patterson, *Pastoral and Ideology*, calls attention to Adam Smith's dichotomy between 'headwork' (thought, invention) and arduous toil, a dichotomy that is presumptively inscribed in Beckford's ideology of Creole social order.

33 The obvious texts of Pope that bear relevance to this continuity are 'Windsor Forest' (1713) and the 'Epistle to Burlington' (1731). In a critical reading of the 'Epistle to Bathurst', John Barrell and Harriet Guest identify Pope's attempt to reconcile these older traditional virtues to a new emergent capitalist ethic as a central contradiction in his work. See 'On the Use of Contradiction: Economics and Morality in the Eighteenth Century Long Poem', in *Pope*, ed. and intro. Brean Hammond (London and New York: Longman, 1996), pp. 115–29. In the same volume, Laura Brown's insights in 'The ideology of Neo-Classical Aesthetics: *Epistles to Several Persons*" are also valuable in tracing the roots of Beckford's ideology. Brown defines Pope's method as designed to formulate a 'cultural ideal for the ruling class, constructed from the

superimposition of an abstract and neo-classical system of aesthetic valuation upon a concrete programme for mercantile capitalist economic expansion', p. 140. Ann Bermingham lays out the explicit class-based, exclusivist tendencies in *Landscape and Ideology*, p. 71. The chapter on Janet Schaw in Elizabeth Bohl's *Women Travel Writers and the Language of Aesthetics, 1716–1818* (Cambridge University Press, 1995), pp. 46–65, explores some congruent ideas and relationships using feminist critiques and gendered references.

34 Heinzelman, 'Roman Georgic,' 188.

35 John Barrell remarks that this use of the aesthetic is a personalizing myth, where landscape becomes a theatre where the poet's own moral reflections are acted out', *The Idea of Landscape*, p. 35.

36 Here the ambiguity of picturesque desire and practice is strikingly produced. Beckford desires both the *neg* of 'vulgar adjuncts' with clear material and economic references, and the *otium* of Arcadian 'scenes of rural dance and merriment.' John Murdoch's definition and description of picturesque categories, especially of the picturesque's representation of landscape as 'a real place [having] a social structure, a culture, and a politics' is particularly helpful. See *The Landscape of Labor: Transformations of the Georgic*, in Kenneth R. Johnson (ed.), *Romantic Revolutions*, Bloomington, IND: Indiana University Press, 1990, p. 177.

37. The definitive eighteenth-century writings on picturesque theory are Richard Payne Knight, *The Landscape, a Didactic Poem, in Three Books* (London, 1794), and Uvedale Price, *An Essay on the Picturesque, as Compared with the Sublime and the Beautiful; and, on the Use of Studying Pictures, for the Purpose of Improving Real Landscape* (London, 1810).

38 Paul Gilroy insists, as I show in the ensuing analysis of eruptive/ disruptive phenomena, that the kinds of love, loss and remembrance typically transcoded in performances like the slave woman's song are continually redeemed from total obliteration by the slavery sublime: see *The Black Atlantic: Modernity and Double Consciousness*, Cambridge, MA.: Harvard University Press, pp. 37, 201.)

39 Narratively, this emanation of the sublime should not be understood to occur in the *Descriptive Account* as abruptly as the relative emphases of this study might suggest. The early and widespread incidence of tropes like repetition and amplification in Beckford's descriptive style inscribes the sublime into the 'political unconscious' of the text. See David Morris on the process by which these and other tropes pass from language to action in sublime narratives: 'Gothic Sublime', *New Literary History* 16 (1985), p. 303.

40 Homi Bhabha, *The Theory of Reading*, Frank Gloversmith (ed.), (Sussex: Harvester Press, 1984), p. 204.

41 Said writes: 'The power to narrate, or to block other narratives from forming and emerging, is very important to culture and imperialism, and constitutes one of the main connections between them', 'Intro-

duction', *Culture and Imperialism* (New York: Knopf, Random House, 1993), p. xiii.

42 Longinus identifies this disruptive force as the power of the sublime to take us outside ourselves with the sudden, startling intensity of a lightning flash (*On the Sublime*, trans. A. O. Prickard (Oxford: Clarendon Press, 1949)), I: 3.

43 Jean D'Costa, 'Oral Literature, Formal Literature: the Formation of Genre in Eighteenth-Century Jamaica', *Eighteenth-Century Studies* 27 (1994), 673.

44 The critical literature on Beckford is minuscule, but one article that takes up his use of the sublime is P. H. Knox-Shaw, 'The West Indian Vathek', *Essays in Criticism* 43:4 (1993), 284–307.

45 Martin Price sketches some significant intellectual and aesthetic sources for this notion in 'The Sublime Poem: Pictures and Powers'. *The Yale Review* 58 (1968), 198–99.

46 Beckford's experience of sublime phenomena in colonial Jamaica conflates the Longinian privileges of 'great writing' with the Burkean anticipations of revolutionary terror, his intimations of the latter serving to inform his reactionary mediations with the *negotium*. For a discussion that helps to place this vision in historical context, see David Morris, 'Gothic Sublimity', *New Literary History* 16:2 (Winter 1985), 299–319.

47 Edmund Burke, *A Philosophical Enquiry Into the Origin of Our Ideas of the Sublime and Beautiful* (Notre Dame, Ind.: University of Notre Dame Press, 1968), p. 205.

6 LEWIS: PERSONALIZING THE *NEGOTIUM*

1 Of the authors represented in this study, 'Monk' Lewis is by far the most notable on account of the wide and enduring popularity of his gothic novel *The Monk*. By the same token, Lewis' biographical data are also better known and more accessible than those of the other authors. I have therefore thought it unnecessary to retail the familiar facts, choosing instead to supply only those which pertain particularly to his Jamaican visits and to the *Journal*. Biographical sources for Lewis are Mrs Cornwell Baron-Wilson's *The Life and Correspondence of M. G. Lewis*, 2 vols. (London: Henry Colburn, 1839), a comprehensive work that is especially valuable for its sampling of Lewis' poetry and private correspondence; Louis F. Pecks, *A Life of Matthew Lewis* (Cambridge: Harvard University Press, 1961) provides a modern, more accessible text with by far the most scholarly reading to date, rendering Lewis' life and work thoughtfully and insightfully. Joseph James Irwin's critical study, *M. G. 'Monk' Lewis* (Boston: Twayne Publishers, 1976), is useful for its ample overview of the major genres of Lewis' literary output and for its selection of excerpts from the journal.

2 In the context of slavery, the term 'social death' is understood as the

total erasure of identity and status which the slave suffers as a result of losing his freedom in any of the contingencies that historically could conduce to human bondage. At Cornwall and Hordley, the signs of renewal and rejoicing engendered in the slaves by the master's coming operated ambiguously: the master's presence reaffirms dramatically, if ironically, his lordship and ownership of their persons, and therefore verifies that loss; but presence also inflames the wistful hope that loss could be recuperated, and Lewis' reforms raised that hope immensely. A concept with profound implications for our understanding of slavery as a universal institution, social death has been lucidly defined and illustrated in Orlando Patterson's *Slavery and Social Death*, to which I am indebted.

3 Our search to understand this apparent lack of interest in the objective particulars of the sugar cane must take cognizance of how the peculiar nature of Lewis' text distinguishes his relation to the Creole project from the preceding authors'. The *Journal* is less the traditional colonial text of prospecting and enterprise but is slanted more towards producing knowledge of the self and its own desire. In the context of a discussion on Malthus and Wordsworth, Clifford Siskin suggests some possibilities for historicist interpretation whose nineteenth-century references strengthen their relevance to Lewis: 'The self makes itself by producing knowledge engendered by its own making; the subject is increasingly its own, and only, object of inquiry' (*The Historicity of Romantic Discourse*, Oxford University Press, 1988, p. 167).

4 Known by variant spellings – John-Canoe, junkanoo – the John Canoe were seasonal masquerades staged by West Indian slaves around Christmastime and featured elaborate costumes, dancing and other rites. Orlando Patterson traces their origins back to West Africa and offers an extended interpretation of their cultural and political components in *The Sociology of Slavery*, pp. 239–47.

5 The standard psychological and philosophical denotations of solipsism would be sufficient to justify attribution of that mentality to Lewis here, but the social and political theorist William Godwin, a contemporary of Lewis, includes in his usage of the concept a description of a 'protean' personality, given to 'vagaries' and 'idiosyncracy', terms synonymous with my earlier construction of Lewis' identity. See Kenneth Graham, *The Politics of Narrative: Ideology and Social Change in William Godwin's Caleb Williams* (New York: AMS Press, 1990), p. 142.

6 Louis F. Peck, *A Life of Matthew G. Lewis* (Cambridge, Mass.: Harvard University Press, 1961), pp. 65–6.

7 What David Richards observes about Stedman's journal as an historical critique of European culture both underlines the space Lewis has placed between himself and that traditional version of the *negotium* narrative and vindicates Lewis' interrogating and reformist postures, especially the very non-combative and enlightened stance he adopted

in the face of his own 'revolted negroes' at Hordley (*Journal*, 359–403); according to Richards, Stedman's self-representation in his journal betrays 'above all a sense that European culture is fragmenting into chaos, displayed by its constant wars, its sexual predations and its violent obsessions. It is this riven culture, exported to South America, which Stedman is sent to protect from the 'revolted negroes' of Surinam (*Masks*, 90).

8 Mrs Cornwell Baron-Wilson, *The Life and Correspondence of M. G. Lewis*, p. 121.

9 Orlando Patterson, *Slavery and Social Death*, pp. 62–6. As bourgeois subject, Lewis may here be seen as asserting that subject's authority to locate self in conflictual forces, to explore newly defined public identities, to fashion new roles and new spaces. Implicit in these spaces of self-fashioning is the notion of multiple public spheres, a revisionist interpretation of Habermas which would comprehend an ideology such as Lewis instituted at Cornwall. Such an interpretation rejects any stable, uniform or homogeneous model of the public sphere, amplifying the concept instead to embrace 'the boundaries, structures of the spaces where public debates of political and social issues take place [which] have to be negotiated in accordance with the needs and values of the community', Peter Uwe Hohendahl, 'The Public Sphere: Models and Boundaries', in Craig Calhoun, *Habermas and the Public Sphere* (Cambridge, Mass.: MIT Press, 1992), p. 107.

10 These forms of verbal deceit and subversion, masked as drollery, complaisance or even abject flattery have been thoroughly represented in scholarship on slavery and other kinds of oppression, but Gordon Lewis' definition of them as 'Jamaican creolized language used to dazzle and confuse the figures of authority in a splendidly conducted linguistic game' hints at the slaves' role and Lewis' immersion in the diverse forms of creolization surrounding him, and credits his ability to know the difference (*Main Currents*), pp. 178–9.

11 The term 'transculturation' has been widely used in historical, ethnographic and cultural studies, most commonly to define the transfer and assimilation of values, customs, and ideas, especially in colonialist and imperialist contexts. Typically the term assumes the superior hegemonic force of metropolitan cultures over subject peoples. However, Lewis' work, among others, has demonstrated that transculturation is, as it were, dialogic and certainly reciprocal: the European subject inevitably assimilated and was assimilated into the otherness of colonial experience, both consciously and unconsciously. The very development of a distinct creole class with its own definable creole identity forcefully suggests complex ways in which colonizer/master was influenced by the colonized/slave and autochthonous inhabitant. In Lewis' case the impact is most remarkable in the tropes of empathy and familiarity, the indulgence for the slaves' foibles and idiosyncracies that inform his

textualized experience. Transculturation is the principal enabling factor in Lewis' remarkable sense of congeniality with the human and natural constituents at Cornwall. It also figures in his capacity to deploy the images and ideas aesthetically in the *Journal*. For pertinent discussions of transculturation, see Fernando Ortiz, pp. 97–103; and Mary Louise Pratt, *Imperial Eyes: Travel Writing and Transculturation* (London and New York: Routledge, 1992), p. 6.

12 Chester G. Starr characterizes the *polis* as the political system in which the values of Western civilization were first made explicit and conscious; see his *Individual and Community: The Rise of the Polis (800–500 BC)* (Oxford University Press, 1986), p. 14.

13 Ibid., p. 51.

14 At least one other text in recent cultural criticism of the Americas has given validity to this analogical approach. David Richards invokes the idea of the *polis* to show how its references resonate in the ethnographic constructions of self and other in colonial settings. See *Masks*, p. 47.

15 Benjamin Nathans, 'Habermas's Public Sphere in the Era of the French Revolution', *French Historical Studies* 16 (Spring 1990), 620–44.

16 The suggestiveness of public sphere theory to the broader cultural reach of Lewis' ideas may be assessed from the distinction John Nerone makes between self-interest and civic virtue as formulated in the two schools of political and cultural theory represented by John Locke and Adam Smith. See Nerone's 'The History of the Public Sphere', *Journal of Communication* 42:2 (Spring 1992), 167.

17 Steven E. Levine, 'Seascapes of the Sublime: Vernet, Monet, and the Oceanic Feeling', *New Literary History* 16 (1985), 377.

18 Marie Helene Huet, 'The Revolutionary Sublime', *Eighteenth Century Studies* 28 (1994), 51–2.

19 Raymond Smith, 'Religion in the Formation of West Indian Society, Guyana and Jamaica', *The African Diaspora: Interpretive Essays*, Martin Kilson and Robert I. Rothberg (eds.) (Cambridge, MA: Harvard University Press, 1978), p. 328.

20 For a concise discussion of obeah's origins, uses and cultural meaning in the politics of slavery, see Leonard E. Barrett, *Soul-Force: African Heritage in Afro-American Religion* (New York: Anchor Press/Doubleday, 1974), 68–72. Lively, illustrative sketches and references to obeah's influence on the lives of slave and free may be found in Jean D'Costa and Barbara Lalla, *Voices in Exile: Jamaican Texts of the 18th and 19th Centuries* (Tuscaloosa and London: University of Alabama Press, 1989). An article by Alan Richardson, 'Romantic Voodoo: Obeah and British Culture, 1797–1807', *Studies in Romanticism* 32 (Spring 1993), 3–28, gathers some of the seminal sources and interprets meanings and attitudes associated with its practice in the referenced period.

21 Peck, *Life of Lewis*, pp. 26–8.

22 According to Peck (ibid., 158), one such conversation is noted in

Wilberforce's diary with a date of 1816, and a letter dated 16 October 1817 may be found in *The Correspondence of William Wilberforce*, 2 vols., ed. Robert I. and Samuel Wilberforce (Phildelphia: Henry Perkins, 1841), vol. II, pp. 205–8.

23 John Pollock, *Wilberforce* (New York: St. Martin's Press, 1977), p. 246.

24 Peck, *Life of Lewis*, p. 151.

25 David B. Morris, 'Gothic Sublimity', *New Literary History* 16:2 (1985), 299.

26 Martin Price, 'The Sublime Poem: Pictures and Powers', *The Yale Review* 58 (1968), 219.

27 Clifford Siskin uses the phrase 'metaphysical certitudes' in reference to the object of the sublime's undermining and decentring actions on the post-Burkean subject. This language is apt for thinking about the fate of the *negotium* under the disruptive, defamiliarizing power of the sublime. See 'Gender, Sublimity, Culture', 37–50.

28 Edmund Burke, *Reflections on the French Revolution and Other Essays* (New York: E. P. Dutton, 1951), p. 10.

29 Carl Woodring, *Politics in English Romantic Poetry* (Cambridge, MA: Harvard University Press, 1970), p. 328.

30 With this shift in the social and moral valorization of the *negotium*, we see a further distancing of the sublime from its Burkean-Enlightenment moorings to the link Kant stressed between moral feeling and the sublime. See Neal Oxenhandler, 'The Changing Concept of Literary Emotion: A Selective History,' *New Literary History* 20 (1988), p. 112.

31 Terry Eagleton, *The Ideology of the Aesthetic*, p. 54.

32 Ibid., p. 37.

33 Ibid., p. 32.

34 Guy Oakes, Intro. to Carl Schmitt, *Political Romanticism* (Cambridge, Mass: The MIT Press, 1986), p. xix.

35 Nathans, Rev. of Habermas' *Structural Transformation of the Public Sphere*, *French Historical Studies* 16 (1990), p. 644.

POSTSCRIPT AND PROSPECT

1 Charles de Rochefort, *Histoire*, p.194.

2 Edouard Glissant','Creolization in the Making of the Americas', p. 270.

3 Gordon Lewis, *Main Currents*, p. 27.

4 See James Boswell, *Life of Johnson*, II: 166; III: 166, 400; and Joseph Addison and Richard Steele, *Spectator*, No. 31, *Spectator*, No. 507 and *Guardian*, No. 71.

5 Jurgen Habermas, *The Structural Transformation of the Public Sphere: An Inquiry into a Category of Bourgeois Society* (Cambridge, MA: MIT Press, 1989), pp. 6–7.

6 Ibid., pp. 20–1.

Select bibliography

Adams, Richard N., 'On the Relation between Plantation and 'Creole Cultures'. *Plantation Systems of the New World*, Social Science Monographs VII, Washington, DC: Pan American Union, 1959.

Anon, *The Present State of the British Sugar Colonies Considered*, np, nd.

Althusser, Louis, *For Marx*, London: Allen Lane, 1969.
    Lenin and Philosophy, and Other Essays, London: New Left Books, 1971.

Anstey, Roger, *The Atlantic Slave Trade and British Abolition, 1760–1810*, London: Macmillan, 1975.

Augier, F. R., et al. *The Making of the West Indies*, London: Longman, 1961.

Bailyn, Bernard, *Voyagers to the West: a Passage in the Peopling of America on the Eve of the Revolution*, New York: Knopf, 1986.

Baron-Wilson, Cornwell, Mrs, *The Life and Correspondence of M. G. Lewis, with Many Pieces in Prose and Verse, never before Published*, London, H. Colburn, 1839.

Barrell, John, *The Idea of Landscape and the Sense of Place, 1730–1840; an Approach to the Poetry of John Clare*, Cambridge University Press, 1972.

Beckford, William, *A Descriptive Account of the Island of Jamaica, with Remarks Upon the Cultivation of the Sugar-Cane, Throughout the Different Seasons of the Year, and Chiefly Considered in a Picturesque Point of View; Also, Observations and Reflections Upon What Would Probably Be the Consequences of an Abolition of the Slave-Trade, and of the Emancipation of the Slaves*, London: T. and J. Egerton, 1790.

Benezet, Anthony, *A Short Account of that Part of Africa Inhabited by Negroes*, Philadelphia: W. Dunlap, 1762.

Benjamin, Walter, *Illumination*, trans. Harry Zohn, Hannah Arendt (ed.), New York: Schocken Books, 1969.

Bermingham, Ann, *Landscape and Ideology: The English Rustic Tradition*, Berkeley: University of California Press, 1986.

Bhabha, Homi, 'Representation and the Colonial Text', *The Theory of Reading*, Frank Gloversmith (ed.), Sussex: Harvester Press; Totowa, NJ: Barnes & Noble, 1984.

Bohls, Elizabeth A., *Women Travel Writers and the Language of Aesthetics, 1716–1818*, Cambridge University Press, 1995.

Bolt, Christine, and Seymour Drescher (eds.), *Anti-slavery, Religion, and Reform: Essays in Memory of Roger Anstey*, Folkestone, Eng.: W. Dawson; Hamden, CT: Archon Books, 1980.

Bono, Barbara, *Literary Transvaluation From Vergilian Epic to Shakespearean Tragicomedy*, Berkeley: University of California Press, 1984.

Boomert, Arie, 'The Arawak Indians of Trinidad and Coastal Guiana, 1500–1650', *Journal of Caribbean History* 19:2 (1984), 128.

Boswell, James, *Life of Johnson*, G. B. Hill and L. F. Powell (eds.), 6 vols. Oxford University Press, 1934.

Boucher, Philip, *Cannibal Encounters: Europeans and Island Caribs, 1492–1763*, Baltimore: Johns Hopkins University Press, 1992.

  Les Nouvelles Frances: France in America, 1500–1815, An Imperial Perspective, Providence, RI: The John Carter Brown Library, 1989.

Brathwaite, Edward, *The Development of Creole Society in Jamaica, 1770–1820*, Oxford: Clarendon Press, 1971.

Burke, Edmund, *A Philosophical Enquiry Into the Origin of Our Ideas of the Sublime and Beautiful*, Notre Dame, Ind.: University of Notre Dame Press, 1968.

  Reflections on the French Revolution and Other Essays. New York: E. P. Dutton, 1951.

Burns, Alan Cuthbert, *History of the British West Indies*, London: Allen & Unwin, 1965.

Butler, Judith P., *Subjects of Desire: Hegelian Reflections in Twentieth-Century France*, New York: Columbia University Press, 1987.

Camic, Charles, *Experience and Enlightenment: Socialization for Cultural Change in Eighteenth Century Scotland*, University of Chicago Press, 1983.

Carrington, Selwyn H. H., 'The American Revolution in the British West Indian Economy', in Barbara L. Solow, and Stanley L. Engerman (eds.), *British Capitalism and Caribbean Slavery: the Legacy of Eric Williams*, Cambridge University Press, 1988.

Cartwright, Michael, Rev. of *Les Nouvelles Frances*, by Philip P. Boucher, *Eighteenth-Century-Studies* 26 (1992): 167–70.

Certeau, Michel de, *Heterologies: Discourse on the Other*, trans. Brian Massumi, Minneapolis: University of Minnesota Press, 1986.

Cheyfitz, Eric, *The Poetics of Imperialism: Translation and Colonization from The Tempest to Tarzan*, New York: Oxford University Press, 1991.

  The Writing of History, New York: Columbia University Press, 1988.

Clarkson, Thomas, *The History of the Rise, Progress, & Accomplishment of the Abolition of the African Slave-Trade, by the British Parliament*, Philadelphia: James P. Parke, 1808, repr. London: Frank Cass, 1968.

Cleland, William, *The Present State of the Sugar Colonies Considered; but more especially that of the island of Barbadoes*, London: Printed by John Morphew, 1713.

Clifford, James, 'On Ethnograpohic Allegory', in James Clifford and George E. Marcus (eds.), *Writing Culture: The Poetics and Politics of Ethnography*, Berkeley: University of California Press, 1986.

Copley, Stephen, and Garside, Peter (eds.), *The Politics of the Picturesque: Literature, Landscape; and Aesthetics since 1770*, New York: Cambridge University Press, 1994.

Craton, Michael, *Testing the Chains: Resistance to Slavery in the British West Indies*, Ithaca, NY: Cornell University Press, 1982.

Curtin, Philip, *The Atlantic Slave Trade: A Census*, Madison: University of Wisconsin Press, 1969.

D'Costa, Jean, 'Oral literature, formal literature: the formation of genre in eighteenth-century Jamaica', *Eighteenth-Century Studies* 27 (Summer 1994), 663–76.

Deleuze, Gilles, and Guattari, Felix, *Anti-Oedipus: Capitalism and Schizophrenia*, New York: Viking Press, 1977.

Dobson, David, *Scottish Emigration to Colonial America, 1707–1785*, Athens and London: University of Georgia Press, 1994.

Donald, James, and Hall, Stuart (eds.), *Politics and Ideology: A Reader*, Philadelphia: Open University Press, 1986.

Donaldson, Gordon, *The Scots Overseas*, Westport, CT: Greenwood Press, 1976.

Drescher, Seymour, 'Paradigms Tossed Capitalism and the Political Sources of Abolition' in Barbara L. Solow, and Stanley L. Engerman, (eds.), *British Capitalism and Caribbean Slavery: The Legacy of Eric Williams*, Cambridge University Press, 1988.

Dunn, Richard S., *Sugar and Slaves; The Rise of the Planter Class in the English West Indies, 1624–1713*, Chapel Hill: Published for the Institute of Early American History and Culture at Williamsburg, VA, by the University of North Carolina Press, 1972.

Eagleton, Terry, *The Ideology of the Aesthetic*, Cambridge, MA: Basil Blackwell, 1990.

Edwards, Bryan, *The History Civil and Commercial of the British West Indies*, 5 vols. London 1819.

Ellis, Keith, 'Images of Sugar in English and Spanish Caribbean Poetry', *Ariel* 24 (1993): 149–59.

Equiano, Olaudah (Gustavus Vassa), *The Interesting Narrative of the Life of Olaudah Equiano* (1789) in *The Classic Slave Narratives*, Henry Louis Gates, Jr. (ed.), New York: Penguin Books, 1987.

Ferguson, Adam, *Essay on the History of Civil Society*, Edinburgh, 1767; Boston: Hastings, Etheridge and Bliss, 1809.

Foucault, Michel, *Discipline and Punish: The Birth of the Prison*, New York: Pantheon Books, 1977.

Fowler, Alastair, 'The Beginnings Of English Georgic', *Renaissance Genres: Essays on Theory, History and Interpretation*, Barbara Kiefer Lewalski (ed.), Cambridge, MA: Harvard University Press, 1986.

Gaspar, David Barry, *Bondmen and Rebels: A Study of Master Slave Relations in Antigua*, Baltimore and London: Johns Hopkins University, 1985.

Gikandi, Simon, *Maps of Englishness: Writing Identity in the Culture of Colonialism*, New York: Columbia University Press, 1996.

Gilroy, Paul, *The Black Atlantic: Modernity and Double Consciousness*, Cambridge, MA: Harvard University Press, 1993.

Girard, Rene, *Violence and the Sacred*, Trans. Patrick Gregory, Baltimore: Johns Hopkins University Press, 1977.

Glissant, Edouard, 'Creolization in the Making of the Americas', *Race, Discourse, and the Origins of the Americas: A New World View*, Vera Lawrence Hyatt and Rex Nettleford (eds.), Washington, DC: Smithsonian Institution Press, 1995.

Goveia, Elsa, *Slave Society and the British Leeward Islands at the End of the Eighteenth Century*, New Haven: Yale University Press, 1965.

A Study on the Historiography of the British West Indies to the End of the Nineteenth Century, Washington, DC: Howard University Press, 1980.

Graham, Kenneth W, *The Politics of Narrative: Ideology and Social Change in William Godwin's* 'Caleb Williams', New York: AMS, 1990.

Grainger, James, *The Sugar-Cane! A Poem*, London: Printed for R. and J. Dodsley, 1764.

Greenberg, Mitchell, *Detours of Desire: Readings in the French Baroque*, Columbus: Miami University by the Ohio State University Press, 1984.

Handler, Jerome S. and Frederick W. Lange, *Plantation Slavery in Barbados: An Archaeological and Historical Investigation*, Cambridge, MA: Harvard University Press, 1978.

Heinzelman, Kurt, 'Roman Georgic in the Georgian Age: A Theory of Romantic Genre', *Texas-Studies-in-Literature-and-Language* 33 (1991), 182–214.

Herder, Johann Gottfried, *Uniform: Ideen zur Philosophie der Geschichte der Menschheit*, [*Outlines of a Philosophy of the History of Man*], Trans. T. Churchill, New York: Bergmans, 1966.

Hinnant, Charles H., *Purity and Defilement in Gulliver's Travels*, London: Macmillan, 1987.

Huet, Marie Helene, 'Thunder and Revolution: Franklin, Robespierre, Sade', in Sandy Petrey (ed.), *The French Revolution 1789–1989: Two Hundred Years of Rethinking*, Lubbock: Texas Tech University Press, 1989.

'The Revolutionary Sublime', *Eighteenth Century Studies* 28 (1994), 51–64.

Hulme, Peter, *Wild Majesty: Encounters With Caribs from Columbus to the Present Day: An Anthology*, Oxford: Clarendon Press; New York: Oxford University Press, 1992.

Hume, David, 'Of National Characters', *Essays, Moral, Political*, T. H. Green and T. H. Grose (eds.), 2 vols, London: Longmans, Green, and Company, 1907.

Hume, David, *Treatise of Human Nature*, Oxford: Clarendon Press, 1975.

Hyatt, Vera Lawrence, and Nettleford, Rex (eds.), *Race, Discourse, and the Origins of the Americas: A New World View*, Washington: Smithsonian Institution Press, 1995.

International Conference on Theoretical Orientations in Creole Studies, *Historicity and Variation in Creole Studies*, Ann Arbor, MI: Karoma Publishers, 1981.

Theoretical Orientations in Creole Studies, New York: Academic Press, 1980.

Irwin, Joseph James, *M. G. 'Monk' Lewis*, Boston: Twayne Publishers, 1976.

Jacquin, Philippe, 'The Colonial Policy of the Sun King', *The Sun King and The New World*, Robert McDonald (ed.), New Orleans: Louisiana Museum Foundation, 1984.

Joppien, Rudiger, *Philippe Jacques de Loutherbourg, RA, 1740–1812*, London: Greater London Council, 1973.

Kidd, Colin, *Subverting Scotland's Past: Scottish Whig Historians and the Creation of an Anglo-British Identity, 1689–c. 1830*, Cambridge University Press, 1993.

Kilson, Martin L, and Robert I. Rotberg (eds.), *The African Diaspora:Interpretive Essays*, Cambridge, MA: Harvard University Press, 1976.

Knox-Shaw, P. H., 'The West Indian Vathek', *Essays in Criticism* 43:4 (Oct 1993), 284–307.

Kolodny, Annette, *The Lay of the Land: Metaphor as Experience and History in American Life and Letters*, Chapel Hill: University of North Carolina Press, 1975

Le Page, R. B., *Acts of Identity: Creole-Based Approaches to Language and Ethnicity*, Cambridge University Press, 1985.

Lenman, Bruce, *Integration, Enlightenment and Industrialization: Scotland 1746–1832*, University of Toronto Press, 1981.

Lery, Jean de, *Histoire d'un Voyage Fait en la Terre du Bresil: Autrement Dite Amerique*, Lausanne: Bibliotheque Romande, 1972.

Levine, Steven E., 'Seascapes of the Sublime: Vernet, Monet, and the Oceanic Feeling', *New Literary History* 16 (1985), 377–400.

Lewis, Gordon K., *Main Currents in Caribbean Thought: The Historical Evolution of Caribbean Society in Its Ideological Aspects, 1492–1900*, Baltimore: Johns Hopkins University Press, 1983.

Lewis, M. G., *Journal of a West-India Proprietor, Kept During a Residence in the Island of Jamaica*, London: J. Murray, 1834.

Ligon, Richard, *A True & Exact History of the Island of Barbadoes. Illustrated with a map of the island, as also the principal trees and plants there, set forth in their due proportions and shapes, drawn out by their several and respective scales. Together with the ingenio that makes the sugar, with the plots of the several houses, rooms, and other places, that are used in the whole process of sugar-making*, London: P. Parker and T. Gily, 1673.

Longinus, *On the Sublime*, Trans. A.O. Prickard, Oxford: Clarendon Press, 1949.

McKendrick, Neil, *et al. The Birth of a Consumer Society: The Commercialization of Eighteenth-Century England*, Bloomington, IN: Indiana University Press, 1982.

McKeon, Michael, 'Andrew Marvell and the Problem of Mediation', *Andrew Marvell*, Harold Bloom (ed.), New York: Chelsea House, 1989.

Meyer, Duane Gilbert, *The Highland Scots of North Carolina, 1732–1776*, Chapel Hill, NC: University of North Carolina Press, 1961.

Mims, Stewart Lea, *Colbert's West India Policy*, New Haven: Yale University Press, 1912.

Mintz, Sidney Wilfred, *Sweetness and Power: The Place of Sugar in Modern History*, New York: Viking, 1985.

Morris, David B., 'Gothic Sublimity', *New Literary History* 16 (1985), 299–319.

Murdoch, John, 'The Landscape of Labor: Transformations of the Georgic', Kenneth R. Johnson (ed.), *Romantic Revolutions*, Indiana University Press, 1990.

Nathans, Benjamin, Rev. '*The Structural Transformation of the Public Sphere*, by Jurgen Habermas'. *French Historical Studies* 16 (1990), 620–44.

Nerone, John, 'The History of the Public Sphere', *Journal of Communication* 42 (1992), 167.

Nettleford, Rex M., *Caribbean Cultural Integration: The Case of Jamaica: An Essay in Cultural Dynamics*, Los Angeles: Center for Afro-American Studies and UCLA Latin American Center Publications, University of California, 1979.

Nichols, John, *Illustrations of the Literary History of the Eighteenth Century. Consisting of authentic memoirs and original letters of eminent persons; and intended as a sequel to the Literary anecdotes*, London: Nichols, Son, and Bentley, 1817–58.

Oakes, Guy, Intro. *Political Romanticism*, by Carl Schmitt, Cambridge, Mass: The MIT Press, 1986.

Ortiz, Fernando, *Cuban Counterpoint; Tobacco and Sugar*, New York: A. A. Knopf, 1947.

Oxenhandler, Neal, 'The Changing Concept of Literary Emotion: A Selective History', *New Literary History* 20 (1988), 105–21.

Pagden, Anthony, *Lords of All the World: Ideologies of Empire in Spain, Britain and France c. 1500–c. 1800*, New Haven, CT: Yale University Press, 1995.

Patterson, Annabel M., *Pastoral and Ideology: Virgil to Valery*, Berkeley: University of California Press, 1988.

Patterson, Orlando, *Slavery and Social Death: A Comparative Study*, Cambridge, MA: Harvard University Press, 1982.

   The Sociology of Slavery: An Analysis of the Origins, Development, and Structure of Negro Slave Society in Jamaica, Rutherford, NJ: Fairleigh Dickinson University Press, 1969.

Peck, Louis F., *A Life of Matthew G. Lewis*, Cambridge, MA, Harvard University Press, 1961.

Plant, Marjorie, *The Domestic Life of Scotland in the Eighteenth Century*, Edinburgh University Press, 1952.

Pollock, John, *Wilberforce*, New York: St Martin's Press, 1977.

Pope, Alexander, *Epistle to Bathurst; A Critical Reading With an Edition of the Manuscripts*, Earl R. Wasserman (ed.), Baltimore: Johns Hopkins Press, 1960.

Price, Martin, 'The Sublime Poem: Pictures and Powers', *The Yale Review* 58 (1968), 194–219.

Priestley, Herbert Ingram, *France Overseas through the Old Regime*, New York and London: D. Appleton-Century Company, Inc., 1939.

Ragatz, Lowell J., *The Fall of the Planter Class in the British Caribbean, 1763–1833: A Study in Social and Economic History*, New York and London: The Century Co, 1928.

Rice, C. Duncan., *The Rise and Fall of Black Slavery*, Baton Rouge: Louisiana State University Press, 1976.

Richards, David, *Masks of Difference: Cultural Representations in Literature, Anthropology, and Art*, New York: Cambridge University Press, 1994.

Richards, Eric, 'Scotland and the Uses of the Atlantic Empire', in *Strangers within the Realm: Cultural Margins of the First British Empire*, Bernard Bailyn and Philip D. Morgan (eds.), Institute of Early American History and Culture, Williamsburg, Virginia Chapel Hill and London: University of North Carolina Press, 1991.

Roberts, Walter Adolphe, *The French in the West Indies*, New York: Bobbs-Merrill, 1942.

Rochefort, Charles de, *The History of Barbados*, London: Printed for John Starkey and Thomas Dring Jr., 1666.

Ryan, Michael T., 'Assimilating New Worlds in the Sixteenth and Seventeenth Centuries', *Comparative Studies in Society and History* 23:4 (1981), 519–38.

Said, Edward W., *Culture and Imperialism*, New York: Knopf, Random House, 1993.

Sandiford, Keith, "Our Caribs" are not Barbarians: The Use of Colloquy in Rochefort's *Natural and Moral History of the Caribby Islands'*, *Studies in Western Civilization* 2:1 (Fall 1993), 69–85.

Scammell, Geoffrey *The First Imperial Age*, London; Boston: Unwin Hyman, 1984.

Schaw, Janet, *The Journal of a Lady of Quality*, Evangeline Walker Andrews and Charles McLean Andrews (eds.), New Haven: Yale University Press, 1934.

Shinagel, Michael, *Daniel Defoe and Middle-Class Gentility*, Cambridge, MA: Harvard University Press, 1968.

Siskin, Clifford, 'Gender, Sublimity, Culture: Retheorizing Disciplinary Desire', *Eighteenth Century Studies* 28 (1994), 37–50.

Siskin, Clifford, *The Historicity of Romantic Discourse*, New York: Oxford University Press, 1988.

Smith, Adam, *An Inquiry into the Nature and Causes of the Wealth of Nations*, 1772, New York: Modern Library, 1937.
   Theory of Moral Sentiments, 1759, Intro. E. G. West, Indianapolis: Liberty Classics, 1976.

Smith, Raymond, 'Religion in the Formation of West Indian Society, Guyana and Jamaica', in *The African Diaspora: Interpretive Essays*, Martin Kilson and Robert I. Rotberg (ed.), Cambridge, MA: Harvard University Press, 1978.

Solow, Barbara L. and Engerman, Stanley L. (eds.), *British Capitalism and Caribbean Slavery: The Legacy of Eric Williams*, Cambridge University Press, 1988.

Starr, Chester G, *Individual and Community: The Rise of the Polis, 800–500 B.C.*, Oxford University Press, 1986.

Stedman, John G., *Narrative of a five years' expedition, against the revolted negroes of Surinam, in Guiana, on the wild coast of South America; from the year 1772, to 1777: elucidating the history of that country, and describing its productions . . . with an account of the Indians of Guiana, & negroes of Guinea*, London: J. Johnson and T. Payne, 1806–13.

Stephen, James, *The Crisis of the Sugar Colonies; or, An enquiry into the objects and probable effects of the French expedition to the West Indies, and their connection with the colonial interests of the British empire, to which are subjoined sketches of a plan for settling the vacant lands of Trinidada. In four letters to the Right Hon. Henry Addington*, New York: Negro Universities Press, 1969.

Thomas, Dalby, *An Historical Account of the Rise and Growth of the West-India Colonies*, New York: Arno Press, 1972.

Tracy, James D., Review of *The First Imperial Age*, by G .V. Scammell, *The Sixteenth Century Journal* 22 (1991), 387–88.

Tribe, Keith, *Land, Labour, and Economic Discourse*, London and Boston: Routledge & K. Paul, 1978.

Tryon, Thomas, *Tryon's Letters upon Several Occasions for the Merchant, Citizen, and Countryman's Instructor*, London: Printed for Geo. Conyers and Eliz. Harris, 1700.

Virgil, P., *Georgics*, Cambridge University Press, 1988.

Wallace, Anne D., *Walking, Literature, and English Culture: The Origins and Uses of Peripatetic in the Nineteenth Century*, Oxford: Clarendon Press; Oxford University Press, 1993.

'Farming on Foot: Tracking Georgic in Clare and Wordsworth', *Texas-Studies-in-Literature-and-Language*, 34:4 (Winter 1992), 509–40.

Ward, J. R., *British West Indian Slavery, 1750–1834: The Process of Amelioration*, Oxford: Clarendon Press; Oxford University Press, 1988.

White, Hayden V., *The Content of the Form: Narrative Discourse and Historical Representation*, Baltimore: Johns Hopkins University Press, 1987.

Williams, Eric Eustace, *Capitalism & Slavery*, New York: Russell & Russell, 1961.

From Columbus to Castro: The History of the Caribbean, 1492–1969, London: Deutsch, 1971.

Williams, Raymond, *Keywords: A Vocabulary of Culture and Society*, Oxford University Press, 1985.

Wilson, Kathleen, *The Sense of the People: Politics, Culture, and Imperialism in England, 1715–1785*, Cambridge University Press, 1995.

Woodring, Carl, *Politics in English Romantic Poetry*, Cambridge, MA: Harvard University Press, 1970.

Worrall, David, 'Agrarians against the Picturesque', Stephen Copley and Peter Garside (eds.), *The Politics of the Picturesque: Literature, Landscape, and Aesthetics since 1770*, Cambridge University Press, 1994.

Wynter, Sylvia, '1492: A New World View', Vera Lawrence Hyatt and Rex

Nettleford (eds.), *Race, Discourse, and the Origins of the Americas: A New World View*, Washingto, DC: Smithsonian Institution Press, 1995.

Young, Robert J. C., *Colonial Desire: Hybridity in Theory, Culture, and Race*, London: Routledge, 1995.

Index

abolition, 9, 123
Abolition Act, 11, 15
Abolition Committee, 124
Abolition Society, 15
absenteeism, 3, 9, 16
Achilles, The (ship), 26
Acosta, Jose de, 44
Adam (Jamaican slave), 166
aesthetics, forms of in slave society, 8–9
Africa, 28
Africans (*see* slaves)
American Revolution, effects on Creole
    plantation society, 122–23
Antigua, 14, 100, 102
anti-saccharite movement, 9, 35, 124
anti-slavery, 35, *see also* abolition
Asiento, 14

Bakhtin, Mikhail, 1
Barbados, 1, 7, 24, 175
    as aesthetic source, 35
    boiling houses, 36
    early econ. growth/dev., 30
    early plantations, 11
    early settlement, 11–12
    plague outbreak, 24
    sugar production, 1, 12, 30
Barker, Francis, 36
Baron-Wilson, Cornwell, 156
Barthes, Roland, 18
Beckford, William (Alderman), 14
Beckford, William, 2, 118
    as author 165
    critique on English liberty, 129
    as political reactionary, 121
    as publicist, 119
    works: *Descriptive Account*, 118–22; *Remarks
    on the Situation of the Negroes in Jamaica*,
    118
Behn, Aphra, 33
Belley, 41

Bellin, Jacques, 30
Benezet, Anthony, 14
Bermingham, Ann, 20
Bhabha, Homi, 18
bodies
    in historical narrative theory, 17–18
    as property, 8
boiling houses, 36, 122; *see also* sugar
    machinery and equipment
Bono, Barbara, 19
Borryau, John, 68
Boswell, James, 67
Boucher, Philip, 6
bourgeois, 3, 6–7
    emulation and display, 125, 157
    formation of consciousness, 38
Brathwaite, Edward (Kamau), 5–6, 21, 152
Bridewell prison, 26
Burke, Edmund, 170–71
Burt, Miss Daniel Mathew, 68
Butler, Judith, 71
Byron, George Gordon, Lord, 152

Cape Verde Islands, 31, 33
Caribbean, 4, 7
    cultural history, 5, 21, 177–80
    historiography, 5–6
    intellectual history, 4, 21, 177–80
Caribs, 17, 22, 44–5
    critique of European civilization, 54–5
    discursive recovery in Beckford, 126
    distinguished from cannibals, 56–7
    origins mythicized, 56–57
    relations with French, 13, 45–6
Carlisle Bay, 28
Cheyfitz, Eric, 75, 134
    and exchange values, 75
    and translation, 65; *see also translatio*
Cicero, Marcus Tullius, 159
Clarkson, Thomas, 124
Clifford, James, 50

217